|| FEARING THE IMMIGRANT ||

Fearing the Immigrant

RACIALIZATION AND URBAN POLICY
IN TORONTO

Parastou Saberi

University of Minnesota Press

Minneapolis

London

Portions of chapters 2 and 3 were published in a different form in "Preventing the 'Paris Problem' in Toronto: The Evolution and Pitfalls of Community Policing in 'Immigrant Neighbourhoods,'" *Race & Class* 59 no. 2 (2017): 49–69; copyright 2017 Institute of Race Relations, https://doi.org/10.1177/0306396817717892.

Published by the University of Minnesota Press
111 Third Avenue South, Suite 290
Minneapolis, MN 55401–2520
http://www.upress.umn.edu

ISBN 978-1-5179-0983-3 (hc)
ISBN 978-1-5179-0984-0 (pb)

A Cataloging-in-Publication record for this book is available from the Library of Congress.

Printed in the United States of America on acid-free paper

The University of Minnesota is an equal-opportunity educator and employer.

UMP BmB 2022

For Farzaneh and Himani

Contents

Beginnings

ON URBAN POLICY AND INTERNATIONAL RELATIONS

PUBLIC ENEMY NUMBER ONE

On January 15, 2015, just a week after the fatal shootings at the office of the satirical magazine *Charlie Hebdo* in Paris, on the other side of the Atlantic Ocean Christopher Hume, the top urban affairs columnist of the *Toronto Star,* penned an article entitled "Suburbs of Paris and Toronto More Alike Than You'd Think" (Hume 2015a). Hume warned readers of Canada's highest-circulation newspaper about the similarities between "the French capital's notorious *banlieues* [suburbs]" and "the old inner suburbs of Toronto"—what in public and official discourses are referred to as *immigrant neighborhoods.* He reminded readers that the Kouachi brothers, who executed the attacks, were born and raised in the *banlieues* of Paris, where they "faced lives of poverty, frustration, anger and alienation" (Hume 2015a). Toronto's "old inner suburbs . . . are not as bleak as those around Paris," yet Hume emphasized that "they can be just as isolating—physically, economically, and socially. The building stock—mostly concrete and highrise—offers little in the way of a public realm, and what does exist is often degraded and dangerous." While Toronto is "more tolerant and inclusive" than Paris, "many [of its] highrise suburban communities desperately need to be remade to twenty-first-century standards." Hume went on to applaud the latest place-based housing redevelopment policy of the City of Toronto, Tower Renewal. "We need," he signed off his article, "more programs like tower renewal" (Hume 2015a). A month later, Hume reiterated that "It's Time to Transform the Suburbs" (Hume 2015b). Urban policies such as Tower Renewal, he underlined, are the solution to the isolation of "a growing population of under-employed immigrants living in aging residential towers throughout the post-war inner suburbs" (Hume 2015b).

In those winter days of 2015, Hume was not alone in warning about the positionality and locationality of the Kouachi brothers—their being male, non-White, children of (Algerian) immigrants, and from the *ban-lieues*. On both sides of the Atlantic Ocean, from *The Guardian* to the *New York Times,* a wave of commentators warned of the "lost children of the [French] Republic" in the *banlieues,* who have become the internal enemy of the Republic (Chrisafis 2015; Callimachi and Yardley 2015). One is tempted to write off these statements as sensational journalism. After all, sensationalism and journalism have been longtime bedfellows, not least at the time when more than forty world leaders marched arm-in-arm under the banner of "*Je suis Charlie*" in central Paris to show unity against what they have declared as the international enemy of the West (fundamentalist Islamism and its terrorism) and the public-enemy-number-one *in* the West, the so-called homegrown radicalized citizens. Sensational journalism, however, is hardly the story here.

There is a deep environmental determinism at play in the picture that Hume paints for his audience. Particular aspects of the urban fabric of the *banlieues* of Paris and of Toronto's postwar suburbs, from their morphological and architectural forms ("highrise," "concrete," "suburban") to their socioeconomic marginality and racialized demography ("under-employed," "alienated," "immigrants"), we are told, have made them so "bleak," "degraded and dangerous" that they are now a potential threat to urban *and* international security. The solution, we are reminded, is nothing less than a civilizational overhaul of their urban fabrics in order to "transform" these marginalized neighborhoods "to twenty-first-century standards" and to pacify the threat their "immigrant" inhabitants, assumedly, pose to peace, order, and security. Such a form of environmental determinism is also at the heart of Hume's (and many other commentators' and experts') shrinking of the morphological diversity of the *banlieues* and that of postwar suburbs to a particular geographical imaginary of highrise concrete buildings. In reality, neither the *banlieues* of Paris nor Toronto's postwar suburbs are reducible to one particular urban form.

Environmental determinist conceptions of deprived neighborhoods as dangerous and calls for their renewal have a long history, a history that goes back to the liberal and colonial conceptions of poverty, danger, disease, rebellion, and insurrection that flourished in the contexts of the extremely unevenly developed industrial cities and the colonies in the eighteenth and nineteenth centuries. The emergence of social and health policies and urbanism in the imperial metropole, along with colonial pacification and urbanism in the colony in the second half of the nineteenth and early twentieth centuries, are rooted in this history.[1] Precisely because of this long and complex history, the force of environmental determinism behind Hume's likening of the *banlieues* of Paris and Toronto's so-called immigrant neighborhoods and his explicit linking of urban policy and international security begs our attention. It is the force of the racialized geographical imaginaries of danger in such environmentally determinist logic and what that means for social justice that are the concern of *Fearing the Immigrant: Racialization and Urban Policy in Toronto.*

The international context of the time—a major calculated attack in Paris by self-proclaimed supporters of Daesh (the Islamic State) on the *Charlie Hebdo* magazine, which itself was quickly represented as a cultural symbol of French *laïcité* (secularism) and freedom, was imperative in bringing Paris and Toronto together. The 2015 Paris attacks and the subsequent attacks in European cities brought a shift in the urban geo-politics of the War on Terror in terms of the hegemonic geographical imaginaries of the enemies of the West. When in the mid-2000s the boomerang consequences of the War on Terror came to haunt Europe—recall the Madrid bombing and the murder of Theo Van Gogh in Amsterdam in 2004 and the 2005 London bombing—security strategists, policymakers, and academics quickly represented Western cities as the victims of terrorism executed by foreign attackers who managed to penetrate "our cities" from the outside of "our" national and regional borders (see Coaffee, Wood, and Rogers 2008; Graham 2010). The attacks that shook several European cities from 2014 to 2017, however, were carried out by European citizens living in Europe. The locationality and positionality of these attackers shifted the geographical imaginaries of the figure of the enemy in urban security politics in Europe and North America. As individual attackers such as the Kouachi brothers became the face of "public enemy number one," the so-called home-grown radicalized, so too their localities— not their cities (Paris or Brussels), but rather their neighborhoods (the likes of Gennevilliers, Saint-Denis, and Molenbeek)—turned into the new frontiers of the War on Terror *inside* Europe. I have examined this shift elsewhere and underscored the centrality of environmentally determinist conceptions of the urban fabrics of these neighborhoods in this ideological shift in the politics of war that, in turn, has strengthened the convergence of security politics, racialization, and urban governance (Saberi 2019). Territorialized, racialized, and homogenized as "immigrant," "segregated," and "breeding grounds," these marginalized, majority non-White neighborhoods, we are told, are threats to social cohesion, the so-called Western way of life, security, and peace. "A territorial, social, ethnic apartheid has spread across our country," then French prime minister Manuel Valls quickly declared in the aftermath of the *Charlie Hebdo* attack. Hume's warning about Toronto's so-called immigrant neighborhoods was a rearticulation of this security fixation with the assumed ungovernability of the Other at the urban and international scales.

The rearticulation of this security politics in Toronto, however, was not a sudden burst of sensational reaction to the 2015 Paris attacks. Without the longer histories behind the production of the racialized geographical imaginaries of the *banlieues* of Paris and Toronto's so-called immigrant neighborhoods as dangerous spaces, such rearticulation would have not been sensible to an average reader. The term *banlieue* denotes more than its literal meaning, an urban geography, a suburb. *Banlieue* is an ideological term, one that, since the 1980s, has come to signify a racialized and territorialized urban space with links to former French colonies. In public and official discourses, *banlieue* is characterized by ungovernability, ossified in the imaginaries of urban deprivation, highrise concrete social housing, immigration, rioting, violence, and disorder (Hargreaves 1996). This geographical imaginary of *banlieues* as the spaces of racialized ungovernability is rooted in the histories of French colonialism, Republicanism, and urbanism (Dikeç 2007, 2017; Silverstein 2018) (Figure 2). The formation of French urban policy with its emphasis on urban renewal, social mixity, and policing in the *banlieues* since the 1980s, as Mustafa Dikeç (2007) underlines, has been central to the production of this racialized and territorialized geographical imaginary of the *banlieues* as the "badlands" of the French Republic. This longer history is paramount to Manuel Valls's warning about "apartheid" and to the increasing security fixation with the *banlieues* as the spatial focus of French foreign policy and national security, evident in Emmanuel Macron's National Radicalization Prevention Plan (Government of France 2018). These particular racialized and territorialized geographical imaginaries of the *banlieues* have reduced the morphological diversity and everyday life realities in these urban spaces to a particular form of highrise concrete residential building (Figures 1 and 2), one that Hume mobilized in his warning about Toronto's so-called immigrant neighborhoods.

FIGURE 1. A view of Rue de la République in Saint-Denis, an extremely stigmatized *banlieue* in the northern part of the Paris Region. Saint-Denis came into the media spotlight worldwide (and particularly in North America) in the aftermath of attacks in European cities from 2015 to 2017. The image here depicts the everyday vibrant street life in Saint-Denis, an everyday reality that is erased from the representations of *banlieues* by Hume and other media pundits. Photograph credit: Stefan Kipfer, March 2017.

In *Fearing the Immigrant,* I examine the making of Toronto's so-called immigrant neighborhoods as spaces of racialized ungovernability and underline the central roles of urban policy, liberal multiculturalism, and liberal humanitarianism in this process of making. At its core, the book is about the spatiality of the processes of racialization and securitization at the urban and international levels by historicizing a major form of urban policy—place-based or area-based policy—that is specifically designed to target the geographical concentration of non-White poverty in Toronto. The book provides a critical examination of the processes and forces involved in the making of policies of social development, urban redevelopment, and policing in Toronto's so-called immigrant neighborhoods from the early 1990s to the late 2010s. Engaging with the genealogies of major policy concepts, I situate these policies in a historical and multiscalar comparative context, one that encompasses global development and

FIGURE 2. A view of a highrise concrete building in Le Luth, Gennevilliers, a *banlieue* northwest of the city of Paris. Gennevilliers came into international media spotlight in the aftermath of the attacks on the *Charlie Hebdo* magazine office. The racialized and territorialized geographical imaginaries of this form of residential space have haunted the diverse realities of the French *banlieues.* Photograph credit: Stefan Kipfer, April 2010.

security circles such as the World Bank, the World Health Organization (WHO), and Western counterinsurgency doctrines, along with Canada's colonial and imperial geographical imaginaries of danger as well as American, British, and French urban policy histories. A central message of the book is about the relational formation of urban policy and international relations in various geographies and temporalities. At the heart of this relational formation, I argue, sits the continuous reconstruction of the racialized geographical imaginaries of the Other as danger. In analyzing these geographical imaginaries of danger, a key argument of *Fearing the Immigrant* is that the geo-political fear of the figure of the immigrant is central to *Racialization and Urban Policy in Toronto.* Rather than providing the grounds for a socially and racially just urban life, urban policy, so far, has functioned as a force of normalizing racism and racialization.

The genealogy of the geographical imaginaries of immigrant neighborhoods in Toronto, as chapters 1 and 2 recount, goes back to the racialized and territorialized security ideology at the heart of the figure of the "undesirable immigrant" in Canada that originates in the nineteenth century and, more immediately, to what has become known as the "Paris problem" in Toronto. The former dates back to the settlement strategies of the British White-settler colonies (the Dominions), in our case, the White Canada Policy, which was Canada's official immigration policy into the 1960s. The latter way of situating Toronto and Paris in relation to each other originated in 2005, when France witnessed one of the most intense rebellions of her *banlieues* against state violence and racism, one that pushed then president Jacques Chirac to declare a state of emergency for three weeks. Quickly thereafter, the "Paris problem" became a code for so-called race riots in Toronto's urban policy circles. If Hume's fearmongering has a history, so has his urban policy solution—Tower Renewal—to prevent the prospect of violence in Toronto. Since its emergence in the 1960s in the United States and its later transplantation to Europe (particularly to England and France), place-based urban policy has long been used as a state strategy to nullify the threat of urban unrest and so-called race riots.[2] Pathological and racialized conceptions of urban deprivation, unrest, and violence have been central to the logic of place-based urban policy and its focus on injecting development to provide peace and security.

In critical urban research less attention has been paid to how this developmental logic of place-based urban policy parallels well-established arguments in foreign policy and the intellectual field at the heart of it, namely, international relations.[3] A common foundation of international development, humanitarianism, and counterinsurgency is based upon the belief that state intervention in the form of development is necessary to nullify insurgency, revolution, violence, and civil war in the global South; hence to sustain the peace, order, and security of the established order (see Cowen and Shenton 1996; Duffield 2007; Wilson 2012; Feichtinger, Malinowski, and Richards 2012). This common logic sits at the heart of the nexus of security, racialization, and development (see Wilson 2012). As I argue in this book, engaging with this nexus directs us to think through how urban policy and international relations have historically formed in relation to each other. International relations and urban policy are deeply rooted in the state's need to govern what it designates as ungovernable, that is, a population that refuses reverence toward the dominant order and authority and thus becomes a security threat in need of pacification.

As the recent decolonial turn in the academic field of international relations has shown, since its birth as a specialized field in the late nineteenth century one of the major concerns of what today we call *international relations* has been the governing of antagonistic class and racial relations of imperialist capitalism at home and abroad (van der Pijl 2014; Wilson 2012; Vitalis 2015; Davis, Thakur, and Vale 2020). Urban policy, as we know it today, emerged in the long mid-twentieth-century conjuncture of decolonization, civil rights movements, and Black radicalism on both sides of the Atlantic Ocean, in the United States and the United Kingdom. It was not accidental that urban policy targeting deprivation became a state strategy to nullify the threat of the so-called race riots and the real urban crisis they exposed, first in the United States (1960s), shortly thereafter in the United Kingdom (1960s and 1970s), and later in France (1980s). The histories of state community development and community policing, two central pillars of both place-based urban policy and counterinsurgency, tell a story of strategic, albeit ad hoc, policy mobilities at the international and urban scales to govern the ungovernability of the racialized Other (Immerwahr 2015; Roy, Schrader, and Crane 2014; Light 2003). These policy mobilities have been central to the formation of urban policy. Ideologically and strategically, urban policy practitioners draw on colonial pacification (or what today is called *counterinsurgency*) to make their spaces of intervention. It is precisely because of the shared concern of urban policy and international relations to govern the violent racial and class relations of imperialist capitalism at various scales that I suggest understanding the fear of the immigrant in geo-political terms. This geo-political fear, I contend, has made the comparison between Paris and Toronto possible and sensible.

Fearing the Immigrant: From Paris to Toronto

Paris and Toronto are different, yet related, geographies, as are France and Canada. One national geography is located in the heart of Europe; the other is stretched across the northern part of the Americas. Each national geography has its own specific histories of state formation, colonialism, imperialism, nationalism, immigration, and urbanization. Contemporary French Republicanism, with its explicit Christian and White imaginary, is different from Canadian liberal multiculturalism, which, while deeply holding on to Whiteness and Christianity, purports to recognize and celebrate the racialized Other—the "visible minorities"—in the national polity (see Bannerji 2000). Specificity, however, is born within a whole rather than outside of it. The present national geography of Canada could not have materialized outside of the history of capitalism and, in particular, French and British White settler colonialism in the so-called New World and the resulting systematic genocide, displacement, and exploitation of the Indigenous peoples and their lands. *Fearing the Immigrant* starts from the premise that this colonial history is imperative to the security politics around Toronto's immigrant neighborhoods in the twenty-first century.

The contemporary realities and geographical imaginaries of Toronto's immigrant neighborhoods and the *banlieues* of Paris are also rooted in what I refer to as the *conjuncture of decolonization,* a period from 1945 to 1975. In the midst of the volatile geo-politics of the decolonizing world in the decades after World War II, France (similar to other European countries) was in dire need of cheap labor to reconstruct its devastated national economy and geography. Cheap labor meant bringing workers from the colonies and former colonies. The morphology of the *banlieues* is the product of a particular articulation of modernist architecture and planning (highrise concrete building and suburban landscape) as a solution to the other problem at the time, the *bidonvilles* (literally "tin can cities," the slums), themselves the products of state racism and lack of adequate housing for the increasing number of former colonial subjects coming to rebuild postwar, post-colonial France.[4] We will see in chapter 1 how the postwar-economy labor needs and Canada's foreign policy ambitions to become an imperial power of its own in the conjuncture of decolonization pushed the Canadian state to end the White Canada Policy in the early 1960s. This relational formation of immigration and foreign policies, along with the later introduction of multiculturalism policy, brought together the governing of non-White populations inside and outside of Canada's national and emerging imperial geographies. The production of Toronto's postwar suburbs and its so-called immigrant neighborhoods, as chapters 1 and 6 document, are the result of the transplantation of similar European modernist urban planning visions (which formed French *banlieues*), along with Canada's labor, immigration, and settlement policies in the decades after the 1960s. It is within and out of these broader histories that, in spite of their differences, the contemporary social geographies of Paris and Toronto come to represent a great deal in common, morphologically, aesthetically, and socioracially.

Contemporary Paris and Toronto are both global cities within their respective national geographies. Both cities have heavily invested in their urban cores in order to establish themselves as competitive nodes for attracting capital. If central Paris stands for the grandiose urban landscape of French culture and imperial glory, on the other side of the Atlantic Ocean downtown Toronto has come to portray the pretentious self-image of liberal multiculturalism and its commodified way of life, erasing the fact that White (settler-colonial) wealth and power have always had a stronghold there. The inherent core-periphery relations of capitalism have meant that the other side of this coin of urban prosperity is the production of peripheralized geographies of exploitation and marginalization, that is, *banlieues* and postwar suburbs. If since the 1980s, the *banlieues* of Paris have come to represent the badlands of poverty and violence, in Toronto, the concentration of historically White wealth[5] in downtown has been increasingly circled by half-rings of concentrated non-White[6] poverty in postwar suburbs, where so-called immigrant neighborhoods are mostly located. The social composition, built form, and morphology of these suburban geographies of the postwar era stand in contrast to the cliché imaginary of North American postwar suburbia and its Fordist urbanism anchored on the mass production of privately owned, detached, single-family housing (see Hayden 2003; Gans 2018). In Toronto, the horizontality, Whiteness, and middle-class ethos of Fordist urbanism is frequently ruptured by the verticality of some 1,200 highrise residential rental apartments—all resurrections of Le Corbusier's "tower in the park"—and by their majority non-White working-class inhabitants (Figures 3 and 4). These highrise rental apartment blocks, not the privately owned bungalow areas, are what Hume likened to the cliché image of the *banlieues* of Paris.

When the residents of the *banlieues* of Paris and other major French cities staged their biggest revolt in French history in fall 2005, Toronto was in the midst of a spike in gun-related murders among its non-White youth across the city's postwar suburbs; indeed, 2005 was called "the year of the gun" in Toronto. In Paris, Nicolas Sarkozy, then French interior minister, referred to the revolting *banlieues* youth as "racaille," a racially pejorative term translated into English as scum or rabble, and called the authorities to "power-wash" ("nettoyer au Kärcher") their

FIGURE 3. An aerial view of part of Rexdale in the northwest end of Toronto. Clusters of highrise rental apartments cut through the low-rise, privately owned bungalow landscape of Toronto's postwar suburbs. These highrise buildings are the ones Hume referred to as "degraded" and "dangerous." Photograph credit: Parastou Saberi, July 2021.

FIGURE 4. One of the incarnations of Le Corbusier's "tower in the park" in Rexdale, located in the northwest end of Toronto. It is the geographical imaginary of these buildings that Hume mobilized and compared to the *banlieues* of Paris. Photograph credit: Parastou Saberi, July 2021.

neighborhoods and housing projects. In Toronto, media pundits and politicians drew similarities between Toronto's "growing immigrant underclass" and those who ignited the "ethnic uprisings" in the *banlieues* of Paris (Valpy 2005; Jouanneau 2005). Shortly after the uprising of the *banlieues,* the accidental death of a White woman, caught in a shootout in downtown Toronto, shook the city and Canada. Then prime minister Paul Martin warned that "we cannot take our peace or our understanding of it for granted" (quoted in *Toronto Star* 2005). It was out of this context that, as we will see in chapter 2, a new problem was named in Toronto: the "Paris problem." More than temporal proximity, as I document in *Fearing the Immigrant,* it was a security ideology focusing on the perceived racialized ungovernability of so-called immigrant neighborhoods that brought Toronto and Paris together in that particular year and after.

In the decade that followed, influential forces, from media pundits to the Toronto Board of Trade (the major voice of capital in local and regional politics), the United Way (the major philanthrocapitalist body in regional and urban politics), along with policymakers, the police, architects, urbanists, and academics, all implicitly or explicitly pointed to the "Paris problem" as a threat to Toronto's peaceful diversity, competitiveness, and world-class reputation. Highlighting the "best practices" of place-based urban policy in the United Kingdom and France, these sociopolitical forces aggressively advocated for state intervention through urban policy in Toronto's so-called immigrant neighborhoods. In early 2006, the City of Toronto and United Way rolled out Toronto's first place-based urban policy in targeted neighborhoods across the postwar suburbs. The policy was composed of a social development strategy, the Priority Neighbourhoods Strategy, accompanied by a policing strategy, the Toronto Anti-violence Intervention Strategy (TAVIS). It was not a coincidence that, a decade later, Hume (2015a, 2015b) extended Toronto's "Paris problem" to so-called home-grown radicalization and advocated Tower Renewal. Tower Renewal, as chapter 6 documents in detail, is the continuation of the above-mentioned place-based urban policies.

To date, scholars have only examined limited aspects of place-based urban policy in Toronto, namely, public housing redevelopment (Kipfer and Petrunia 2009; August and Walks 2012) and targeted policing (Heroux 2011) in the downtown; racialized criminalization in postwar suburbs (Siciliano 2010); and the shortcomings of territorialized designation in urban policy (Cowen and Parlette 2011). *Fearing the Immigrant* provides the first comprehensive critical analysis of urban policymaking in Toronto from the 1990s to the late 2010s. The book provides a thorough engagement with the genealogies and contemporary developments of major policy techniques involving mapping and policy concepts such as poverty, security, policing, development, empowerment, social determinants of health, equity, and prevention drawn from the corridors of the City of Toronto and Public Safety Canada to those of the WHO and the World Bank and on to the doctrines of Western counterinsurgency. A major claim of the book is that the geo-political fear of the immigrant, as embodied in the state fear of the unrest of non-White working class, is central to the formation of urban policy in Toronto. This geo-political fear builds upon the long history of perceiving the figures of the immigrant and the racialized excluded as a threat to peace and security and the object of state intervention in the West, a history that is deeply entangled with the histories of colonialism, international relations, and urbanism.

Before starting the story of Toronto, however, let me explain my theoretical and methodological approach to historicizing the relations of urban policy, international relations, and racialization. In the remaining part of this introduction, I will briefly engage with the importance of bringing into our analysis the ways state intervention at the urban and international levels form and function in relation to each other as part of the broader strategies of pacifying racialized ungovernability. I will then move to my methodological approach and the methods I mobilized to investigate urban policymaking and racialization in Toronto, and finish with a brief outlook of the chapters.

URBAN POLICY, INTERNATIONAL RELATIONS, AND GEO-POLITICAL FEAR

The form of urban policy that is under investigation in this book, that is, place-based or area-based policies of social development, housing redevelopment, and policing, are not new. Since the 1990s, place-based urban policy has increasingly become the mantra for state intervention in metropolitan centers across North America and Western Europe. The solution to geographical and racialized concentrations of poverty and extreme uneven development in imperial metropoles is, we are told, to target problem localities and to craft certain policies, from development to policing, to address their particular plights; hence the adjective *place-based.* In English-language critical urban literature, scholars have linked the recent popularity of place-based approaches in urban policy to neoliberalization (Harvey 1989a, 1989b; Jessop 2002; Brenner and Theodore 2005; Brenner 2004; Smith 1996, 2002; Peck and Tickell 2002; Peck 2004). The premise of these studies is that the crisis of Fordist capitalism in the 1970s resulted in the prominence of neoliberalism as the political ideology of the state to manage the inherent contradictions of capitalism. Focusing on the political economies of urban policy and capitalism, scholars have underlined the key role of place-based policy in the neoliberal processes of state rescaling and restructuring, as well as the strategic role of cities in capital accumulation both locally and globally. While constructive particularly in demystifying the flowery justifications of neoliberal policies in the name of the so-called free market, participation, and progress, the sole focus on political economy and a resultant reading of politics off of economic crisis have come at the expense of erasing the racial dimension of state intervention, sidestepping the ways such processes at the urban and international scales function in relation to each other as part of the broader governing of racial and spatial relations of imperialist capitalism in our time.

Loïc Wacquant's (2008, 2009; Wacquant and Slater 2014) work in this regard stands out as an exception. Focusing on the geographical concentration of non-White poverty in the U.S. "Black ghetto" and the French *banlieues,* Wacquant underlines the central roles of the state, racism, and environmentally determinist rationalities in the production of territorial stigmatization around these peripheralized urban geographies. Policymakers, in turn, use territorial stigmatization as a justification for state intervention in the form of place-based urban policy. Following his mentor Pierre Bourdieu, Wacquant (2009) conceptualizes the territorial stigmatization of the "Black ghetto" in the United States and the *banlieues* in France as variegated forms of symbolic violence enacted by the U.S. and French states. The state, as we will see, also plays an important role in the production of the racialized realities and geographical imaginaries of Toronto's immigrant neighborhoods, yet not exactly in the ways that Wacquant formulates; there are some shortcomings in Wacquant's analysis. First, he takes for granted the welfare state's universalist claims and thus not only separates the penal and social dimensions of the state but also sidesteps the racialized and antirevolutionary histories of the welfare state (see Katznelson 2005; Neocleous 2008). Second, Wacquant's (2009, 116–17) conceptualization of symbolic violence is exclusively focused on state coercive strategies of abjection to the point of leaving aside the productive power of the state as a force of abjection (Pattilo 2009). Such a premise severely limits our understanding of the complex forms of state violence, including the violence of racism. In *Fearing the Immigrant,* I underline the force of the productive power of the state in the case of Toronto's immigrant neighborhoods, where territorial stigmatization and racialization also build upon the liberal humanitarian ethos of compassion, inclusion, and empowerment.

Third, similar to the abovementioned political-economic-inspired studies, Wacquant takes neoliberalism as his point of departure. It is the processes of neoliberalization and the de-socialization of labor since the 1970s that, for him, are the roots of the problems (Wacquant 2008, 2009). We cannot, however, explain the importance of the "Paris problem" in Toronto's urban policy or Hume's comparison of Paris and Toronto in his linking of urban policy and international security with a sole focus on neoliberalization and the economic crisis of Fordist capitalism. Antonio Gramsci's insights are useful here. Writing, from inside Mussolini's prison system, on the rise of fascism instead of socialism in Italy, Gramsci warned about limiting our understanding of politics to economic crisis. "It may be ruled out," he underlined,

> that immediate economic crises of themselves produced fundamental historical events; they can simply create a terrain more favorable to the dissemination of certain modes of thought, and certain ways of posing and resolving the entire subsequent development of national life. . . . The specific question of economic hardship or well-being as a cause of new historical realities is a partial aspect of the question of the relations of force, at various levels. (1971, 184–85)

The point is not to dismiss the force of neoliberalization in the formation of place-based urban policy. As chapter 2 shows, place-based urban policymaking in Toronto emerged in the late 1990s and early 2000s, that is, at the time that the neoliberal restructuring and rescaling of the state had already been consolidated. The powerful role of the nongovernmental organization (NGO) and humanitarian forces in urban policymaking in Toronto, as other chapters also highlight, could not have been materialized without the consolidation of the neoliberal state. Gramsci's insights underline the importance of prioritization in historicizing the politics of state problematization, racialization, and intervention. A comprehensive understanding of the politics of state intervention requires an engagement with the dialectics of the relations of force at a multiplicity of scales, geographies, and temporalities.

In *The Badlands of the Republic,* Dikeç (2007) shows the significance of going beyond the concept of neoliberalism and engaging with the questions of politics, space, and ideology in examining urban policy, underlining the role of other political ideologies besides neoliberalism, namely, French republicanism and colonialism, in building and normalizing the political fear of the *banlieues,* which in turn sits at the heart of French urban policy targeting *banlieues.* Others have also emphasized the transformed continuity of French colonial strategies of racialization and spatial intervention in targeting *banlieues* through urban policy and policing (Blanchard 2011; De Barros 2005; Rigouste 2011). Inspired by Dikeç's (2007, 2017) work on French urban policy and his emphasis on the political nature of the urban rage of the excluded, I emphasize the paramount force of Canadian national *and* foreign ideologies, namely, liberal multiculturalism and liberal humanitarianism, in making the racialized geographical imaginaries of Toronto's immigrant neighborhoods as the spaces of the internal enemy and as the targets of urban policy.

What I refer to as the *immigrant* is not limited to those with official immigrant status. The term *immigrant neighborhoods* does not have factual accuracy in a literal sense of the word. The majority of the residents of these racialized urban geographies are citizens of their respective national geographies, be it in Canada or France. What I refer to as the *immigrant* is an ideological figure, one that is demarcated as the Other, racially, socially, and geographically. In public and official discourses, the *immigrant* in immigrant neighborhoods functions as a code for what such neighborhoods have in common: a high concentration of low-income, non-White residents, many with kinship ties to former colonies. Media images of these neighborhoods are saturated with their non-White demography, youth unemployment figures, homicide incidents, *hijabi* women, even their urban design and architecture, all reinforcing visible social, racial, and morphological differences with, indeed segregation from, the so-called Western city, be it Toronto or Paris. In such urban depictions, media and official discourses represent the immigrant as an internal enemy, as a racialized and territorialized security subject that needs to be disciplined and pacified. The immigrant as such is an ideological figure, one that has a long history, going back to the politics of labor mobility in England at the dawn of capitalism (see Anderson 2013).[7] As we will see, the immigrant as an ideological figure has geo-political, imperial, and (neo-) colonial dimensions; it is a historically specific articulation of the racist, gendered, and class-based sociospatial structures of imperial and (neo-)colonial national geography and economy. To emphasize the term's racialized and territorialized connotations, I use *immigrant neighborhoods* instead of *low-income, majority non-White neighborhoods* throughout this book. I also use *the immigrant* in the singular and definitive to underline the recomposed historical continuities in the production of this figure across various geographies and temporalities, historical continuities that are embedded in the core-periphery relations of capitalism, (neo-)colonial imperialism, and war.

The core-periphery relations of capitalism are imperative to the making of the immigrant. Following the insights of Karl Marx (Marx and Engels [1848] 2002, 37) and marxist scholars (Arrighi 2007; Wood 2005; Harvey 2005; Gilroy 1987; Amin 1974, 1973) on the global nature of capital, I understand imperialism as the ensemble of core-periphery relations (economic, social, political, territorial, and military relations) that have been essential to secure the global conditions for the expansion and accumulation of capital in favor of the imperial cores. The specific nature of imperialism is not fixed; rather, it is determined by the dominant mode of capital accumulation of each era (i.e., mercantile, colonial, neocolonial). By *colonial relations* I refer to the particular form of domination that was developed through the core-periphery relations of European colonialism from the late fifteenth century and particularly since the eighteenth century, a form of domination that is based on hierarchical racial and territorial relations of subordination and dehumanization in order to facilitate the dispossession and exploitation of the racialized Others (the colonized) and their territories (the colony) for securing capital accumulation (Fanon [1961] 1967, 2004; Mamdani 2020). Colonial relations have been essential to the survival of capitalism through the forceful integration of vast geographies of the globe outside of Europe, along with their inhabitants, into the imperial relations of capitalism. Colonization, as Mahmood Mamdani argues, was central to the relational formation of the modern state and "the making of permanent minorities, and their maintenance through the politicization of identity" (2020, 18).

This relational formation of the modern state, colonization, and racialization, which has been vital for sustaining the core-periphery relations of capitalism, is crucial to understanding the politics of racialization in Toronto and Canada more generally. "The entire Canadian project," as Tyler Shipley writes, "was premised on the idea that the English were a superior race and should therefore expand the reaches of their empire, conquer all who stand in the way and grow the capitalist world markets as widely as possible to their own advantage" (2020, 2). The hegemony of this colonial ideology, and the conception of the Whiteness at the heart of it, facilitated the genocide and displacement of the Indigenous peoples in Canada, the commodification of their land, and, as chapter 1 documents, gave birth to the figure of "the undesirable immigrant" by the early twentieth century. In those years, "White Canada Forever" was a popular pub song of the common White men, who would collectively sing "We welcome as brother all white men still, but the shifty yellow race, whose word is vain, who oppress the weak, must find another place" (quoted in Shipley 2020, 103). This ideology of Whiteness, as we will see, is still central to the making of the figure of the immigrant in Canada, albeit in a recomposed form.

By the mid- and second half of the twentieth century, modern European colonialism formally shattered vis-à-vis the global forces of anti-colonial struggles and the economic devastation of European imperial heartlands at the end of World War II. I refer to this period, roughly from 1945 to 1975, from the end of World War II to the moment of the official decolonization of the world as we know it, as the *conjuncture of decolonization*. When it comes to the politics of this period, the Western imagination is fixated on the violence of World War II and the Cold War. Largely erased from this imagination is the violence that ravaged the geographies of the colonial world to pacify decolonialization. Writing in the midst of the anti-colonial upheaval of the time, Frantz Fanon ([1961] 1967, 2004) depicted the centrality and relationality of violence in the projects of colonization and decolonization. European colonial powers, from France and Britain to Belgium and Portugal, violently opposed, suppressed, and eventually settled for manipulating and pacifying the real promises of decolonization (independence, self-determination, socialism, and emancipation) in their respective colonial territories. From C. L. R. James (1958) and Frantz Fanon ([1961] 1967, 2004) to Achille Mbembe (2001) and on to Mahmood Mamdani (2020), anti-colonial intellectuals have resolutely criticized how, through colonial racialization and the proxy of the national bourgeoisies, trained and backed by former colonial powers, neocolonial relations have come to indirectly manage the transition from formal to informal colonial domination and exploitation in former colonies. I use the term *neocolonial* to refer to this process, that is, to refer to the *recomposed continuity* of colonial relations in the aftermath of the shattering of modern European colonialism.

In Canada, while Indigenous peoples are still subjected to the settler-colonial relations of the Canadian state (Coulthard 2014), the conjuncture of decolonization was imperative to both the eventual demographic composition of the country and its changing international image as the "humanitarian middle power," one different from European colonial powers. Neocolonial relations have since been central to both the national image of tolerant and the international image of peacekeeper Canada. Throughout the 1950s and 1960s, while the Canadian state firmly held on to the White Canada Policy, it actively portrayed an international image of itself as a supporter of former colonies struggling for independence. In 1957, the year that Lester B. Pearson—who, in those days, was a supporter of the White Canada Policy and later became a celebrated prime minister (1963–1968)—won the Nobel Peace Prize for his role in resolving the Suez Canal Crisis, was also the year in which he defended the integrity and the right of the European colonial powers over their colonies (Shipley 2020, 255). On the ground, Canada firmly stood in the way of decolonization; Canada voted against the independence of Morocco and Tunisia at the United Nations in 1965 and loyally supported the violent atrocities of the apartheid regime in South Africa, the British state in Kenya, the French state in Algeria, and the Belgian state in the Congo (Shipley 2020, 249–93). Chapters 1 and 2 document how the relational formation of Canadian immigration and foreign policies in the conjuncture of decolonization and thereafter would come to consolidate neocolonial relations in the making of racialization and urban policy in Toronto and Canada.

I take this most-often ignored multiscalar and multidimensional history seriously and emphasize the force of geo-political fear in the making of racialization and urban policy in Toronto. By *geo-politics* I do not refer to the traditional concern with statecraft, national borders, and relations with other nation-states. Rather, inspired by critical debates in the field of political geography, my usage problematizes geo-politics. In highlighting its parts, *geo* and *politics,* my aim is to emphasize the ways in which geographical discourses, ideologies, and practices have measured, described, assessed, and constructed particular imaginaries of the world and hence spaces of world politics at various scales (Ó Tuathail and Dalby 1998; Dodds 2005; Agnew 2007; Dalby 2008). Geo-politics as such is an intellectual terrain concerned with and influenced by the nexus of space, ideology, and politics as part of the broader imperial relations of capitalism. Politics, as Gramsci (1971, 175–90) emphasized, is the dialectical outcome of the relations of force at various scales—urban, regional, national, and international. To understand politics as such means to go beyond a narrow focus on the economic and to unsettle the liberal separations between the domestic and the international, the police and the military, war and peace, and the state and civil society. In this sense, my reference to the geo-political throughout this book is not about the outside of the state, but about *the constitution of the geographical imaginaries and boundaries* of inside and outside, here and there, the domestic and the foreign, the enemy within and the enemy without.

Geo-political cartographies of fear are central to making and normalizing the assumed racialized ungovernability of immigrant neighborhoods. As Simon Dalby (1990, 2007) has argued, cartographies of political fear within and without the domestic space are central to rendering Others as threatening, as enemies. The nexus of space, politics, and ideology plays a crucial role in turning particular geographical imaginaries of insecurity into common sense and thus in naturalizing the geo-political cartographies of fear. More than half a century ago, the French marxist philosopher and sociologist Henri Lefebvre (1991) argued that space is not a tabula rasa. Space is a social product; it is the ultimate locus and medium of struggle. "There is a politics of space," Lefebvre famously emphasized, "because space is political" (2009, 167–85). Expert knowledge on urban and political issues, as Dikeç underlines, is "guided by particular ways of imagining space, and different ways of imagining space have different implications for the constitution of perceived problems and proposed solutions" (2007, 171). Dikeç's insights on urban policy parallel the insights of Dalby and other scholars in the subfield of critical geopolitics who have emphasized the role of geographical imaginaries and practices in producing the spaces of politics and the changing perceptions of threat in world politics. In other words, neither geo-politics nor urban policy simply acts on space as a thing; rather, they produce their spaces of intervention based on particular geographical imaginaries. In the following chapters, we will see how geo-political ideologies and neocolonial relations have come to define the figure of the immigrant and the territoriality of immigrant neighborhoods in Toronto as spaces of the enemy within, and thus as spaces of urban policy. Chapter 2, in particular, shows how these geo-political ideologies of immigrant neighborhoods have become central to normalizing racialization, as sections of the youth living in these peripheralized urban spaces have internalized them to the point that their identities are not only racialized but also territorialized, by the state and by themselves, albeit for different reasons.

Any focus on state policy requires a clear conceptualization of the state, not least because in our neoliberal time the term *state* has become one of the most mystified concepts. My conceptualization here follows the insights of Gramsci (1971) and Lefebvre (1976, 1991, 2009). Recasting the conceptual distinction of the state and civil society in liberal Hegelian thought and so following Marx, Gramsci (1971) conceptualized the bourgeois state form as the "integral State." The integral state is not limited to the machinery of government and legal institutions, but includes the latter; the concept captures the dialectical unity of civil society and political society embodied by the bourgeois state form in capitalist liberal democracy (Gramsci 1971, 206–75).[8] Gramsci's concept of the integral state is all the more important in our neoliberal era, as NGO and philanthrocapitalist forces have become major players in policymaking and implementation. *Fearing the Immigrant* engages with the role of the integral state and its increasingly organized multiscalar political and expert forces, namely, the roles of NGO, philanthrocapitalist, urbanist, academic, and security forces in making particular visions of reality as proofs of racialized ungovernability in policymaking.

The spatiality of the integral state goes beyond that of the state institutions. Lefebvre's (1976, 1991, 2009) insights on the spatiality of the state, that is, the state's relation to the spaces of the national territory, the core-periphery relations, and the state's own territorial-institutional form, are complementary to those of Gramsci (1971). Bringing Gramsci and Lefebvre together is constructive for understanding how the integral state mobilizes diverse spatial policies to manage the intensely volatile racial, social, and spatial relations of imperialist capitalism on worldwide, national, and local scales. Observing the politics of space in the midst of the conjuncture of decolonization, Lefebvre (2009, 181) pointed to the ways that the French state mobilized urban policy in order to sustain domination over the post-colonial (im-)migrant by confining their lives to what he termed "the internal colonies" of French cities—urban spaces that soon would capture public and official imaginations as *banlieues* and immigrant neighborhoods. In Toronto, as chapters 2 and 3 document, "the internal colony" is a lived experience. Many residents of immigrant neighborhoods explicitly link their experiences of police raids to those of the Palestinians, Iraqis, and Afghans living in their respective war zones of imperialism and settler colonialism. Such comparison is not a rhetorical one; rather, it is one based on the lived experiences of violence, marginalization, criminalization, dehumanization, and domination.

Urban policy has been central to state security governance, and not just due to the power of militarized policing and the penal state. Following the insights of Michel Foucault (2003) and other scholars in critical security studies, namely, Mark Duffield (2001, 2007), Mark Neocleous (2008), and Colleen Bell (2011a, 2011b), I emphasize the complementary nature of security and development in state intervention at a multiplicity of scales, from the urban to the international. This complementary dimension is imperative in going beyond the separation of the penal and social arms of the state, as well as that of the domestic and foreign in state intervention. One upshot of engaging with the complexities of the nexus of security and development in the formation of urban policy is that, as chapter 3 underlines, policing is not the opposite of urban policy (understood solely as social and urban development interventions). Policing is integral to urban policy; they are the two sides of the same coin of state urban intervention (Saberi 2017). We will see, for example, how the recent social turn in policing in Toronto, far from being a progressive move, has reinforced the geo-political fear of the immigrant through policy mobilities among police, security, development, public health, and counterinsurgency forces. The book, thus, extends the works of Wacquant and Dikeç on the politics of state urban intervention. Its claims are also correctives to the current emphasis on the police state, in academic and activist circles, understood most often as a repressive/coercive state that functions mainly on surveillance and militarized policing.

In emphasizing the relational formation of urban policy and international relations, *Fearing the Immigrant* offers two original contributions to academic debates on place-based urban policy and racialization in North America and Western Europe, which for activists will bring to the fore the importance of engaging with urban policy and its neocolonial dimension. First, in prioritizing the conjuncture of decolonization, I underscore the geo-political fear of the immigrant as a major force in racialization and urban policymaking. This geo-political fear builds upon environmentally deterministic imaginative geographies of racialized ungovernability: geographical imaginaries that are based on dualistic racialized conceptions of civilized and uncivilized, urbanity and rurality, developed and underdeveloped. Even when wrapped with the ethos of liberal humanitarianism, the rationale of urban policy, similar to that of counterinsurgency, functions upon the blurring zones between concepts and notions of the domestic and the international, war and peace, and security and development. The case of Toronto highlights how through place-based urban policy, the state not only plays an important role in producing the immigrant as the target of geo-political fear, as the racialized and territorialized security subject, but also aims to secure the production of a neocolonial urban order by simultaneously recomposing and supposedly humanizing racialization through moderating the inherent violence of racialized exploitation and domination. Place-based urban policy is thus not reducible to being a sole product of neoliberalization. Strategically and ideologically, place-based urban policy is a rearticulation of counterinsurgency in the imperial metropole with the aim of pacifying and discipling racialized ungovernability.

Second, I underline that a historical-materialist understanding of racism and racialization in Western metropolitan centers requires critical engagement with the relational formation of urban policy and international relations. The territorialized and racialized security ideology at the heart of urban policy has been central to the construction of the immigrant as the object of ruling classes' geo-political fear and as the target of state intervention. The intertwined histories of place-based urban policy and counterinsurgency sit at the core of the relational formation of urban policy and international relations.

Elsewhere, I have examined the role of colonial urbanism in French colonial counterinsurgency in the late nineteenth and early twentieth centuries (Saberi 2017). Here, by historicizing urban policymaking in Toronto, I argue colonial history and the logic of counterinsurgency breathe forcefully in state urban intervention in the twenty-first century. In a manner similar to counterinsurgency, international development, and humanitarianism, place-based urban policy, I contend, builds upon the nexus of security, racialization, and development to recompose colonial relations of domination with the aim of pacifying perceived threats to the existing order. This is what I call the *neocolonial dimension* of urban policy that has reinforced and reified racism and racialization. The goal of intervention is neither the reform of social relations of racialization nor the eradication of poverty and uneven development. Rather, the goal, similar to that of an old colonial logic at the heart of counterinsurgency and humanitarianism, is amelioration, that is, the moderation of the violence of uneven development, systemic racism, racialized exploitation and domination, and so to transform the immigrant into a liberal subject more resilient and less threatening to the functioning of imperialist capitalism.

What makes the case of Toronto important for students of urban and international politics, in my view, is the hegemony of liberal multiculturalism and humanitarianism in Canada. Far from eradicating the security politics around the immigrant, liberal multiculturalism, as we shall see, has facilitated the articulation of the geo-political fear of the immigrant within the boundaries of a liberal humanitarian ideology, one that renders non-White working-class spaces as spaces simultaneously in need of securitization and tutelage. This rendition parallels the perceptions of so-called ungoverned spaces in humanitarian wars and the War on Terror. The predominance of this liberal humanitarian ideology in urban policy is the outcome of the force of liberal multiculturalism as Canada's national ideology and that of liberal humanitarianism as the main ideology of Canada's foreign policy (Razack 2004; Bell 2011a, Shipley 2020), along with the increasing ascendency of liberal humanitarianism in international relations (Weizman 2011; Wilson 2012), including in imperialist wars (Duffield 2007; Dillon and Reid 2009; Foley 2010). Liberal humanitarianism is an ideology shot through uneven geographical imaginaries and a moral economy of the suffering of the wretched of the world, whether at home (the poor, the immigrant, the homeless, the youth) or further away (the slave; the colonized; the victims of famines, epidemics, and wars) (Fassin 2012). Amelioration, understood as the necessity of moderating violence, has been central to liberal humanitarianism. The genealogy of amelioration can be traced back to eighteenth- and nineteenth-century liberal colonial thought and the attempts of fractions of the bourgeoisie, colonial authorities, and their missionary allies to ameliorate the violence of industrial capitalism, slavery, and colonization in order to sustain the rise of colonial imperialist capitalism (Lester and Dussart 2014).

Amelioration has also been imperative to the politics of colonial recognition. In his quest to understand the construction of the colonial subject, Fanon ([1961] 1967, 2004) emphasized the necessity for moderating violence in order to sustain colonial rule. Colonial rule, Fanon underlined, was never based solely on naked force; rather, it was heavily contingent on the more complex and mediated form of violence that is the recognition of the colonized. Far from being a source of human emancipation for the colonized, colonial recognition is itself a force that reproduces colonial relations of domination (Fanon 2004; Coulthard 2014). A not dissimilar politics of recognition is at play in liberal humanitarianism and its quest for amelioration. If the condition of possibility for a humanitarian politics of compassion is, as Fassin (2012) notes, the recognition of the wretched Others as humans (albeit still subordinated), what necessitated the birth and survival of such compassion (albeit in different forms) is rooted in the securing of domination through the moderation of violence (Lester and Dussart 2014; Wilson 2012; Weizman 2011). This is why humanitarian recognition has never recognized the wretched Others as equals. Humanitarian recognition has always worked within the limits of colonial-liberal recognition, and that is precisely why it has been central to pacifying threats to imperialist capitalism. In our case, we will see how liberal humanitarianism has become the hegemonic ideology of urban policymaking, fueled by philanthrocapitalist forces such as United Way since the late 1990s. Chapter 6 takes this discussion further and shows how liberal humanitarianism has become the mantra of urbanists and architects behind Tower Renewal.

Scrutinizing the force of liberal humanitarianism in urban policy and its links to international relations is imperative for those concerned with social and racial justice in Toronto and elsewhere. The contemporary shift toward humanitarian ways of war and development is not limited to the zones of neocolonial occupations and extractions in former colonies. The American gurus of counterinsurgency in the War on Terror, such as David Kilcullen (2013) and John Nagl (2014), have already underlined the necessity of amelioration (moderating violence) in the peripheralized spaces of metropolitan centers worldwide. Grasping the fact of an increasingly urbanized world and grounding their analyses in a Malthusian conception of surplus population, a Hobbesian notion of war of all against all, and a social-Darwinian politics of the survival of the fittest, Kilcullen and Nagl argue that future insurgencies will increasingly spring from the slums of the global South and the *banlieues* of the global North rather than from the mountains of Afghanistan. The military, we are told, should shift its focus to urban counterinsurgency and resiliency, as well as to learning and appropriating lessons from the fields of community policing through to urban planning and community development.

The failure of amelioration as a goal of urban policy has come to haunt Western cities with the sudden unfolding of the Covid-19 pandemic since early 2020. After decades of urban policy implementation to ameliorate the conditions of immigrant neighborhoods, the uneven urban geography of the pandemic has hit *banlieues* and immigrant neighborhoods hard, from Paris to Toronto and on to London and New York (Willsher 2020; Public Health Ontario 2020; Kibry 2020; Keating, Cha, and Florit 2020). There are significant lessons to take away from Toronto as the current pandemic and its resultant public-health crisis have brought a new wave of attention to the concept of social determinants of health in policy and activist circles alike. Chapters 3 and 5 document how the concept of social determinants of health, with its revolutionary roots in the conjuncture of decolonization, returned to prominence in a recomposed form in international public health politics in the early 2000s. A decade later, the concept traveled from the corridors of the WHO to those of the City of Toronto in 2013 and has since become central to making urban policy for immigrant neighborhoods. Seven years into policy implementation, what we have witnessed by the first half of 2021 is that the very same immigrant neighborhoods targeted by urban policy in the name of social determinants of health have been hit the hardest by the pandemic in a city that has chosen "Diversity Our Strength" as its motto since 1998. This is not accidental; rather, as readers will see, it is the logical result of a quantitative and de-historicized conception of the social determinants of health in policymaking from the international to urban levels.

ON METHODOLOGY

My methodological approach is greatly influenced by the insights of marxist, antiracist feminist sociologist Himani Bannerji on ideology, colonial discourse, racism, Whiteness, identity, and nationalism (1995, 2000, 2011, 2014, 2016). For Bannerji (1995) the processes of racialization include the simultaneous production of Whiteness and Othering. She locates these processes in the context of Marx's concepts of ideology, social relations, and capitalism in an "attempt to create a method of social analysis in which the different social moments can retain both their specificity and reveal their implications and constitutive relations to all other specific social relations" (Bannerji 1995, 51). Ideology, in the sense that Marx and Engels ([1848] 1976) defined it in *The German Ideology,* is not only about representations or a constellation of a body of ideas and discursivities; as Bannerji emphasizes, ideology is "an epistemological procedure rather than merely an amalgamated content" (2016, 210). We need, Bannerji argues, to understand "race" and racism as ideology and thus to pay attention "to the complex relationship between discourses, texts, and social relations in syntactical terms, as a kind of grammar of thought involving practice." "The form of thought," she underlines, "not just its content, becomes important for us by understanding not just the word but its placement in speech or writing" (2014, 132–33). Ideology, in this sense, "is the process of creating a dehistoricized and desocializing body of content—of representations of reality" that simultaneously also erases and distorts reality (Bannerji 2011, 236). While ideology is a mystification, "it is a mystification that arises from—and thus corresponds to—a particular moment in the historical development of human social and productive relations" (Bannerji 2016, 210). "Race," for Bannerji,

> is a word that has evolved and been used in the context of social
> relations of domination in order to manage difference based on
> power, as well as to obscure and obfuscate that with the help
> of reified categories or ideas. The idea of "race," therefore, is
> an ideological instrument produced in relations of ruling and
> justification. (2014, 134)

It is through a critique of ideological knowledge that I write about urban policy. Why such an emphasis on ideology and urban policy? The question of ideology is at the heart of the question of knowledge. The ideological dimension of a crisis, as the late Stuart Hall emphasized in *Policing the Crisis* (1978, 219), is crucial in producing consent to "the interpretations and representations of social reality generated by those who control the mental, as well as the material, means of social reproduction," and, "to the measure of control and containment which this version of social reality entails" (1978, 221). Today, in comparison to state policies of austerity, the state's mobilization of urban policy to target concentrated (non-White) poverty in imperial metropolitan centers and its relation to everyday struggles of the working class hardly occupies any space in Left politics. For the most part, the urban question is relegated to the realm of specialists: geographers, urbanists, architects, planners, and policymakers. It is the forms of knowledge produced in these specialist realms about immigrant neighborhoods, urban policy, and security that are the focus of my analysis. This is not to say that any form of specialist knowledge is ideological in essence. The point is to scrutinize the ways state power is ideologically legitimized in a modality of scientific technique by examining the specific relations between science–knowledge and dominant ideologies.

Following Bannerji's insights, here I have engaged with the forms and contents of ruling ideas in the formation of urban policy and international relations. I show how certain fundamental concepts—at the heart of the geographical imaginaries of danger—function ideologically in urban policy and international relations. From the problematized subjectivity of the immigrant as threat to the conception of poverty as risk, from empowerment to policing, from development to security, from social determinants of health to equity, from participation to prevention, I engage with the ways these concepts operate in place-based urban policy, counterinsurgency, and humanitarian interventions. Tracing these policy lineages requires an active engagement with various disciplines and subdisciplines. Discipline is centripetal, "it isolates, it concentrates, it encloses," to quote Foucault (2004, 46). Going beyond the enclosed borders of disciplines, I have engaged with debates in urban studies, political geography, critical geopolitics, critical security studies, social and political theory, and anti-colonial discussions. Urban policymaking, as we will see, travels across geography, scale, time, and the constructed borders of academic disciplines, and its travels are greatly influenced by the broader geo-political imaginaries of danger. In this sense, the book also contributes to critical debates on policy mobilities (Ong 2011; McCann 2011; McCann and Ward 2015; Ward 2006), in particular what Jennifer Robinson (2015) has emphasized as the "topographical and topological spatial imaginations" of urban policy mobility.

I mobilized three tools of investigation: textual analysis, key informant interviews, and participant observation. Textual analysis of policy and media sources, published between 1990 and 2020, is one of the major methods in this book. My analysis of policy texts is based on a close reading of relevant documents published by a variety of institutions and organizations, including the City of Toronto, United Way, University of Toronto Cities Centre, Toronto Public Health, E.R.A. Architects, the Center for Urban Growth and Research, Toronto Police Service, Ontario Provincial Police, Public Safety Canada, Ontario Government, Government of Canada, Department of National Defense, World Bank, and WHO. Following Dorothy Smith (1990), I approach texts as constituents of social relations. The aim of textual analysis is to uncover the ideological practices that produce a certain kind of knowledge practical to the task of ruling. Textual analysis is thus more than an interpretation of the utterances of policymakers. The objective of analysis is to uncover the social relations that allow such utterances to become common sense—to speak with Gramsci.

I used the media as a source for analyzing the public discourse pertaining to the questions of racialization, non-White poverty, the immigrant, postwar suburbs, policing, security, and violence in Toronto. Here my main focus was on major Canadian and Toronto news outlets, including the *Toronto Star, Globe and Mail, National Post, Sun, Toronto Life,* and *Torontoist.* My analysis is also based on fifteen participant observations from December 2012 to April 2015. In the span of three years, I attended events organized by major actors in urban policy in Toronto, including public meetings, community consultations, town halls, and a design workshop organized by Architecture for Humanity Toronto and Ryerson University (see Appendix B). Between June 2013 and July 2014, I conducted forty key informant interviews with a variety of stakeholders, including policymakers at the City of Toronto, local politicians, main figures at the United Way and Toronto Police Services (TPS), academics, staff at community organizations and the Public Interest research institute, urbanists, activists, and landlords of rental highrise buildings. From early 2017 to mid 2019, I followed up with some of my interviewees and spoke to five new key informants, in particular those working at community centers through which many of these policies are implemented.

THE BOOK IN BRIEF

Chapter 1 sets the broader historical and socioracial context of the making of the figure of the immigrant as threat and danger in Canada and Toronto. It begins with a summary of the evolution of immigration policy from the White Canada Policy to the period of 1962–1976, when Canada gradually opened up its immigration policy. I then follow the ramifications of this history in the urban conditions of Toronto in the late twentieth and early twenty-first centuries. I underline how the relational formation of Canadian immigration policy and foreign policy in the conjuncture of decolonization, along with ongoing struggles for racial and social justice, have been central to the making of the post-colonial immigrant and their geographical imaginaries in Toronto. I continue this discussion in chapter 2 by examining the ideological construction of non-White poverty as a security threat, one that eventually led to the birth of the "Paris problem" in Toronto. Here my focus is on the sociopolitical forces central to the emergence of a powerful liberal humanitarian ideology, focused on the figure of the immigrant, and its links to the broader trends in international relations.

Chapters 3 to 6 are based on the period from 2005 to 2017, during which time place-based urban policy became *the* policy solution to the problematic of concentrated non-White poverty in Toronto. I examine the ways that the nexus of development, security, and racialization plays out in place-based urban policy, starting with the ideological formation of various state strategies of policing in chapter 3. One of the major premises of this chapter is that police power has both coercive and productive dimensions. In engaging with major policing strategies and ideologies, I highlight the centrality of the geo-political fear of the immigrant in both coercive and productive dimensions of policing in Toronto and Canada. I particularly engage with the ascendency of prevention as the main pillar of the social turn in policing in Toronto's policy circles, and situate the ideological working of prevention in policing in relation to its ascendency in international relations.

Chapter 4 zooms in on the unfolding of the Priority Neighbourhoods strategy (2005–2012) and its link to the geo-political fear of the immigrant and immigrant neighborhoods. Connecting the main concepts of the Priority Neighbourhoods Strategy to those in current policing strategies, as well as to those in international development and humanitarianism, I examine the ideological dimensions of major policy concepts such as empowerment, participation, and economic integration. The rolling out of the Priority Neighbourhoods Strategy also initiated the forceful ascendency of a knowledge production industry about the immigrant in Toronto and Canada. Here, my major focus is on mapping as both a technique and form of scientific knowledge that has simultaneously reified and reinforced the geo-political fear of the immigrant. I continue this discussion in chapter 5 by introducing readers to Toronto's reformed place-based urban policy, Toronto Strong Neighbourhoods Strategy 2020 (City of Toronto 2012a) following its formation from 2011 to 2017. I focus on two new components of the policy: social determinants of health and equity. While both concepts appear to bring a progressive move in place-based urban policy, I argue they build upon a positivist ideology (i.e., the quantification of social problems) that is framed in a liberal humanitarian discourse. Tracing the conceptual and historical roots of these concepts from the conjuncture of the 1960s United States to the policy corridors of the WHO and the World Bank in the twenty-first century, the chapter focuses on the ideological functions of the state's appeals to equity and social determinants of health in the relational formation of urban policy and international relations.

The final chapter takes readers back to the opening lines of the book by zeroing in on the period from 2008 to 2018 and the formation of the Tower Renewal program, the most pervasive place-based housing redevelopment policy in Canada. Following the ascendency of mapping as a scientific technique, chapter 6 documents how the rental highrise concrete buildings would eventually turn into an object of state investigation and intervention. These residential buildings are the ones that Hume described as "bleak," "isolated," and "dangerous." The unfolding of Tower Renewal has brought urbanists, architects, and health authorities into the scene of place-based urban policy-making. The emphasis on "vertical poverty" and highrise buildings, as we will see, has reinforced the geo-political fear of the immigrant and the comparison between Toronto's postwar suburbs and the *banlieues* of Paris. This is most evident in the popularity of Doug Saunders's

(2011) concept of "arrival city" in Toronto's urban lexicon. Engaging with Saunders's internationally celebrated book, *Arrival City: How the Largest Migration in History Is Reshaping Our World,* I show the ways that Saunders's ideas build upon racialized geographical imaginaries of danger and in that parallel the ideas of Kilcullen (2013) and Nagl (2014) mentioned earlier.

Fearing the Immigrant opens up new perspectives on the continuities in and transformations of the politics of state security and development interventions at various scales, geographies, and temporalities, perspectives that are very relevant to the current situation in Europe and North America. The increasing success of hard-Right populism and the fear expressed in discourses of so-called home-grown radicalization linked to imperialist rivalries and wars have created an urban crisis centered on diversity, integration, and security in Europe with immigrant neighborhoods at its spotlight. While the Right has demonized these localities as failed estates of violence and existential threats to the West, on the Left-Liberal spectrum, from the corridors of the European Union and the European Forum for Urban Security to those of European municipal governments, there are liberal-humanitarian calls for place-based state interventions to prevent so-called radicalization in European cities (Saberi 2019). Meanwhile, the current Covid-19 pandemic and the crisis of public health that it has triggered have revealed the violence of the extreme uneven urban geographies of the most celebrated global cities in the West, from New York and Toronto to London and Paris. The nakedness of this violence, from the rapid spread of the virus and the rising number of deaths to the loss of jobs in so-called immigrant neighborhoods, has horrified the mainstream media and the public. *Fearing the Immigrant* alerts us to the ideological mobilization and shortfalls of amelioration, highlighting the fact that the current appeals to development, inclusion, and public health in place-based intervention in immigrant neighborhoods will not go beyond the nexus of security-tutelage if left to those in power. Far from being progressive, such forms of intervention normalize the forms of violence that breathe through the lived experience of racism, uneven development, and precarity, while simultaneously nurturing the neoliberal and neocolonial forces that are perpetually on the verge of birthing a new fascism in the first half of the twenty-first century. It is high time to reenvision urban policy in the name of equality and justice, in the name of a new humanism, to speak with Fanon.

1

Making the Immigrant

POLITICS, IMMIGRATION POLICY, AND FOREIGN POLICY

> Today the world has worked out the curious hybrid of
> judicial equality of states and racial inequality of peoples.
> Australia is determined to remain white; Canada eases its
> conscience by accepting a handful of domestic servants; the
> contemporary slogan is "keep Britain white," . . . . Whatever
> the Commonwealth may be in theory, it is in practice being
> increasingly tainted with racial limitations.
>
> —Eric Williams, speech at the University of New Brunswick

IMMIGRATION POLICY AND FOREIGN POLICY IN THE CONJUNCTURE OF DECOLONIZATION

In the heyday of decolonization in 1965, Eric Williams, the first prime minister of the newly independent Trinidad and Tobago (a former British colony), harshly criticized the hypocrisy of the post-colonial Commonwealth and the existing racist realities of Great Britain and its White settler-colonies like Canada—as quoted in the above epigram. Speaking at the University of New Brunswick convocation ceremony to receive an honorary doctorate of law degree, Williams was no stranger to the histories of British and French empires. His *Capitalism and Slavery* (1944), influenced by C. L. R. James's *The Black Jacobins* (1938), was one of the pioneering works to debunk the moral and humanitarian motives behind British abolitionism by pointing to the role of slave struggles and the declining profitability of slavery as major forces in abolishing the slave trade in the nineteenth century. In pointing to "the curious hybrid of judicial equality of states and racial inequality of peoples," Williams was warning about the recomposed continuity of colonial relations in a neocolonial form under the guise of legal independence in order to undo the geo-political volatility of imperialist capitalism in the conjuncture of decolonization. As regards to Canada, Williams's account of the "racial limitations" of the Commonwealth was a critique of the colonial ideology central to Canada's deeply intertwined immigration policy *and* foreign policy in the 1960s. Unlike many Canadians then and now, Williams, who was well familiar with Canada's imperialist endeavors in the Caribbean (see Houdson 2010; Shipley 2020), was also aware of Canada's intensified diplomatic activities at the United Nations to rhetorically align itself with the newly independent countries in the early 1960s only to safeguard its own evolving imperialist interests and the shaken imperial interests of Britain in the emerging national geographies of the Third World (see McKercher 2014; Shipley 2020). Such "racial limitations" had their roots in the past and they grew into the future; they have been central to the making of the figure of the immigrant in Toronto.

Until the 1980s, the hegemonic story of postwar Canada, backed by prominent immigration scholars, was one of a sudden rupture in the early 1960s as "racial discrimination . . . had become distasteful and impractical to the ruling groups in both major political parties" (Hawkins 1974, 144). It was, we are told, the awakened conscience of liberal-minded bureaucrats at the Department of Citizenship and Immigration that de-racialized immigration policy in 1962 (Hawkins 1991; Knowles 2007). Since the 1990s, a growing number of critical scholars have underscored that neither at the time nor later was racism erased from immigration policy and the Canadian polity (Satzewich 1989; Thobani 2000, 2007; Bannerji 2000; Walcott 2003; Choudry et al. 2009; Maynard 2017). Building on and extending these contributions, I start the story of Toronto by directing readers to the importance of Canada's White settler-colonial history and the relational formation of Canadian immigration and foreign policies in the conjuncture of decolonization and thereafter. These histories are imperative for understanding the urban conditions of the making of the post-colonial immigrant and their geographical imaginaries in Toronto by the late twentieth century.

What we know today as the nation-state of Canada has a much shorter history than that of human settlement, organized trade, and political life on the national territory that we call Canada. Already by 500 BCE–1,000 CE, Indigenous peoples had settled and established trade routes and forms of political governance across what is now called Canada. The nation-state of Canada has its roots in the European colonization of the Americas beginning in the late fifteenth century, particularly in the commercial and territorial rivalries between the French and the British imperial powers in the eighteenth century. By 1756, these imperial rivalries engendered a global war—the Seven Years' War—spanning from India and Europe to the Americas, a global war that lasted until 1763. In North America, the British defeated the French and gained control of "New France," as the 1763 Treaty of Paris proclaimed. Soon after, the ensemble of forces from the loss of settler-colonial territory (the Thirteen British Colonies) in the aftermath of the American Revolution, the rise of the timber trade in the Canadas, along with the need to deal with its rising surplus population in Britain made the mass settlement of British North America the governing colonial policy of the British Empire. And thus was born the expansion of the North American British colonies—Provinces—that in a century would be confederated into one federation and baptized in the 1867 British North America Act as the Dominion of Canada. The displacement and genocide of Indigenous peoples, the birth of Canadian cities, along with the production of a Canadian (English and Québécois) elite, whose wealth and political power was based in industrial and merchant capital by the mid-nineteenth century were the outcomes of this history.

Since the late eighteenth century, the geographical imaginary of cities in Canada has been ingrained in the systematic and violent displacement and erasure of Indigenous peoples (Edmonds 2010). There is a colonial logic of superiority, rooted in an ideology of Whiteness, at the core of how the Canadian state has historically managed the questions of Indigenous and non-White populations. The geographical imaginaries of this ideology of Whiteness was one of making so-called civilization in the heart of wilderness, of expanding the frontiers, of taming and populating the assumedly empty wastelands of the British North America (Baldwin, Cameron, and Kobayashi 2012). The violent erasure of Indigenous peoples and their histories is so profoundly normalized in Canada's national mythology that it is still celebrated in the works of its renowned artists, from Emily Carr's depiction of a dead Indigenous culture and abandoned villages to the novels of Margaret Atwood and on to the empty landscapes in the paintings of the Group of Seven (see Erickson 2013). If the erasure of Indigenous peoples and their histories has been one pillar of the geographical imaginary of cities in Canada, the other pillar has been the fear of the poor and non-White populations.

Immigration policy was central to keeping the geographical imaginary of cities White in Canada. Ideologically and demographically, the White Canada Policy has shaped Canadian politics and polity for much of the country's life since the 1867 Confederation. The policy remained officially the cornerstone of immigration and citizenship laws into the second half of the twentieth century. Reading Ontario newspapers in the mid-nineteenth century, one comes across colonial assertions "that not only were Black people naturally 'savages' in their 'native wilds' of Africa, but also 'reverting rapidly to the savage state wherever relieved from slavery'" (Shipley 2020, 104). In 1885, the federal parliament passed laws to limit and ban the entry of people from China by imposing hefty entry duties that came to be known as "head tax."[1] In 1904, in a speech before the Empire Club in Toronto, Fredrick Barlow Cumberland (vice-president of the Niagara Navigation and author of several books) told the audience, "We are trustees for the British race. We hold this land in allegiance" (quoted in Levitt and Shaffir 2018, 9). "We are all of the opinion," reads Vancouver's *Daily Province* in 1907, "that this province must be a white man's country. . . . We do not wish to look forward to a day when our descendants will be dominated by Japanese or Chinese, or any other colour but their own" (cited in Shipley 2020, 9).

The fear of non-White populations was officially sanctioned in the Immigration Act of 1910, which gave the power to exclude those "deemed undesirable" at the discretion of the governor-in-council and was further expanded in the amending Act of 1919 (Hawkins 1991, 16). The Canadian state introduced the amended 1919 Immigration Act in the context of the rising power of left politics in the midst of the geo-political and economic volatilities of the early twentieth century, particularly the 1917 Russian Revolution and the 1919 General Strike in Winnipeg. The 1919 Act thus aimed to safeguard the social relations of White-settler colonialism and capitalism in Canada. The figure of the "undesirable immigrant" in the amended 1919 Act (Section 38, Clause C) had explicit class, racial, and geographical dimensions. The "undesirable immigrant" was one

> deemed unsuitable having regard to the climatic, industrial, social, educational, labour or other conditions or requirements of Canada or because . . . [of] their peculiar customs, habits, modes of life and methods of holding property, and because of their proba-

ble inability to become readily assimilated or to assume the duties and responsibilities of Canadian citizenship within a reasonable time after entry. (cited in Hawkins 1991, 17)

For non-White populations living in Canada, from Chinese to Black, Japanese, and East Indian peoples, the White Canada Policy meant segregated lives in cities and the denial of the franchise. Canada's first prime minister, John A. Macdonald, had amended that denial to the 1885 Franchise Act. For almost a century, every Canadian prime minister, from the Scottish John A. Macdonald to the Scottish-descendent William Lyon Mackenzie King, the Québécois Louis St. Laurent, and onto the German-descendent John Diefenbaker, all strongly approved of White Canada Policy. No political party came out against it.

This ideology of Whiteness was central to incorporating "anti-Semitism into aristocratic disgust at the working-class movements" in Canadian cities, and, to Canada's "intervention in the global context" in the first half of the twentieth century (Shipley 2020, 180, 104). The geo-political volatility that the ensemble of the 1917 Russian Revolution, the First World War, and the rise of socialism and fascism in Europe produced, made the marriage of racism (particularly anti-Semitism) and anti-Communism a hegemonic force in politics in Canada. William Lyon Mackenzie King, who served as the tenth prime minister of Canada from 1921 to 1948 (excluding 1930–35), was wary of both the poor and the Jews. By the 1930s, fascist organizations and Swastika Clubs were formed across Canada, particularly in Ontario, Quebec, and Manitoba (Shipley 2020, 180). In Toronto, Brigadier General Dennis Draper, who served as the city's police chief from 1928 to 1946, mobilized his police power to form a "Red Squad" to crack down on both the left and non-White populations, to "break up meetings, outlaw organizations and ban Yiddish and other foreign-language newspapers for fear that they were being used to foment revolution" (Shipley 2020, 181; Levitt and Shaffir 2018).

The first and most intense urban unrest in Toronto was born out of this context in the same year that Adolf Hitler came to power in Germany. The forgotten "Christie Pits Riots" took place in 1933, when the youth flying squad of the Swastika Club shouted "Heil Hitler" as they came to protect the community from "undesirable elements" and violently attacked Jewish people during a baseball game for the junior city championship at Willowvale Park (Christie Pits Park) in downtown Toronto (Levitt and Shaffir 2018). Young Jewish and Italian immigrants fought side by side against the increasing number of White supremacists in Toronto at the time. The *Toronto Daily Star* (1933) described the event as "a crowd of more than 10,000 citizens, excited by cries of 'Hail Hitler' [that] became suddenly a disorderly mob and surged wildly about the park and surrounding streets trying to gain a view of the actual combatants, which soon developed in violence and intensity of racial feeling into one of the worst free-for-alls ever seen in this city." Only a few arrests were made, showing the indifference of the Toronto police and mayor to the rise of racism and fascism in the city.

Neither the horror of the Holocaust, nor the end of the Second World War, or Canada's reluctant signing to the United Nations Declaration of Human Rights in 1948 affected the pillars of White Canada Policy. Canadians of Chinese and East Indian origins gained the right to vote in 1947 and those of Japanese origin in 1949, and provinces started outlawing Jim Crow–style racism that had segregated Black, Jewish, and Chinese populations. Yet, the Citizenship Act of 1947 and the Immigration Act of 1952 strongly held on to the White Canada Policy. Except for a strategic rewording of "race" to "ethnic group," the 1952 Act kept the power to exclude those "deemed undesirable," this time based on nationality (Hawkins 1991, 17). In a 1957 confidential memorandum, the Department of Citizenship and Immigration explicitly explained the fear of non-White populations, exposing the deep roots of this fear in a colonial relation of domination that, as mentioned earlier, builds upon hierarchal racial and territorial relations of subordination and dehumanization.

> It has been the long-standing policy of this Department to restrict the admission to Canada of coloured or partly coloured persons. . . . This is partly due to the fact that Canadians are not accustomed to seeing coloured people occupying positions which would place them on a social and economic level with their white neighbours. . . . Immigration must not have the effect of altering the fundamental character of the population and Canada is perfectly within her rights in selecting persons whom we regard as desirable future citizens. (Department of Citizenship and Immigration 1957, quoted in Herzog 2018, 48)

For the Canadian state and public in the late 1950s, non-White populations, their spatial proximity, social mixity, and claims to equality, threatened the White geographical imaginary of cities; Canada had to remain a White settler country with its own imperial power.

At the heart of this vision was the colonial environmental determinist belief that non-White populations are essentially unassimilable, biologically incapable of adaptation, and thus their increased numbers would cause the emergence of so-called race relations problems similar to those in the United States and Britain (see Satzewich 1989; Kierylo 2012; Maynard 2017). It is important to mention that despite the hegemony of White Canada Policy, the policy never stood in the way of the exploitation of non-White labor when the capitalist economy called for it. While the Immigration Act of 1923 banned the (already limited) entry of Chinese populations, in 1925, the Railway Agreement allowed the Canadian Pacific and Canadian National railway companies to temporarily bring in their needed labor power from China (Hawkins 1991, 27). Between 1946 and 1961, Canada accepted 12,841 people from the Caribbean; the majority of them came in as female domestic servants (Satzewich 1989, 79). This was what Williams referred to as Canada's attempt to "ease its conscience" in his 1965 speech at the University of New Brunswick.

The "undesirable immigrant" would come to include other figures depending on the broader geo-political upheavals of the second half of the twentieth century. At the peak of the Cold War in the 1950s, the Canadian state extended the definition of those deemed "undesirable" to the then-designated international enemy of the West, the communist. In 1950, Lester B. Pearson, then secretary of state for external affairs in Laurent's Liberal government, noted, "I do not see why we should in principle assist in any way those Canadians to return to Canada who also have Jugo Slav nationality and who left Canada because of their Communist views" (cited in Herzog 2018, 50–1). In the same year, Canada opened up its borders to those who had directly served the Nazi war machine in Europe (Shipley 2020, 237). In 1951, the Canadian Citizenship Act was amended to give the state the right to revoke citizenship from naturalized Canadians who had returned to their country of origin for more than two years. As Ben Herzog has documented, a confidential 1951 memorandum from Arnold Heeney, then under-secretary of state for external affairs, "recommended that this provision should be invoked when the immigration was from the Soviet Union, Poland, Czechoslovakia, Hungary, Bulgaria, Romania, Albania, or China" (2018, 51).

In the midst of the conjuncture of decolonization in 1962, Diefenbaker's federal Conservative government dropped explicit racial references in the Immigration Act of 1952. Immigration officers were required to treat equally independent would-be immigrants from all over the world based on their potential economic contributions to Canada, a regulatory modification that the Liberal government of Lester B. Pearson formalized into the point system in 1967. The successor Liberal government of Pierre Trudeau, after passing the 1971 Multiculturalism Policy (to mainly nullify the threat of Quebec separatism), finally sanctioned the point system into the Immigration Act of 1976. This gradual opening up of the Canadian immigration policy was the inevitable outcome of three interrelated economic and political forces in the conjuncture of decolonization. First, Canada's postwar industrialized economy and rapid urbanization needed a constant pool of skilled labor. The postwar mass European immigration, mostly from southern Europe and to some extent the refugee camps of central Europe, were essential to kickstart the postwar economic boom in Canada. By the early 1960s, however, there was a recognition that in competition with other booming economies of Europe and the United States for attracting skilled labor, new geographies have to be opened up for labor recruitment to Canada (Thobani 2007). Second, as Williams mentioned in his speech at the University of New Brunswick, the rising political power of "keep Britain White" in the United Kingdom had already started limiting the entry of former British imperial subjects, particularly those from the Caribbean. This was part of the British government's strategy to deal with the movement of former (non-White) imperial subjects in the face of the demise of the British Empire (see El-Enany 2020). To compensate its own refusal of the new Commonwealth citizens, the British state put pressure on Canada to open up its immigration policy to Commonwealth citizens (Satzewich 1989, 84; Vineberg 2018, 239; Virdee 2014). The Conservative government of MacMillan passed the Commonwealth Immigrants Act to "halt black immigration" to the United Kingdom (Solomos 2003, 57–8) in 1962, the same year that Canada attempted to open up its immigration policy.

Third, changes in Canadian immigration policy were deeply in relation to Canada's postwar foreign policy as an evolving imperial power of its own. In order to foster Canada's growing imperialist interests in the newly independent countries of the Third World, there was a recognition that Canada could not continue championing altruism, peacekeeping, and multilateralism while its own territory was under one of the most racist immigration policies worldwide. There was thus a strategic need to align immigration and foreign policies (Vineberg 2018). As recent critical analyses of Canadian foreign policy show, in the conjuncture of decolonization, the country's foreign policy, while deeply tainted with a colonial ideology that non-White people were not ready for independence, aimed for a carefully crafted image of altruism, humanitarianism, and enthusiasm to gain the trust of the newly independent countries in the Caribbean, Africa, and Asia. "There are few," Diefenbaker noted proudly in 1960, "that can speak with the authority of Canada on the subject of colonialism, for Canada was once a colony of both France and the UK" (cited in McKercher 2014, 333). Capitalizing on this distorted image of Canada, the aim of foreign policy in this conjuncture was to pave the way for Canada's imperialist endeavors at the time that former French and British imperial powers were trembling—albeit momentarily (see Webster 2009; Spooner 2009; Gendron 2006; Houdson 2010; McKercher 2014; Shipley 2020).

It was in this context that Ellen Fairclough, then minister of citizenship and immigration, along with her deputy minister, George Davidson (who later went to pick up a position at the United Nations), argued for "placing immigration policy in its proper context as part of foreign policy" (Corbett 1963, 179). Addressing the Social Planning Council of Metropolitan Toronto on the importance of the new regulatory changes in March 1962, Fairclough concluded,

> The world we live in today is a far cry from the one of the turn of the century or even of 15 years ago. The new-emerging nations of the world will be watching with interest to see how sincere we are in applying our new immigration policy and the reception the Canadian people give to the newcomers. We have here a golden opportunity . . . to demonstrate to these people that Canadians too realize that the winds of change are blowing, the maturity we show today can reap big dividends for future generations. (cited in Corbett 1963, 180)

And thus, the winds of change continue blowing thereafter. The Liberal government of Lester B. Pearson that came to power a year later continued this project. The 1966 White Paper on Immigration echoed a similar rationale for brining immigration and foreign policies closer to each other in a push for Canada's "golden opportunity."

While underlining the economic imperatives of opening up Canada's immigration to national geographies outside of Europe and the United States, as well as a brief mention of the humanitarian aspects of such opening up (Government of Canada 1966, 7–17), the White Paper went on to highlight the "international implications" of such reform:

> Canada's willingness to participate generously in refugee programs has important international implications. So also does our basic immigration policy. . . . Any discrimination, in the selection of immigrants, creates strong resentments in international relations. . . . It is the Government's policy . . . to maintain and improve international relations by removing the last vestiges of discrimination from immigration legislations and regulations. (Government of Canada, 1966, 17)

The changes to Canada's immigration policy in the 1960s eventually resulted in today's actual demographic diversity in Canadian metropolitan centers, as well as the celebratory image of Canada and its biggest, most populace, and diverse city, Toronto. These changes did not translate into the eradication of racism and racist discrimination, however. In the mid-1960s, the Canadian state's perception of non-White migrant laborers (particularly from the Caribbean) as security threats to the White geographical imaginary of Canada was a hotly discussed topic in parliamentary debates (Satzewich 1989; Sharma 2006). While explicit racist language was deleted, there remained a consistent preference for the admission of White European immigrants (Choudry et al. 2009; Thobani 2007). The denial of entry to those "deemed undesirable" continued by other means, including bureaucratic techniques of differential treatment of applicants and application processes, as well as the uneven distribution of immigration offices across the Third World (Maynard 2017, 54–55).

Rather than eliminating racist discrimination, the linking together of immigration and foreign policy along with the introduction of multiculturalism policy brought together the governing of the non-White populations inside and outside of Canada's national and emerging imperial geographies. The Canadian state championed multiculturalism, its assumedly de-racialized immigration policy, and bilingualism both domestically and internationally, turning them into the pillars of Canadian altruism and tolerance. After 1963, the Pearson Liberal government quickly capitalized on Canadian bilingualism for gaining ground in the former French colonies, at that time newly independent African countries (Gendron 2006, 140). Three decades later, in 1993, "The Somalia Affair" (the killing of a Somalian teenager by Canadian peacekeepers in Somalia), as Sherene Razack (2000, 2004) has documented, simultaneously ruptured and confirmed central aspects of the entangled immigration and foreign policies of Canada, of racism at home and abroad. "Somalis (both those in Somalia and those who come to Canada as refugees)," Razack notes, "have become the embodiment of disorder and dirt" (2000, 128). As we shall see, from this point on, the figure of the immigrant as the Black Caribbean criminal would come to also include the Somali youth. By the 2000s, Rexdale, a neighborhood in Toronto's northwest, which is associated with residents of Somali background, would become a so-called hotspot of urban policy experimentation.

Canadian peacekeeping in Somalia was an important part of the broader Canadian foreign policy discourse of "Canada the good." Since the early 1990s, as Alison Howell (2005) argues, "Canadian values and culture" have become central to foreign policy intervention in so-called developing, failing, or failed states. To justify its imperialist intervention, Canada has "produc[ed] a narrative of 'Canada the good' that is implicated not only in obscuring histories of violence, but also in the governance of Canadians" (2005, 1). The 1995 Liberal government foreign policy document, *Canada in the World,* proudly echoed Diefenbaker's words in 1960, stating that "Canada's history as a non-colonizer power, champion of constructive multilateralism and effective international mediator, underpins an important and distinctive role among nations as they seek to build a new and better order" (DFAIT 1995, 9). "Canadian values, and their projection abroad," we are told, "are key to the achievement of prosperity within Canada and to the protection of global security" (DFAIT 1995, 34). Altruism and humanitarianism are "the clearest expressions of Canadian values and culture—of Canadians' desire to help the less fortunate and of their strong sense of social justice—and an effective means of sharing these values with the rest of the world" (DFAIT 1995, 40). Starting from the 1990s and increasingly into the twenty-first century, as we shall see in the following chapters, through the work of philanthrocapitalist forces, particularly United Way, altruism and humanitarianism would become major aspects of urban policy targeting immigrant neighborhoods in Toronto.

GEOGRAPHICAL IMAGINARIES, RACISM, AND RACIALIZATION

Changes to the immigration policy in the 1960s and the increasing visibility of non-White populations quickly threatened the White geographical imaginary of Canadian metropolitan centers like Montreal and Toronto. The actual crumbling of this White imaginary in everyday urban spaces brought an explosion of racism and violence against non-White residents. From the mid-1960s and particularly in the 1970s, accounts of racist violence became a common feature of the front pages of newspapers in Toronto (Kierylo 2012, 3). Antiracist activism and demonstrations, along with Black organizations that flourished in this period in Montreal and in Toronto, were also imperative to resisting the White geographical imaginaries of both cities (Graham and McKay 2019; Austin 2013; Walcott 2003; Kierylo 2012). Toronto-based organizations such as the Afro-American Progressive Association, Black Liberation Front, Black Youth Organization, and Black Student Union (at Centennial College) were influential in both countering everyday racism and building political consciousness in the city (Graham and McKay 2019, 133–68). Antiracist and Black-power inspired events were mostly organized by the Black Caribbean and West Indian student and activist groups, who in turn were influenced by the rise of Black Power in the United States and inspired by anti-colonial and liberation movements in the Caribbean and Africa. In the fall of 1968, Black radical figures such as Stokely Carmichael, Walter Rodney, and C. L. R. James spoke at the Congress of Black Writers at McGill University in Montreal (Austin 2013). In the spring of 1969, the Black Liberation Front of Canada and the West Indian Students Organization sponsored a Black Panther Party talk and rally at which Kathleen Cleaver, the first woman in the executive branch of the U.S. Black Panther Party, gave a talk (Kierylo 2012, 162).

In the midst of the abovementioned events, and alerted by the rise of racial tensions and urban unrest in Britain that was reignited by the 1958 Notting Hill unrest, for the first time so-called race relations became a topic of state investigation in Canada. The Ontario Human Rights Commission (OHRC) published the first of these reports on Toronto in 1969, only to deny any form of institutional racism (*Globe and Mail* 1969). Similar to commission reports on urban unrest and racist violence in Britain, the OHRC report squarely blamed racism on a sudden influx of Blacks in Toronto, the popularity of Black Power among Black youths, name-calling, interracial dating, and competition for status. The report also identified the geography of racial tensions, mostly in and around today's downtown and midtown (St. Clair West) Toronto and warned that if racial tensions remain uncontrolled, they would lead to so-called race riots. These claims would be repeated in various government and media reports and commentaries on racism and racial tensions in Toronto into the late 1970s. From the Canadian Council of Social Development (*Toronto Star* 1972), to the Department of Immigration, to the Ontario Human Rights Commission (Government of Canada 1974) and the Metro Toronto Task Force on Human Relations (Pitman 1977), all voiced comparable messages in their reports.

These reports systematically denied the existence of institutional racism in Toronto and Canada. Instead, capitalizing on the new image of Canada as tolerant, altruist, and multicultural, the reports quickly transformed the White geographical imaginary of Toronto into a raceless one. In 1974, then Toronto mayor David Crombie argued that Toronto was different from U.S. cities (which still were feeling the heat of the Black urban uprising of a few years earlier). Toronto, Crombie stated, had "an instinct for law and order" and "tolerance for minority groups" (cited in Kierylo 2012, 219). In a close analysis of debates on racism at the time, Małgorzata Kierylo contends that "public officials used the rhetoric of multiculturalism to argue that claims to racism were absurd as Canada was a nation of acceptance and cultural pluralism" (2012, 228). Canada's international image was at the heart of this denial. In 1970, Mitchell Sharp, then minister of external affairs, argued that "suspicion of racism could damage Canada's relations with the Caribbean" (*Globe and Mail* 1970). The raceless and tolerant geographical imaginary of Toronto was simultaneously built upon blaming non-White populations as the cause of racial tensions. Almost all government reports pointed to the influx of non-White immigrants, the spatial proximity of White and non-White populations, the import of racism and anti-White sentiments from the United States and the United Kingdom, economic conditions, urban sprawl, and the mindless acts of a minority of racist individuals as major causes of racial tensions.

Progressive nongovernmental organizations, such as the Social Planning Council of Metro Toronto and the Urban Alliance on Race Relations, which at the time were run by antiracist activists and leftists, had a different story to tell. In their reports, they argued that institutional racism is real and has severely affected non-White residents' employment and housing conditions in Toronto (Kierylo 2012, 249). By the late 1970s, leftist Canadian periodicals, such as *Canadian Dimension,* also started documenting the effects of racism on immigrants' access to proper employment and housing (see Hout 1978). As Daiva Stasiulis (1989) has documented, by the late 1970s and early 1980s, Toronto's West Indian and South Asian residents collectively organized against rampant racism on the part of the police and in the public school system.

These debates and events were taking place in the context of the changing geography of immigrant settlement in the Toronto region. In the immediate postwar years, central Toronto was the main destination for arriving immigrants from Europe, who were attracted by relatively cheap housing prices as the result of the state-led suburbanization of Canadian middle-income White families. As shown in Figure 5, by 1970, central Toronto was the geography of concentrated poverty, while postwar suburbs marked the geography of middle-income, majority White families. The gradual gentrification of downtown Toronto (beginning in the late 1960s and then systematically accelerated since the 1990s) changed this pattern (Caulfield 1994; Magnusson 1983). Since the mid-1970s, immigrant settlement patterns have undergone an increasing peripheralization, progressively concentrating in the city's postwar suburbs, a trend of peripheralization that is now extended into the regions of Peel and York and particularly in the municipalities of Markham, Mississauga, Vaughan, and Brampton. Already by 1975, parts of the postwar suburbs in Scarborough and Rexdale (particularly the public housing area of Jamestown Crescent) became known as geographies of non-White populations and increasing racial tensions (OHRC 1977). By the 1980s, the figure of

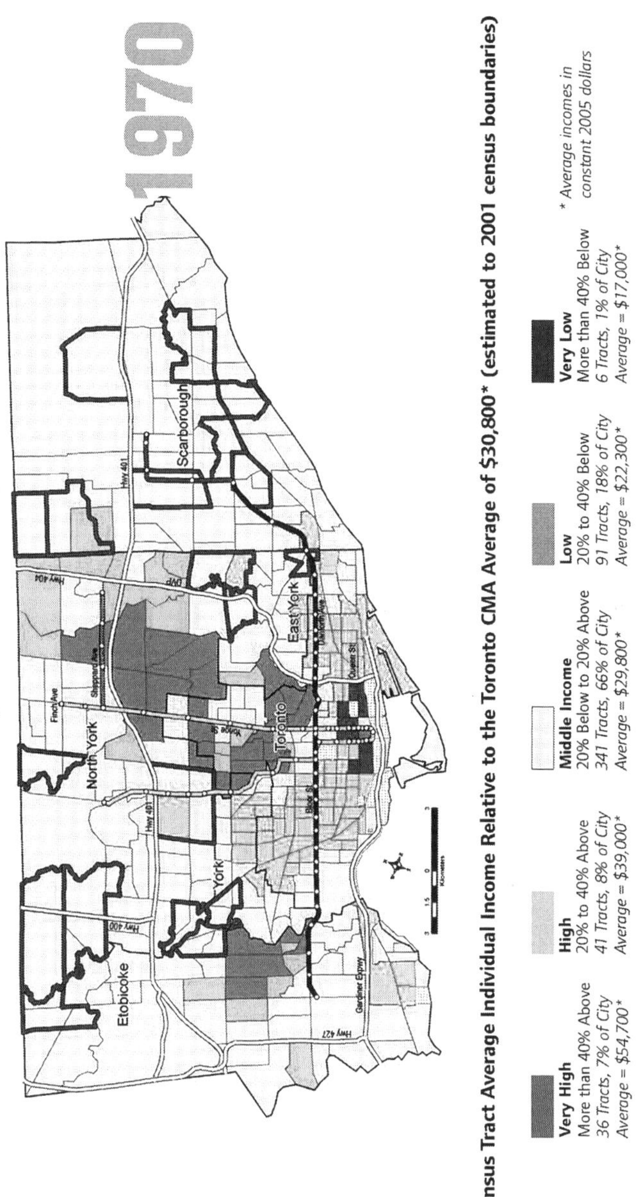

FIGURE 5. The relational geographies of wealth and poverty in Toronto in 1970 shows the concentration of wealth (very high and high income) in the mid-center and upper-center of the map (the current upper-end of downtown and central midtown, which are still wealthy areas) and in a pocket in the midwest end of the city. Postwar suburbs in this map are solidly populated by middle-income populations, while the concentration of low- and very low-income populations is in the center-bottom of the map (the majority of the current downtown area). Source: Hulchanski 2010, 4.

the immigrant in Toronto already embodied the non-White working class, while its geographical imaginary was equated with low-income pockets of postwar suburbs. This territorialization and racialization of the immigrant has had violent effects on the lives of residents of these peripheralized urban geographies. In *Brother,* David Chariandy (2018) vividly depicts the traumatic clash of the everyday violence of living in the immigrant neighborhoods of Scarborough and the daring dreams of their inhabitants, of the racialized excluded, in the 1980s and 1990s.

NEOLIBERALIZATION AND THE CRIMINALIZATION OF THE IMMIGRANT

While deep-rooted systemic racism has been essential to the making of the non-White working class in Toronto, so have the rapid neoliberal state restructuring and economic de- and reregulation since the late 1970s. The 1970s witnessed both the opening up of Canadian immigration policy and the introduction of the preliminary moves toward neoliberalization by the Liberal government of Pierre Trudeau (see Wolfe 1984). The Mulroney Conservative government that came to power in 1984 began the processes of state restructuring by limiting fiscal transfers of equalization payments to the provinces, cutting the federal government's direct spending on social programs, and reorganizing the eligibility criteria for obtaining social assistance (Russell 2000). The changes profoundly affected the housing sector. By 1985, the Canada Mortgage and Housing Corporation reduced its support for homeownership and, more importantly, for mixed rental-housing programs. The federal Liberal government of Jean Chrétien that came to power in 1993 reinforced the neoliberal turn in Canada. In the same year, the Liberals eliminated Canada's national housing program. A year later, in 1994, they slashed unemployment benefits by $5.5 billion over a three-year period. The Liberal federal budget of 1995 drastically reduced federal contributions to social spending to the point that it is often considered to mark the end of the Keynesian welfare state in Canada (McBride 2005; Johnson and Stritch 1997).

The 1980s and 1990s were also a period of increasingly intense anti-immigrant debates about the nature of Canada's multiculturalism and immigration policies, debates that eventually resulted in the changing and tightening of the immigration system with the rolling out of the War on Terror.[2] Nostalgic for the White geographical imaginary of Canada, prominent journalists of the mainstream newspapers in both English Canada and Quebec continued criticism of the official multiculturalism policy (Karim 2002). During the Mulroney government years, attacks on non-White immigrants were frequently voiced in parliamentary debates about the "refugee problem," coded as debates on the flaws of the immigration system and the "diminishing quality" of immigrants (Abu-Laban 1998). The public explosion of racist discourses and ideologies in the 1980s and 1990s should also be seen in relation to the broader anti-immigrant turn in the United Kingdom and continental Europe (Kundnani 2007, 2014; El-Enany 2020; Yılmaz 2016; Lucassen 2005) and the discourses of international migration and human security in international relations, which, by this time had turned the immigrant into a security threat in and for the West (Duffield 2001, 2007; Kaldor 1999).

By the end of the 1980s the flowery promises of free market advocates confronted hard realities. In 1989 Canada entered its most serious economic downturn since the Great Depression of the 1930s (Frisken 2007, 190; Rachlis and Wolfe 1997). The economic recession provided fodder for the public outburst of racist anti-immigrant debates around the "diminishing-returns" and the "human capital quality" of the incoming non-White immigrants (Galabuzi 2006, 143–72). The result was that non-White immigrants were increasingly represented as potential security threats in and to Canada, rather than potential Canadian citizens, voters, and contributors to Canada (Abu-Laban 1998; Sharma 2006; Galabuzi 2006). Building upon the momentum facilitated by the outgoing Conservative federal government, the Chrétien Liberal government (1993–2003) aimed at reforming the immigration policy by problematizing family reunification and putting greater emphasis on the economic self-sufficiency of immigrants. The result, as Yasmeen Abu-Laban put it at the time, was "pitting (good) self-sufficient independent immigrants against (bad) family class immigrants" who then were implicitly blamed for stealing "our" Canadian welfare and "our" Canadian social and educational services (1998, 11). At the same time, the federal Liberal government mobilized a discourse of integration as a "Canadian approach" to the assumed problems of immigration (despite the already wide use of the concept in Europe) (Abu-Laban 1998). In doing so, and similar to the 1960s and 1970s, non-White immigrants rather than state restructuring, government policies, and systemic racism became the problem to be solved.

The other side of the coin of integration was the elimination of the "undesirable immigrant," a practice, as we saw, with roots in the White Canada Policy and its later use to eliminate the communist threat in the 1950s and 1960s. As Liberals held up the flag of multiculturalism, altruism, and humanitarianism in foreign policy interventions, they made it easier to deport permanent residents who were deemed security threats to Canadian society. In 1995, Bill C-44 amended the Immigration Act to include new provisions that allowed for the deportation, without a right of appeal, of permanent residents deemed a "danger to the public." The government introduced Bill C-44 in the context of intensified anti-Black racism around the "Jamaican criminal" in Toronto as a security threat to the (White) public (D'Arcy 2007). Bill C-44 resulted in increased deportation of Jamaican nationals from Canada and particularly from Toronto (Barnes 2009; Burt et al. 2016).[3] Media pundits quickly characterized the "Jamaican criminal" in Toronto as "the barbarians [who] are inside the gates" (Valpy 1994, also see D'Arcy 2007). Such characterization, followed by actual deportations of Jamaican permanent residents, cemented the geographical imaginaries of neighborhoods such as Regent Park and Jane and Finch, spaces where a large number of Black residents with links to Jamaica resided, as so-called dangerous neighborhoods. The same influential media commentators, such as Michael Valpy and Rosie DiManno, who furiously penned about Toronto's "Paris problem" in 2005 and after (see Beginnings and chapter 2), were also viciously vocal in racializing and stigmatizing Black residents as "barbarians" (Valpy 1994), as ones who "pillaged" Toronto's "innocence" in the mid-1990s (DiManno 1994). As we will see in chapter 3, the figure of the Black criminal, particularly following the "Somalia Affair," would come to include those from Somalian background and would play an important role in place-based policing strategies in Toronto.

The 1990s experienced the intense bursting of the contractions of systemic racism, uneven urban development, and neoliberalization. The decade turned into a politically intense time in Toronto. From around 1989, a series of killings or injuring of several Black people by the Toronto Police once again brought the questions of "race," racism, and crime into the public eye (Jackson 1994). The issue of "race and crime" became a hot topic in the 1991 municipal election. In 1992, following the Rodney King verdict in Los Angeles, a solidarity march on Toronto's downtown Yonge Street, organized by Black activists, turned into confrontations between the police and the demonstrators. Influenced by the burning images of unrest in South Central Los Angeles, the media called it the "Yonge Street Riot," and it became Toronto's version of so-called race riots. By this time, the history of Toronto's Christie Pits Riot was erased from the public memory. The "Yonge Street Riot" shook Toronto's self-constructed and self-congratulatory image of diversity and tolerance (Jackson 1994). It was followed by an unprecedented series of official reports, including a commissioned report on *Race Relations in Ontario* (Lewis 1992) and an audit of the race relations practices of the then Metropolitan Toronto Police Force (Andrews 1992). The short-term result of the reports was place-based policy: the Ontario New Democratic Party government of the time introduced Fresh Arts, an arts program for non-White youth in poor neighborhoods. The policy did little to change the actual racist practices of policing. On the contrary, community policing intensified in Toronto's low-income neighborhoods. A year after the "Yonge Street Riot," by the fall of 1993, Toronto Police introduced one of the first targeted policing programs—Project 35—into poor downtown neighborhoods. In the summer of 1994, Toronto Police extended Project 35 to public housing projects in the postwar suburbs of Scarborough and York. Project 35 became the precursor of targeted policing in Toronto—a policing strategy that, as we will see in chapter 4, has reinforced the geographical imaginaries of crime by equating violence, non-White youth, poverty, and suburbs (Heroux 2011; Siciliano 2010).

The criminalization of the immigrant was also accompanied by the state's emphasis on knowing the immigrant. Since the mid-1990s, state-sponsored production of knowledge about immigration and integration in Canada's metropolitan centers has become a bustling intellectual industry for universities, NGOs, policy institutions, and think tanks. In a manner similar to the United Kingdom (see Kundnani 2007), the concept of social cohesion helped frame and camouflage the inherent racism of this state-intellectual collaboration. In 1996, the Department of Canadian Heritage identified social cohesion as part of critical policy challenges that would arise over the next decades. In 1997, the Department of Justice Canada and Canadian Heritage co-initiated the Social Cohesion Network (SCN) of the Policy Research

Initiative. The SCN has been an imperative force in knowledge production about social cohesion since the late 1990s (see Jeannotte 1999, 2003; Stanley 2003).

The economic recession, coupled with racist and class-based discourses targeting the immigrant, facilitated the election of the Conservatives under the leadership of Mike Harris in the 1995 Ontario provincial election. Under the populist banner of the "Common Sense Revolution," the provincial Conservative government of Harris (1995–2002) implemented a Thatcherite-style program that qualitatively transformed the political, socioeconomic, and spatial structures in Ontario and Toronto (Keil 2002; Boudreau, Keil, and Young 2009). Their neoliberal interventions drastically affected the lives of many residents and were influential in the production of poverty, specifically among non-White working-class populations (see Khosla 2003). In 1996, the Conservatives shattered the already troubled affordable housing sector in Toronto. They canceled the construction of seventeen thousand units of social housing and downloaded the cost of social housing, public transit, ambulances, and other social programs to municipalities. In January 1998, in one of its most dramatic and undemocratic structural changes in the name of cost saving, accountability, economic competitiveness, and local democracy, the Harris government dissolved the regional government of Metropolitan Toronto (formed in 1954) and its six municipalities (the postwar suburbs of East York, Etobicoke, North York, Scarborough, York, and the former City of Toronto, now referred to as downtown) and amalgamated them into a single municipality called the City of Toronto (see Boudreau, Keil, and Young 2009). In June 1998, the Tenant Protection Act came into effect in the newly amalgamated City of Toronto. The hallmark of the Act was the introduction of "vacancy decontrol"—which effectively removed rent control on units that became available and made it easier for landlords to increase rent and evict tenants. The Act paved the way for the gentrification of downtown Toronto and affected housing affordability in the city for years to come (Slater 2004).

The racial and class tensions of the early 1990s were followed by a series of popular protests against the Harris government. From 1995 to 1997, impressive waves of popular mobilization against the Common Sense Revolution changed the rhythms of life and politics in Toronto.

Unprecedented in the city's political history, popular mobilizations brought together labor unions, community groups, social justice activists, teachers, and students, and culminated in a week-long quasi-general strike in 1996, known as the Metro Days of Action, followed by a province-wide political strike by teachers in 1997 (Kipfer 1998; Camfield 2000). These popular mobilizations were followed by another round of political mobilization in 1997, both in the downtown and postwar suburbs, this time against forced municipal amalgamation (see Boudreau 2000). In the same year poverty became a major policy topic in Toronto. The publication of a series of reports by United Way was influential in pushing poverty to the table of policymakers at the City.[4] It was not a coincidence that these reports, with their message of poverty as risk, came out in 1997. As we will see in chapter 2, the 1990s was also the conjuncture of the comeback of poverty in international relations, as evident from the agendas of the supranational institutions such as the World Bank and the International Monetary Fund (IMF). Particularly the second half of the 1990s also marked the period in which the figure of the immigrant was cemented as a threat to social cohesion by the Canadian state and its intellectuals.

AN URBAN AGENDA FOR THE CITY OF IMMIGRANTS

With the hard collapse of its real estate market in 1989, Toronto underwent a deep recession that continued into the early 1990s. The systematic gentrification and privatized, market-led transformation of downtown Toronto—through national and international capital and facilitated by various levels of the government—were major forces in the recovery of the real estate market (Lehrer and Wieditz 2009). The economic recession turned into a cause for the acceleration of the restructuring of the local state, a process that by the end of the 1990s resulted in the consolidation of the competitive city model of urban governance (Kipfer and Keil 2002). The 1990s also witnessed an increase in the number of immigrants arriving and settling in Toronto and its surrounding areas. Between 1991 and 2001, immigration-induced labor force growth was 132 percent for Toronto in comparison to 70 percent for Canada and 97 percent for Ontario. In Toronto, immigrants composed 37 percent of the total population in 1991, 42 percent in 1996, and 44 percent in 2001. By 2006, immigrants were

45.7 percent of the total population, while non-White population made up 42.9 percent of Toronto's population (Boudreau, Keil, and Young 2009, 91).

The consolidation of city competitive politics in this broader context accelerated socioeconomic and racial polarization and uneven urban development in the city (Ornstein 2000; Filion 2000; Kipfer and Keil 2002; Boudreau, Keil, and Young 2009). From 1991 to 1996, poverty increased from 18.9 percent to 28 percent in Toronto (United Way 1999, 5). Given the already existing systemic racism in the labor market (Henry and Ginzberg 1985; Galabuzi 2006; Pendakur and Pendakur 2011), non-White working-class populations, and particularly non-White women, were severely affected by the state neoliberal restructuring in the name of competition and the free market (Khosla 2003). By the mid-1990s, Toronto witnessed the most visible human costs of the neoliberal revolution: an explosion of homelessness and a crisis of affordable housing in downtown (see Heroux 2011). In the fall of 1998, while developers were ecstatic about the recovery of Toronto's real-estate market, civil society organizations declared homelessness a national disaster in the city (TRDC 1998). By the end of the 1990s, the concrete manifestations of Canada's "economic apartheid" (Galabuzi 2006) became extremely visible in the country's major global city and its most diverse metropolitan center.

The targeting of poverty, disorder, and the immigrant in the late 1990s coincided with the formation of a coalition of pro-urban bourgeois sociopolitical forces that, as we shall see in the following chapters, would gain momentum in the early 2000s and would eventually become an influential force in urban politics and in the knowledge production industry on place-based urban policy in Toronto. While the Harris Conservative government was closely linked to metropolitan corporate transnational capital, its electoral and political bases were mostly located in the newly built, sprawling suburban and exurban districts of southern Ontario (Walks 2004; Dale 1999). The Harris Conservatives rode to their victory on an antiurban ideology, which they mobilized through populist discourses focused on tax cuts, family life, urban crime, and antielite sentiments. The decade-long rule of the Conservatives in Ontario set the stage for political competition between two fractions of the bourgeoisie in the Toronto region with two different visions for economic competitiveness of Canada's major global city. One fraction was celebratory pro-urban, emphasizing the role of cities in economic competitiveness; the other was deeply antiurban, riding on the demonization of cities as centers of vice and crime and an antitax rhetoric of small government. This competition within the ruling class, as we will see in the following chapters, would come to influence the fate of urban politics and policy in Toronto in decades to come.

Beginning in the second half of the 1990s, pro-urban, business, and community-based forces in metropolitan centers began voicing concerns about the political neglect of Canadian cities and how such neglect would affect Canada's economic power and competitiveness in the future (see FCM 2001; TD Bank Financial 2002a, 2002b; Rowe 2000). This emerging pro-urban movement was influenced by the broader neoliberal emphasis on city–regional competitiveness in a globalized economy, on the one hand; on the other hand, it was influenced by the works of Jane Jacobs (a central figure in Toronto's urban reform movement of the 1960s and 1970s) and benefited from the political power of Toronto-based pro-urban philanthrocapitalists—including the United Way. Alan Broadbent, a powerful Toronto-based businessman, civic entrepreneur, and philanthropist, and an advocate of targeting the poor rather than the rich (see Broadbent 2013),[5] was an influential figure in initiating the new urban agenda in Canadian politics and public discourse (Allahwala 2011, 104). In October 1997, Broadbent organized a conference, *Jane Jacobs: Ideas that Matter,* which was followed by a small invitation-only event, *The Evolution of Toronto,* in the spring of 1999. The two events resulted in the publication of the book, *Toronto: Considering Self-government* (Rowe 2000), which galvanized a concerted Toronto-based discussion about the future of cities within the Canadian state architecture. The 1998 forced municipal amalgamation and the subsequent political marginalization of the Toronto-centered pro-urban bourgeois forces reinforced the need for building a coalition around this urban agenda.

The Toronto-centered calls for a renewed national urban policy found supportive echoes in the corridors of Parliament Hill in Ottawa, albeit mostly in rhetoric. In 2001, the federal Liberal government of Jean Chrétien established the *Prime Minister's Caucus Task Force on Urban Issues.* By November 2002 the task force published its final report, *Canada's Urban Strategy: A Blueprint for Action.* The report promised a "significant presence of the Government of Canada in urban regions" (Prime Minister's Task Force 2002). In 2003, the federal

Liberal government under Paul Martin released the New Deal for Cities. At its official introduction in 2004, Martin (2005) proclaimed the "New Deal is a national project for our time." The New Deal came in the context of global city formation and city–regional competitiveness as part of the Liberal government's agenda as articulated in the 2002 Speech from the Throne:

> Competitive cities and healthy communities are vital to our individual and national well-being, and to Canada's ability to attract and retain talent and investment. They require not only strong industries, but also safe neighbourhoods; not only a dynamic labour force, but access to a rich and diverse cultural life. They require new partnerships, a new urban strategy, a new approach to healthy communities for the 21st century. (Government of Canada 2002)

For the most part, the New Deal for Cities remained a policy discourse rather than a policy implemented. The 2006 federal election of a minority Conservative government led by Stephen Harper buried the Liberal urban agenda; the Harper government's strategies were based heavily on resource extraction, trade, and finance capital. Nonetheless, the introduction of the New Deal for Cities, with its emphasis on an "urban and community lens" and collaboration with the local state, gave a political boost to Toronto-centered pro-urban bourgeois forces and their push for place-based urban policy. The 2003 provincial and municipal elections changed the balance of forces in Ontario and Toronto to the benefit of the pro-urban bourgeois forces. In Ontario, the Liberal party under the leadership of Dalton McGuinty ousted the Conservatives. Meanwhile in Toronto, David Miller, who ran on a neoliberal social democrat platform, won the mayoral election.

In the early 2000s, as various levels of government embraced city–regional competitiveness, these levels also pushed for the securitization of immigration policy by distinguishing between preferred and nonpreferred immigrants in the political climate of the War on Terror (Bell 2011a). The Anti-Terrorism Act of October 2001 and the Immigration and Refugee Protection Act of June 2002 equated foreign nationals with the internal enemy. Since then, refugees, immigrants, and citizens of Arab and Muslim descent have increasingly become the chief targets of Canada's national security agenda (Bell 2011a). At the same time, both provincial (Liberal) and federal (Conservative) governments increasingly shifted their labor market strategy toward the labor of temporary migrants rather than permanent residents (Sharma 2006). While this trend had already started in the mid-1980s, the growth of Canada's imperial power in the following decades consolidated this shift in Canada's labor market strategy by the turn of the twenty-first century (Sharma 2006; Gordon 2006; Shipley 2017). The political effects of changes to immigration policy have gone beyond policy circles. Debated and popularized through mainstream media, parliamentary sessions, and official statements, the state targeting of non-White populations as the internal enemy has affected public discourses and reinforced the conception of the immigrant as disorder and a security threat in and to Canada.

In 2003, the victory of David Miller in the mayoral election shifted the political landscape of the city and opened the way for the consolidation of a Third Way regime in Toronto (see Kipfer and Keil 2002). Miller managed to gain support from an array of influential forces in urban politics, including organized labor, centrist and social democrat (sub-)urban politicians, downtown-based liberal professionals and gentrifiers, people in the culture industry, environmentalists, and those in finance, development, philanthropy, and the nonprofit sector. While his Third Way regime retained a progressive and culture-friendly façade (particularly in terms of environment, transit, and street festivals), Miller's policies expanded neoliberal policies and authoritarian initiatives that had already begun under the former conservative mayor, Mel Lastman. Partly as the result of the earlier strategies, partly as the result of Miller's initiatives, the social geography and morphology of Toronto were qualitatively transformed in the first decade of the twenty-first century.

During his two terms (2003–2006 and 2006–2010), Miller systematically facilitated the gentrification and privatized, market-led development of downtown Toronto and strategic nodes, such as the North York and Scarborough centers, in the postwar suburbs; the destruction and gentrification of public housing developments in the downtown (at Don Mount, Regent Park, and later Lawrence Heights) under the rubrics of social mixity and intensification; the monetization of City assets and public lands through Build Toronto;[6] the shift in the tax base from corporate, industrial, and commercial taxes to residential property taxes and user fees; and the commodification of culture as a competitive asset of Toronto's multicultural creative city status. Despite the progressive façade of his Third Way politics, Miller continued austerity policies, budget cuts, and union busting while advocating for public–private partnerships, and he deepened law-and-order policies by expanding the police budget and the militarization of the police force (i.e., TAVIS in 2006 and the G20 security apparatus in 2010). While real-estate and finance capital, developers, gentrifiers, cultural corporations, and the police force were the main beneficiaries of these processes, Miller's strategies reinforced the territorialization and racialization of wealth and political power in the city. By 2010, the contradictions of Miller's eight-year regime were so ripe that the late hard-right populist Rob Ford easily tapped into these contradictions, mobilized a territorialized war-discourse of "city versus suburbs," presented himself as the savior of the ordinary suburban people, and surprised political elites by his victory as the sixty-fourth mayor of Toronto (Kipfer and Saberi 2014). Ford's victory brought a blow to the respectability of Toronto's liberal and red-Tory establishment. In reaction, they blamed "Toronto's angry (non)-white voters" (*National Post* Editorial Board 2010) for what they considered a national and international embarrassment. *Globe and Mail* commentator Michael Valpy called Ford's victory an "immigrant-led working-class uprising" (Valpy and Leblanc 2010).

When Christopher Hume (2015a) warned about Toronto's immigrant neighborhoods, their "degraded and dangerous" "building stock," and the "poverty, frustration, anger, and alienation" of their youths, and went on to champion for their "desperate need to be remade to twenty-first-century standards," he was not simply sensational. The sensibility of his vision and mission builds upon the long history of the making of the geographical imaginaries of the immigrant as threat and danger to Toronto and Canada. Hume's altruism and humanitarianism has a lot in common, geo-politically, with the altruism and humanitarianism of *Canada in the World* that outlined Canadian foreign policy two decades earlier. One is aimed at governing racialized ungovernability in Canada's national geography, the other is aimed to do the same in Canada's imperial geographies. In the following pages, we will see how since the 1990s urban policy has gradually played an important role in this form of governing.

2

The "Paris Problem" in Toronto

RACIALIZATION AND GEOGRAPHICAL IMAGINARIES OF DANGER

> Space is not a scientific object removed from ideology and politics. . . . Space is political and ideological. . . . There is an ideology of space. Why? Because space, which seems homogeneous, which appears given as a whole in its objectivity, in its pure form, such as we determine it, is a social product.
>
> —Henri Lefebvre, "Reflections on the Politics of Space"

THE GEO-POLITICAL FEAR OF NON-WHITE POVERTY

The publication by the United Way Toronto of *Poverty by Postal Code* in 2004 and the reference to 2005 as the "year of the gun" are most often understood as the major events that led to the formation of place-based urban policy targeting non-White poverty in Toronto's postwar suburbs. Both moments were influential in the normalization of a racialized geographical imaginary of poverty and gun violence in public consciousness in Toronto and of a subsequent need for immediate state intervention. Voices affiliated with United Way often credit the philanthropic organization and its 2004 report with the discovery of geographically concentrated poverty in Toronto (I23 2013; I4 2013; I17 2013).[1] As we saw in the previous chapter, however, the production of racialized geographical imaginaries of poverty in Toronto has a longer history. In the 1970s and 1980s, reports on racial tensions were the major force behind the making of racialized geographical imaginaries in Toronto only to deny systemic racism. By the end of the 1990s, as we will see in this chapter, poverty would become the topic of state-led inquiries problematizing the immigrant. This shift did not take place in a vacuum. The conjuncture of the turn of the twenty-first century was one when, domestically and internationally, Western states and international institutions such as the World Bank increasingly targeted poverty and migration from the global South as security threats. And Toronto was no exception.

In the tense context of the late 1990s, as Toronto's restructured economy was slowly recovering from the shocks of the 1989 recession, the specter of a poverty crisis haunted the city. The crisis was as real as it was ideologically constructed and appropriated—appropriated for criminalizing poverty and declaring a humanitarian war on poverty. In the second half of the 1990s, poverty and its increasing visibility in Toronto became a subject of investigation for philanthrocapitalists and the local state. In 1997, United Way Toronto brought poverty to the agenda of policymakers through the publication of three reports: *Metro Toronto: A Community at Risk* (1997a), *Beyond Survival: Homelessness in Metro Toronto* (1997b), and *Way Ahead: Focus on the Future* (1997c). The reports warned about Toronto's rising poverty rate, the growing concentration of "households at risk," the threats of a "jobless recovery" from the recession, the "demographic change" framed as "the changing origins of Toronto's immigrant population,"[2] and "the capacity of the social services infrastructure to respond to social needs." These reports planted the seeds of what would become the dominant conception of poverty in urban policy in Toronto: poverty-as-risk.

The conceptualization of poverty-as-risk in these reports paralleled the dominant ideological conceptualization of poverty in international development and humanitarian interventions as propagated by the World Bank and IMF at the turn of the century, a conceptualization that would become hegemonic in the twenty-first century. In this ideological framing, poverty is understood as integral to growth (i.e., capitalist development) rather than a peripheral issue (which was the dominant framing in the 1980s). Poverty here is seen as the result of a disconnection from the market and thus conceived of as a risk to the security of both the market and society (Best 2013). Solving the problem of poverty is, in turn, contingent on reintegrating the poor into the market economy (see World Bank 2000, 2005, 2012, 2013, 2014; United Nations 2005).

Despite the new terminology of risk, the ideological foundations of poverty-as-risk have a long genealogy. Poverty-as-risk builds upon the eighteenth- and nineteenth-century bourgeois conception of order and the historical association at that time of the poor, the indigent, and the idle with disorder, precisely because of their lack of proper integration into capitalist social relations (see Neocleous 2000). This association has been at the heart of the bourgeoisie's political fear of the poor and the indigent and the formation of a bourgeois colonial order and policing since the eighteenth century (see chapter 3). Poverty-as-risk is a reiteration of this political conception wrapped in a language of neoclassical economics, one that conceives poverty as a quantitative phenomenon and as a security threat to the political stability of imperialist capitalist order. The identification of poverty-as-risk as a social problem in Toronto also paralleled the emerging worldwide political concerns with international migration as a security threat in the 1990s. This was not a coincidence. A common conception of integration works in the immigrant and poverty debates. Integration, disintegration, and exclusion, in both debates, are defined in relation to imperialist-capitalist sociospatial relations. The subjects of both debates—the poor and the immigrant—are conceived of as internal enemies, as security threats to the political stability of Canada.

The 1997 United Way reports were also important for building the ideological ground for framing the unfolding poverty crisis in Toronto as a double crisis, as a humanitarian crisis and a security crisis. As we shall see in the next chapter, the 1990s was also the period when poverty became the target of place-based policing in downtown Toronto (Heroux 2011). At the same time that poverty was equated with disorder and criminalized accordingly, the visibility of homelessness in downtown Toronto became a justification for a humanitarian cry for state intervention. With the United Way report *Way Ahead* (UWT 1997c), the philanthrocapitalist agency established itself as a leading organization for addressing the problem of poverty through its launch of four funding priorities with explicit liberal humanitarian focus: Giving Yong Children a Healthy Start; Addressing Hunger and Homelessness; Assisting Abused Women and their Children; and Helping Newcomers to Settle and Integrate. In *Beyond Survival,* the United Way (UWT 1997b) emphasized its leadership role and called for the creation of a task force on homelessness in Toronto. A few months after, in early 1998, the conservative mayor Mel Lastman (the first mayor of the newly amalgamated City of Toronto) appointed Anne Golden, then CEO and president of the United Way, to head a task force to investigate Toronto's growing homelessness problem. The choice of members of the task force gives us a glimpse into the local state's twin target: poverty and security. Besides Ann Golden, the other two members of the task force were William Currie, at the time a member of the Ontario Provincial Police (OPP) and the OPP Regional Commander for the Greater Toronto Region since 1995,[3] and Elizabeth Greaves, then executive director of Dixon Hall, a long-time community center at the heart of east downtown Toronto servicing public housing neighborhoods such as Regent Park and Moss Park, neighborhoods that were already associated with the "Jamaican criminal" and had become the targets of policing since 1993 (see chapters 1 and 3).

By the end of 1998, Mel Lastman had given the green light to Toronto police to declare a war on street poverty, targeting and removing young panhandlers, squeegee kids, and the visibly poor from downtown public spaces in order to clean up downtown Toronto for gentrification (Esmonde 2002; Gordon 2006, 92; Kipfer and Keil 2002). With the support of the Ontario Crime Control Commission (OCCC), appointed by the Conservative Ontario premier Mike Harris in April 1997, Mel Lastman's "war on squeegees" would become a translation of then mayor Rudy Giuliani's war on the poor in New York City in the same period (see DeKeserdy 2009). According to Jim Brown, then the Conservative member of provincial parliament representing Scarborough West and co-chair of the Ontario Crime Control Commission, "Mayor Mel's war on squeegees . . . [was] a war on bad behaviour" (Brown 1998), one that was synonymous with "social disorder" and would "cause fear and are precursors to crime and community decay" (OCCC 1998).

By the end of the twentieth century, racial tensions, as the topic of investigation, gave its spot to poverty in the newly amalgamated City of Toronto. A report by the Canadian Council on Social Development (CCSD 1999), *Summary Statistics on Poverty in Toronto,* was followed by a United Way (UWT 1999) report entitled *Toronto at a Turning Point: Demographic, Economic and Social Trends in Toronto.* The publication of *Toronto at a Turning Point* indeed marked a turning point in cementing a particular geographical imaginary of non-White poverty and the immigrant as threats in and for Toronto. The report set the problem of poverty against three backgrounds: (1) A mythic construction of Toronto as a city "built on a foundation of rich cultural diversity, healthy neighbourhoods, clean and safe streets, a modern and efficient infrastructure, and social cohesion"; (2) Toronto's economic competition "on the global stage"; and (3) the city's immigrant problem, referred to as "the demographic change" (United Way 1999, 1). As with the United Way's reports in 1997 and the many reports on race relations in the 1970s, "the demographic change" was a code word for non-White populations. In many ways, Toronto's mythic image in this report resembled the raceless tolerant geographical imaginary of Toronto in the 1970s, even though by this time poverty, rather than racial tensions, was problematized, the report was not immune from a racialized gaze.

Toronto at a Turning Point (UWT 1999) was the first report to explicitly frame a particular geographical imaginary of poverty as the problem of non-White poverty located in the city's postwar suburbs. What is important about this report and the many others that would follow are the cartographies of fear that they helped produce by disassociating the increasing concentration of poverty in specific localities and among particular groups from the broader sociospatial and political relations at the heart of the production of concentrated non-White poverty and concentrated White wealth in the city. Even though *Toronto at a Turning Point* mentioned the economic recession in the 1990s and structural changes in the labor market as the broader causes of poverty, these changes were presented as the new reality of globalization—a reality to be taken for granted and to be adapted to rather than questioned or changed. In the absence of any engagement with the explicit and implicit racist structures of Canada's labor market and polity and the neoliberal assault on the welfare state, the report's emphasis on "the changing origins of Toronto's immigrant population," along with their changing settlement destinations in "Scarborough and North York in particular," normalized a geographical imaginary of non-White poverty that became associated with the figure of the immigrant in Toronto.

The production of this territorialized and racialized geographical imaginary was also influenced by the immediate political context of the time: the debates about immigrant integration and social cohesion in the 1980s and the 1990s and the amalgamation of Toronto in the late 1990s (see chapter 1). The report was published less than two years after the 1997 antiamalgamation mobilizations. One of the lasting political effects of amalgamation was a defensive territorialism both in the old City of Toronto (referred to as "the city") and its postwar suburbs. Having its aesthetic and ideological roots in the urban reform movement of the 1970s and heavily influenced by the ideas of Jane Jacobs, this defensive territorialism was anchored on ideological conceptions of the city and suburb as dualistic, fragmented, homogenized, and hierarchized spaces with their own ways of life, culture, and civility—or the lack thereof. As Stefan Kipfer (1998) has argued, this defensive territorialized politics was deeply normalized and reified by the triumph of localism in the antiamalgamation forces, best evident in their appeals to local democracy and local control over the city and suburbs. In this context, the territorialized and racialized geographical imaginary of poverty that the United Way provided helped rescale and rearticulate the immigrant debates in Canada and Europe in relation to the specificities of Toronto. It provided a cartography of immigrant poverty in the newly amalgamated postwar suburbs (now called inner suburbs) as a threat to Toronto (itself represented as a peaceful city of neighborhoods) and its competitive economic power.

The authors of *Toronto at a Turning Point* ended their first chapter on "the demographic trends in the City of Toronto" with a humanitarian call. The report proudly emphasized that "providing temporary support to new immigrants and refugees in the form of orientation services, housing help and language skills is a key ingredient in *reaping the benefits* of this valuable human resource" (UWT 1999, 15; emphasis added). At first glance, this statement appears as yet another compassionate plea to ameliorate the plight of the racialized excluded in Toronto. But it also reveals the contradictory logic of liberal humanitarianism. The political economy of liberal humanitarianism is best captured in the phrase "reaping the benefits of this valuable human resource." It shows that the humanitarian cry around the poverty crisis at the turn of the twenty-first century in Toronto was less about the everyday violence of living in poverty and abjection than it was about how non-White poverty would affect "our peace," "our way of life," and "our" economic competitiveness. Built upon a neoliberal economic rationale of city–regional competitiveness and a geo-political fear of non-White populations, as we will see in the following pages, the mission of this liberal humanitarian ideology is conceived as the tutelage of the poor, the colonized, and the underdeveloped. Tutelage in this liberal humanitarian ideology is a form of neocolonial trusteeship; it is, above all, about making the immigrant less threatening to and more profitable for "our" economy and polity. These themes were also influential in international and urban politics at the dawn of the twenty-first century. An abstract emphasis on integration into global economy became central to international development as well as humanitarian and military interventions in the so-called underdeveloped countries with their assumedly failing and failed states. Similar arguments were also central to the emerging urban agenda in Toronto.

In March 2002, United Way and the Canadian Council on Social Development published an influential report on poverty in Toronto. The report, *A Decade of Decline: Poverty and Income Inequalities in the City of Toronto in the 1990s* (UWT 2002), set the tone for the famous *Poverty by Postal Code* report (UWT 2004). The explicit focus of *A Decade of Decline* was on "the geographical segregation of poverty" (mostly in Toronto's postwar suburbs and also in downtown public housing developments), which the report saw as "a serious threat to the social and economic health of the city and its residents" (UWT 2002, 3, 37–43). In contrast to the 1970s reports that denied any similarities between Toronto and cities in the United States and the United Kingdom, *A Decade of Decline* gave cautionary accounts of their growing resemblances. The specter of Toronto turning into a city fragmented by "immigrant ghettos" was influential in making Toronto's poverty crisis an urgent topic for policymakers. The report built on the literature on the growth of ghettoization in Canada as a justification for its focus on spatial and racial segregation in Toronto (UWT 2002, 36)—a literature that is deeply linked to the debates on the so-called Black ghetto in the United States and the social-cohesion turn in debates on immigrants in Canada and Europe (see Hajnal 1995; Kazemipour and Halli 2000). Warning about the possibility of a ghettoized Toronto, United Way shifted its focus toward "alienated youth" and "growing violence in the streets" (UWT 2002, 43–46). This shift paralleled then-mayor Mel Lastman's war on the poor and the consequent policing strategies since 2000 toward targeting "youth violence" and "gangs and guns" that followed the tenure of the conservative police chief Julian Fantino (see Gordon 2006). The report also emphasized the role of the United Way as the humanitarian trustee "in addressing community problems" and called for "a suburban funding strategy" (UWT 2002, 7, 48).

Representatives of capital in Toronto and Canada (such as the TD Bank and the Toronto Board of Trade) quickly backed the United Way's call for "a suburban funding strategy" by providing it with extra economic logic. As we saw in chapter 1, major representatives of corporate capital in Toronto (who by now had fully embraced city–regional competitiveness) became active promoters of an urban agenda, linking Canada's economic prosperity to public–private investment in cities. In 2002, TD Bank Financial (2002a, 2002b) and the Toronto Board of Trade (2002) published a series of reports on the importance of cities to Canada's economic competitiveness. Similar concerns were also raised in the OECD (2002) report, *Territorial Reviews: Canada, Canada.* Almost unanimously, these reports emphasized city–regional competitiveness as the cornerstone of economic growth, linked the economic prosperity of Canada to that of Toronto, and advocated for the greater involvement of the private sector in urban governance. These reports gave a seemingly scientific economic rationale to place-based state intervention to solve the problem of concentrated non-White poverty while reifying the production of poverty.

We have already seen in chapter 1 how the aborted support of the federal Liberal government for the New Deal for Cities gave another layer of legitimacy to the calls of the pro-urban bourgeois forces for place-based urban policy. At the local-regional scale, the pro-urban bourgeois coalition received a political boost with the formation of the first Toronto City Summit under then mayor Mel Lastman in June 2002 and later supported by Mayor David Miller. The City Summit was led by an alliance of Toronto-based capitalists, philanthrocapitalists, the city's community sector (under the leadership of United Way), and members of Ontario's old Red Tory regime (who had been marginalized since the 1995 victory of the Harris Conservatives). As an important step in the consolidation of a new city–regional regime in Toronto, the 2002 City Summit aimed to forge a strategic alliance among a downtown-oriented business elite and representatives of the city's community sector as well as Toronto-based pro-urban politicians (Social Democrat, Liberal, and Red Tory) (Boudreau, Keil, and Young 2009, 47).

In the aftermath of the Toronto City Summit, Frances Lankin, then CEO and president of United Way, wrote an important essay entitled *Two Solutions for Urban Poverty,* published through the Centre for Urban and Community Studies at the University of Toronto (Lankin 2002). The Centre would soon become the influential academic space for knowledge production on poverty and urban policy in Toronto (see chapter 4). Lankin's essay reads as yet another call for urban policy in zones of non-White poverty (2002, 4–9). She identified "the concentration of urban, immigrant poverty" as an imminent threat to the economic and political security of Toronto (2002, 3). The economic logic of her argument echoed previous reports on poverty-as-risk by the United Way and TD Bank, the debates on immigrant integration and social cohesion, and Richard Florida's work on urban economic competitiveness and quality of life (Lankin 2002, 1, 3–4). Recalling the history of "racial tensions" in U.S. inner cities, Lankin (2002, 10–11) closed her essay by warning about the specter of so-called race riots in Canadian cities, and particularly in Toronto:

> The remarkable, peaceful, at times joyful co-existence of people that are racially, ethnically, religiously, linguistically and economically diverse is our country's greatest accomplishment. . . . But the greatest threats to this remarkable achievement are also found in our large cities. . . . Should we squander the triumph of peaceful diversity, we will lose much more than a good feeling about our country. Should the social cohesion of our large cities be lost, the standard of living of every single Canadian—no matter where they live—shall suffer the consequences. (Lankin 2002, 11)

This orchestrated political effort in making a geographical imaginary of so-called race riots emanating from immigrant neighborhoods would facilitate the turning of the geo-political fear of the immigrant into common sense and a pillar of urban policy in Toronto.

UNITED WAY: THE FORCE OF LIBERAL HUMANITARIAN IDEOLOGY

The year 2003 was a landmark for the coalition of pro-urban bourgeois forces in Toronto. Their political and ideological power gained considerable legitimacy by the victories of David Miller in the 2003 municipal mayoral election and Liberal Dalton McGuinty in the Ontario provincial election in the same year. The coalition quickly and successfully represented itself as a progressive force that would voice the concerns of the citizens of Toronto. This shift was important in turning the coalition's version of an urban agenda into the dominant ideology among policymakers, community organization staff, and progressive forces. At first glance, the coalition's concerns seemed to echo the messy everyday-life realities of those living in the most marginalized parts of the city. Frances Lankin (2003) proudly announced United Way's "new strategic plan, called Community Matters" and highlighted the organization's

> plan to accomplish this by building public awareness of the issues affecting our city, strengthening the capacity of local organizations to meet the needs of their communities, and bringing together partners to find solutions to the social problems that are threatening Toronto's stability and livability, now and in the future. (Lankin 2003)

In April 2003, the Toronto City Summit Alliance (TCSA 2003) released its first policy platform, *Enough Talk: An Action Plan for the Toronto Region.* It read as a political attack on the Harris Conservative Ontario government despite itself being heavily indebted to neoliberal economic competitiveness. At the time of its release, David Pecaut (2003), then the chair of the Toronto City Summit Alliance, wrote: "There is a crisis being created in the city as a result of the Common Sense Revolution and the federal government's downloading. If we want to maintain a sustainable city, we have to reinvest." But in contrast to the popular Left-leaning anti-Harris mobilization from 1995 to 1997, the Toronto City Summit Alliance strategically and successfully used a neoreformist vocabulary (focusing on quality of life and local democracy) to advance its neoliberal agenda of enhancing Toronto's economic competitiveness in attracting footloose national and international capital (Boudreau, Keil, and Young 2009, 205).

The Toronto City Summit Alliance actively built an ideological consensus about the superiority of civil society as the ideal terrain for policy activism, a consensus that is anchored in classical liberal thought that understands civil society as separate from the state. The other side of this neoliberal ideology is the propaganda that government cannot solve social problems alone and thus the private sector needs to be involved. Building upon this ideological twist and mobilizing a populist politics, the pro-urban bourgeois forces have consistently and to a great extent successfully constructed a public image of themselves as part of civil society conceived in this liberal mold, as representing the concerns of ordinary citizens and the voiceless poor. The Alliance actively attempted to represent the pro-urban bourgeois forces as "strictly non-partisan" and as an "inclusive coalition" of Toronto's civic leaders. Pecaut, for example, referred to the participants of the 2002 City Summit, which included high-profile philanthrocapitalists, CEOs of major Canadian banks, insurance companies, and corporations as well as elite politicians, as "citizens" (2007). This identification of influential politico-economic players within Toronto's ruling circles as ordinary citizens de-historicizes class, gender, and racialized dimensions of power relations and the role of the state in the production of racialization, uneven urban development, and urban policy.

The Toronto City Summit's action plan was followed by a United Way report, *Torontonians Speak Out on Community Values and Pressing Issues* (UWT 2003). Published just before the 2003 municipal election, the report reinforced the populist representation of the pro-urban bourgeois forces and legitimized its statements not in the name of research per se, but in the name of Torontonians. The message implied that it was no longer just United Way or policymakers—those who live farthest away from poverty—that see poverty as a threat to Toronto's prosperity and security; rather, Torontonians themselves—presumably those affected by poverty—conceive of "social problems at the neighbourhood level" as "threats to Toronto's stability and livability" (UWT 2003, 4). The report prepared the ground for the Priority Neighbourhoods Strategy, particularly on its focus on the neighborhood scale and the links among non-White youth, violence, and so-called suburban poverty by reiterating the poverty-as-risk ideology and focusing on the territorialized and racialized geographical imaginaries of poverty in Toronto.

For the first time, as Figure 6 shows, maps were used in the report as a visual technique for materializing the geographical imaginary of the so-called youth problem, one that is only located in postwar suburbs and had already been associated with non-White poverty and gun violence (UWT 2003, 19, 33).[4] One comes across the explicit geopolitical fear of the immigrant in the report's naming of poor neighborhoods as "hot spots" and "stressed communities" (UWT 2003, 11–14), a language very similar to the imperialist military language of targeting "weak and failing states" as "hot spots for civil conflict and humanitarian emergencies" (see Wyler 2008). The so-called hot spots of poverty in Toronto were identified, more explicitly than before, as "threatening" to "the cohesion and strength of community life" in the city (UWT 2003, 11).

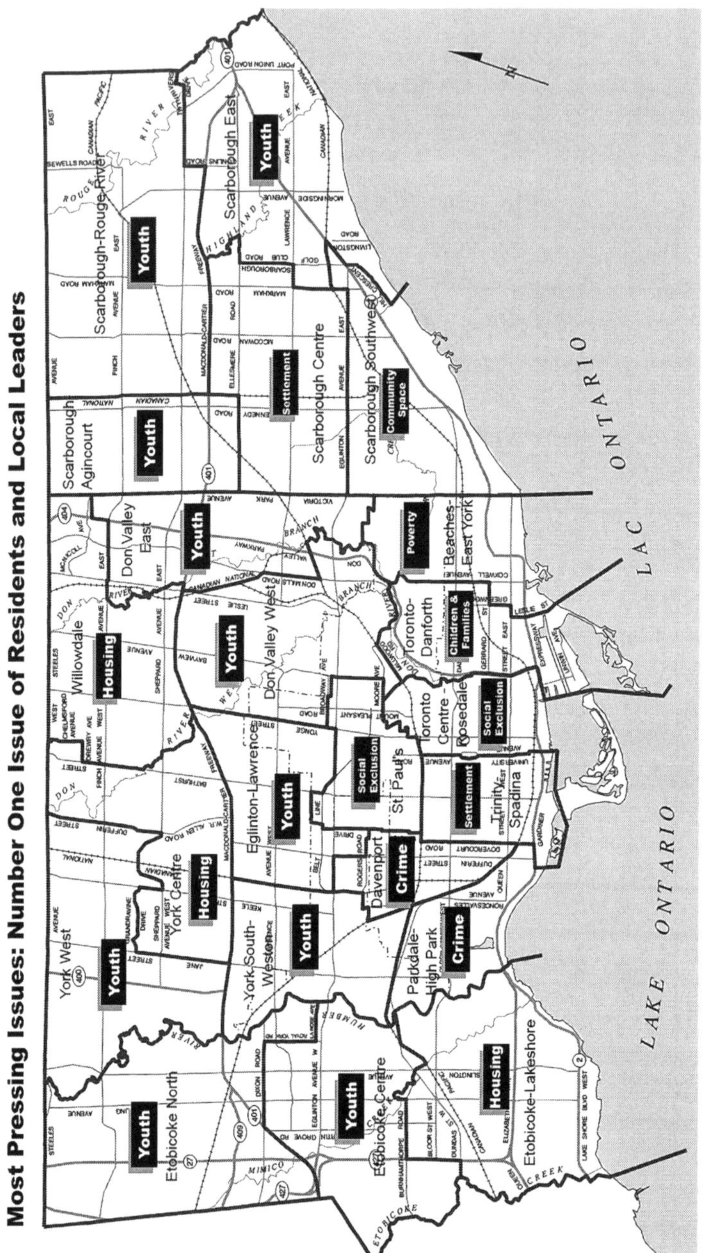

FIGURE 6. One of the first mappings of social problems in Toronto in 2003. Published in *Torontonians Speak Out,* the map provided a geographical image of the locationality of the youth problem in the city. Source: United Way, *Torontonians Speak out on Community Values and Pressing Issues* (Toronto: UWT, 2003): 33. Courtesy of United Way Greater Toronto.

A closer reading of the report, however, reveals that the rosy picture of Toronto's "great diversity," "livability," and "cultural celebrations and festivals" was the picture painted not by the poor living in the city's postwar suburbs, but by those fractions of Torontonians living away from the so-called hotspots of poverty (see UWT 2003, 7–9). Calling for "the need to rebuild community" before it gets too late, the report suggested that senior levels of government should facilitate funding for large-scale investment in the targeted localities (UWT 2003, 40). Highlighting the humanitarian trusteeship of the United Way, the report publicized the organization's mission "to meet urgent human needs and improve social conditions by mobilizing the community's volunteers and financial resources in a common cause of care" (UWT 2003, 3) and ended by identifying United Way as the community's trustee:

> One way that United Way could help is to become the "human voice" for the community. . . . A better "voice" to represent the ongoing daily interests of our people. (UWT 2003, 46)

There is a deep neocolonial humanitarian conception of trusteeship in the way the United Way portrays its image, as "the 'human voice,'" "a better 'voice,'" for the community. This self-image of the organization as "the voice for the community" would become hegemonic in a decade. When in the fall of 2013 I interviewed a former United Way policy analyst about the importance of the organization, she reiterated the closing lines of *Torontonians Speak Out:*

> What United Way was able to provide was to be the voice of the community and to verbalize those sorts of insights that the government is not close enough to reality to be able to say and to recognize emerging program initiatives that would be promising. (I4 2013)

The turning of the United Way into a neocolonial humanitarian trustee of the wretched of Toronto did not happen in a void. The evolution of United Way Toronto, starting from a local branch of the U.S.-based United Way in Toronto in 1973 to a major regional and urban policy lobbyist by the 2000s, was greatly facilitated by neoliberalization and the ascendency of humanitarianism and the NGOization of community activism. The United Way managed to survive the neoliberal austerity attack on the nonprofit sector beginning in the 1990s by becoming the fittest of all, transforming itself into "the largest source of nongovernmental funding for its member agencies" across Toronto (UWT 2003, 44). In the context of systematic cuts to public funds for social and community services across the city (Social Planning Council of Metropolitan Toronto 1997; Evans and Shields 1998), United Way funding has increasingly become the main source of survival for many community organizations, particularly in low-income neighborhoods where accessible social services such as settlement, after-school, and youth-centered programs are in dire need (I31 2013; I6 2013). As United Way has become the major source of nongovernmental funding in Toronto, so has grown its authoritative power. Even though many community workers are aware of the contradictions of United Way politics and practices, they are reluctant to vocally criticize the organization, fearing the loss of funding to their own organizations and consequently their jobs (personal correspondence).

One of the City of Toronto's senior policymakers explained to me how this move was as strategic on the part of United Way as it was facilitated by the neoliberal restructuring of the local state:

> I would say that they [United Way] very intentionally moved towards more policy development. . . . They've really managed to raise a lot more funds. . . . Don't forget that the last head of the organization [Frances Lankin] used to be an MPP [member of provincial parliament in Ontario]. And I have heard the phrase, out of that CEO's mouth, "United Way and the other orders of government." That tells you a little bit about how she saw that organization. They intentionally built a policy capacity. I don't think that's necessarily a bad thing. I think the bigger problem is that our capacity for research, evaluation, and policy development is actually relatively small. When they [United Way] do research, they have so many more resources. . . . I think they very intentionally built that capacity and their ability to intervene in policy at the local, the provincial, and the federal levels. . . . We're less and less organized around the idea of a government doing things, and more and more relying on those who can contribute money to develop the policy agenda. And the worst case of that is, of course, people who are very wealthy are the ones driving the policy

agenda. I think United Way's participation in the policy sphere is part of this broader trend. . . . I think their participation in the policy sphere is not any better or worse than the [right-wing] Fraser Institute's participation in the policy sphere. It's part of that same trend. (I25 2013)

This double strategic choice of being an active part of the integral state would facilitate and normalize the framing of the geo-political fear of the immigrant in a liberal humanitarian discourse in Toronto.

NEIGHBORHOODISM AND GEOPOLITICAL IDEOLOGIES

A few months after the publication of *Torontonians Speak Out,* in early 2004 United Way published its now famous and influential report *Poverty by Postal Code: The Geography of Neighbourhood Poverty, 1981–2001* (UWT 2004). Highlighting that the number of poor families in Toronto increased by almost 69 percent between 1981 and 2001, *Poverty by Postal Code* was the first report to provide an explicit focus on "the spatial dimension, or the 'geography of poverty,'" mapping the "suburbanization" of concentrated non-White poverty and warning about its destructive effects in Toronto (UWT 2004, 4). The concept of neighborhood was central to *Poverty by Postal Code.* On the one hand, references to neighborhood were used to reinforce the mythic image of Toronto as a "city of neighbourhoods" and to pay political due to Toronto's pro-urban bourgeois forces. The report's opening lines were ornamented with the words of Jane Jacobs, calling a "successful city neighbourhood . . . a place that keeps sufficiently abreast of its problems so it is not destroyed by them" (quoted in UWT 2004, 1). Later on, the report quoted David Miller's inaugural speech of December 2, 2003. A follower of Jacobs, Miller declared: "Neighbourhoods are what make this city great. We must value what is distinct about our neighbourhoods, and recognize that which has value beyond its cost" (quoted in UWT 2004, 5). On the other hand, the report mobilized particular geographical imaginaries of poor neighborhoods that were extensively built upon the growing literature on the neighborhood effects of poverty.

The 2004 report differentiated its humanitarian discourse about the rise of concentrated non-White poverty in postwar suburbs from previous reports by incorporating visualization, policy competitiveness, scientism, and localism into the logic of its arguments. First, visualization (the reliance on maps and pictures) was perhaps the one characteristic that visibly differentiated *Poverty by Postal Code* from previous reports. For the first time, as Figure 7 shows, black-and-white and color pictures of different neighborhoods of Toronto decorated the front cover of the report and the margins of every single page. This visualization, through the display of selective pictures of neighborhoods and their residents, would soon become a major feature of the United Way's reports, conveying to readers that United Way is indeed "the voice of community." One can detect a similar form of visualization in the United Way's headquarters, located at the heart of downtown Toronto. Upon my arrival at the United Way head office in fall 2013, what quickly grabbed my attention was the politics of interior design. The space was decorated in a neomodernist rendition of the 1970s modernist interior and furniture design: solid bright colors, ornamented with images of non-White people much reminiscent of the advertisements of the United Colors of Benetton. An endless collection of large- and small-print images of smiling, beautiful non-White faces, some in their assumedly traditional outfits, decorated the walls or hung from the ceiling of the lobby and office rooms of the head office. It was hard to miss how the interior design heavily builds upon the ethos of Canada's imperial policy of neocolonial trusteeship and the aestheticized politics of Canada's liberal multiculturalism (see Bannerji 2000). The visual message of the interior space conveyed that the philanthrocapitalist organization is the voice and the hope of Canada's multicultural Others living in Toronto. In turn, these multicultural Others owe their success, displayed through their smiling faces, to the humanitarian benevolence of United Way.

Another layer of visualization in *Poverty by Postal Code* was maps of poverty and its associated social problems in Toronto. Figure 7 displays how maps provided a cartographic image of changes in neighborhood poverty over three decades from 1981 to 2001 (UWT 2004, 7–10). I will discuss in more detail the role of maps and mapping in solidifying the geo-political fear of the immigrant in the next chapters. For now, it suffices to say that color-coded maps gave a two-dimensional visual form to the hitherto text-based territorialized discussion of concentrated non-White poverty. By giving an illusion of *revealing* Toronto's urban problems, color-coded maps cemented a geographical imaginary of those problems in specific localities of postwar suburbs.

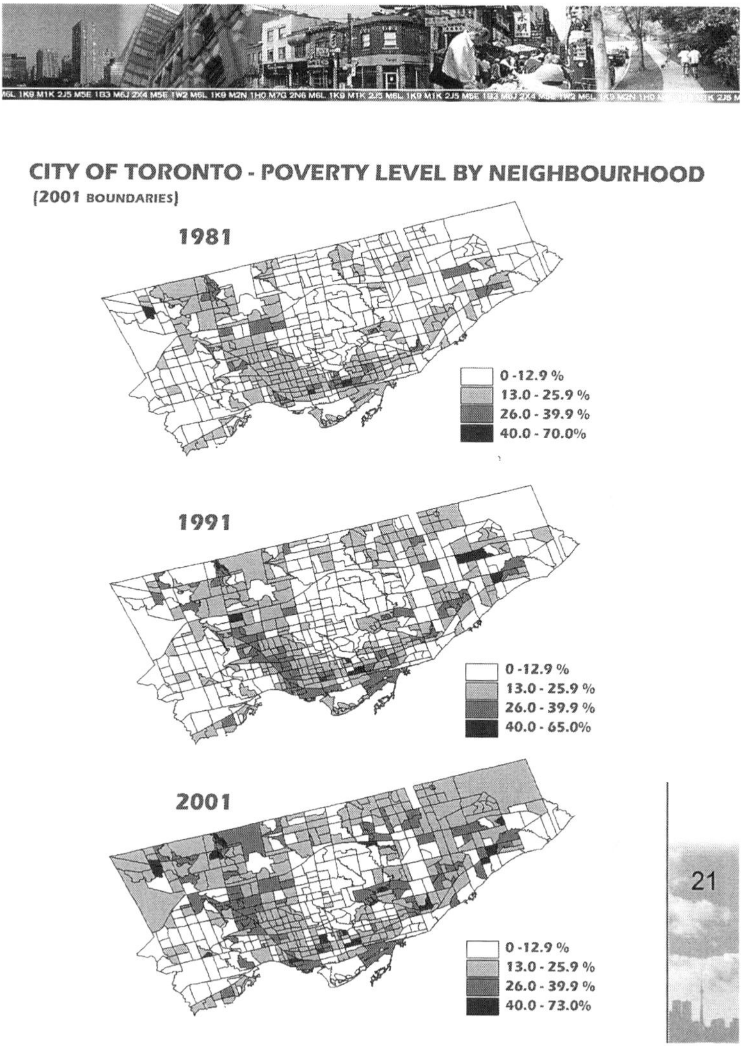

FIGURE 7. A page from *Poverty by Postal Code,* illustrating United Way's mobilization of visual techniques, including the use of neighborhood images and mapping. The images in the page header are from downtown Toronto, while maps showing the growth of neighborhood poverty throughout three decades emphasize postwar suburbs as the location of the poverty problem. Source: United Way, *Poverty by Postal Code: The Geography of Neighbourhood Poverty, 1981–2001* (Toronto: UWT, 2004): 21. Courtesy of United Way Greater Toronto.

The second shift in the report was the explicit way that *Poverty by Postal Code* situated place-based urban policy targeting postwar suburbs as part of Toronto's quest for competitiveness. The report praised the unfolding "renaissance of public policy attention to poor neighbourhoods" in the United Kingdom and the United States.[5] "Canadian cities," the report warned, "have not enjoyed the same kind of public policy attention," which in turn would pose a threat to "the economic and social vitality of an entire region and everyone's quality of life" (UWT 2004, 2). This logic of lagging behind in urban policy mobilities was important to creating a sense of urgency for place-based urban policy in Toronto. A decade later, one of the City's senior policymakers explained:

> Canada, to some extent, lags behind a bit in terms of international trends. Internationally . . . [place-based policy] has been a bit of a focus. Certainly, work taking place in Britain informed the Strong Neighborhoods Task Force. It's one of the reasons it was launched. (I25 2013)

The third shift was an appeal to presumably scientific, evidence-based research, in particular with reference to the growing literature on the neighborhood effects of concentrated poverty and ghettoization in the United States, the United Kingdom, and Canada. The contemporary history of academic attention to concentrated poverty is of particular interest here, not least because this history is explicitly linked to the geo-political fear of so-called race riots. Originated in the United States, the neighborhood effects literature has its roots in the 1987 publication of William Julius Wilson's *The Truly Disadvantaged: The Inner City, the Underclass and Public Policy.* It was in the aftermath of the 1992 Los Angeles unrest of mostly Black and Latino residents, however, that research on the geographical concentration of poverty took off and became an academic subfield of its own with a focus on neighborhood effects of poverty (Burton 1992). The major tenets of the neighborhood effects literature were already at the heart of the broken windows theory that was introduced by James Q. Wilson and George L. Kelling in 1982 and became central to rationalizing the criminalization of poverty and homelessness in New York and Toronto in the 1990s and later was transplanted into the U.S. counterinsurgency strategies in occupied Iraq by the mid-2000s (see Long 2006). By establishing a correlation between location and socioeconomic outcomes, the neighborhood effects literature postulates that living in neighborhoods with high levels of poverty has a negative impact on social development and as such emphasizes the multiplying effects of concentrated poverty in producing poverty and violence (Wilson 1987). Epistemologically, the neighborhood effect literature rearticulates the environmentally determinist discourse of human security in international relations onto the unevenly developed urban spaces of imperial metropoles. Coming to prominence in international relations in the 1990s, human security discourse postulates that "bad neighborhoods" like the Horn of Africa, the Middle East, and other former colonies, provide breeding grounds for violence that could spread to the world's "good neighborhoods" (see Kaldor 1999; Kaldor and Beebe 2010).

As critics have argued, the tautological logic of the neighborhood effects literature easily turns correlation into causation (see Cowen and Parlette 2011). In its emphasis on the cycle and multiplying effects of poverty, the neighborhood effects literature does not go beyond the culture of poverty thesis of the mid twentieth century (see Harrington 1962). A key difference, as Cowen and Parlette (2011) have mentioned, is that the responsibility for poverty is now assigned to the neighborhoods themselves and only indirectly to the poor as individuals. What has remained intact here is the pathologization of poverty and the behavior of those who live in neighborhoods with a high concentration of poverty (Bauder 2002). In its obsessive focus on place and the physical attributes of poor neighborhoods, the neighborhood effects literature rationalizes a particular geographical imaginary of poverty by reiterating the ideological tenets of the early twentieth-century Chicago School of Urban Sociology, in particular the social-Darwinist-inspired and environmentally deterministic idea that the particularities of spatial form, geography, and demography determine social relations. In a similar manner to human security discourse, poverty here is de-historicized; it is disassociated from the processes of the production of uneven urban development and socioeconomic polarization under imperialist capitalism. The focus instead is upon the territorialized geographical imaginaries of poverty (i.e., neighborhoods) rather than poverty as a social relation.

Such conceptions are not limited to the world of academic research. In 2013, I asked a social democratic city councilor about the main problems affecting the priority neighborhood in his riding. He quickly

replied "poverty, poverty, isolation, single-parent families" (I2 2013).
He explained:

> What poverty creates is a neighborhood context where it's tough
> for people to move out of it. . . . From a security perspective,
> poverty creates a number of social ills. You have kids organizing
> themselves into gangs or into groups. Those groups then fight for
> turfs; they fight for a neighborhood base where it'll be their area
> for selling drugs or other activities that they might be involved
> in . . . and that creates all kinds of issues for the people in the
> neighborhood. (I2 2013)

The abovementioned councilor was not alone in pointing to turf politics and its related violence among youths as evidence that poverty
and violence are geographically bounded and territorialized problems.
The ascendency of the neighborhood effects literature into a policy rationale has resulted in the fourth shift in addressing poverty: localism.

Associating poverty with turf politics, gangs, and violence is common among the police, politicians, and the majority of policymakers
with whom I talked (I11 2013; I2 2013; I20 2013; I25 2013). Turf politics, or rather "neighborhoodism" as a youth criminal justice worker
put it, is a reality—and most often a violent reality—for youth from
poor neighborhoods (I31 2013; I16 2013). This neighborhoodism is
related to, yet very different from, the neighborhoodism of Jane Jacobs
and the pro-urban bourgeois forces in Toronto. While the latter builds
upon a celebration of particular aesthetic characteristics of a locality,
the former is indispensably attached to the everyday violence and
contradictions of living within the arbitrary confines of territorially
stigmatized neighborhoods:

> In those larger [public housing] complexes young people tend
> to stay within those complexes, and they have this whole thing,
> not forming gangs per se, but ownership of those neighborhoods,
> and because of the ownership they have in those neighborhoods,
> they [believe they] represent those neighborhoods. . . . I will
> give you the example of Alexandra Park and Regent Park [public
> housing projects], very publicized through the media over the last
> few years in terms of their rivalry. Yonge Street is the boundary.
> Neither one [i.e., certain youth from each area] can go past the

boundary. Their neighborhood issues, their isolation is real. In fact, young people from Alexandra Park [public housing] fear going to the Eaton Centre [shopping mall] because they may be running into someone from Yonge Street or from Regent Park [public housing] who can target them just because they live in Alexandra Park [public housing]. It doesn't even have to be a targeted "You killed my brother, so I'm gonna kill you." It could be as simple as "You're from the neighborhood that killed my brother, so I'm gonna kill you." It's that [kind of] reality [that kids from poor neighborhoods are subjected to]: "I have to stay in my hood to be safe." And that happens all over the city. If you ask people in Scarborough or Malvern Galloway . . . [they] have a similar issue. If you go up to Jane-Finch and Rexdale . . . [they] have a similar issue. . . . They are literally stuck in their four corners. (I31 2013)

How this specific form of neighborhoodism is produced, however, has less to do with poverty and youth gangs per se than with systemic racism, economic marginalization, political alienation, territorial stigmatization, and the criminalization of poverty by the state (the police, urban policy, and the justice and education systems) (I31 2013; I13 2013; I16 2013; see also James 2012a, 2002b).

A youth activist involved with organizing against police brutality in the Jane and Finch neighborhood explained to me how such neighborhoodism is in relation to the geographical imaginaries of non-White poverty and facilitates violence among the youths, which is worth citing in length:

The violence in the community, what we like to term *horizontal violence*—so violence between youth in the community, often youth from the same nationality, is definitely a big concern in these neighborhoods. It's tragic to see that many young people living in the same conditions, and the violence is between each other, . . . instead of against the power structures that are really putting them in those conditions in the first place. . . . Such horizontal violence is a result of those conditions and is the result of, I think, quite a deliberate policy of placing young people in situations and conditions in which that's the only outcome. . . . But the resulting impact of that on young people, who are then involved in illegal forms of survival, or who are pushed out of the

> school system at a very young age, or who are even turned against
> each other by policing . . . is a situation in which there's a lot of
> horizontal violence, a lot of—whether you call it Black-on-Black
> crime, or whatever, but that is definitely a huge concern in the
> neighborhood. I would say that it [i.e., violence] would be on
> people's minds, probably number one. But the number two secu-
> rity concern for people in these communities would be the police,
> whether it's the carding policy that the police have or just stop-
> ping kids, not just kids but really anyone in the neighborhood.
> (I16 2013)

In reaction to the systematic violence that the youth from poor neighborhoods are subjected to on an everyday basis, these youth take refuge in building a sense of ownership in their neighborhoods to the
point of grounding their identities within the geographical limit of
their immediate localities within which they are obliged to live.

The more the violent force of geographical imaginaries of non-
White poverty determines and contains the lives of these youth, the
more they define themselves in territorialized terms. In his studies
of Black postsecondary students living in the Greater Toronto Area
and those living in the Jane and Finch neighborhood (one of Toronto's poorest neighborhoods and a target of urban policy), Carl James
(2012a) observes two different geo-political imaginaries in Black
youth's identity politics:

> The Toronto-wide second-generation Black youth defined "com-
> munity" in racial terms—Blackness. . . . The Jane-Finch youth—of
> Caribbean and African origin—talked of their community first in
> terms of geography, with fixed physical coordinates or boundaries,
> and second in terms of ethno-racial identities. (75–76)

James (2012a, 2012b) relates such neighborhoodism to the territorial
stigmatization and the geographical imaginaries of Jane and Finch
produced not just by the media, politicians, and the police, but also
by the place-based education policies targeting so-called at-risk youth
in neighborhoods having high concentrations of poverty. While education is sold to kids from poor neighborhoods as the only way to get
out of the misery of poverty and violence, the content and politics of

that education reproduce and normalize the socioeconomic, spatial, racialized, and gendered relations that have caused their marginalization and alienation in the first place. The construction of the at-risk designation, James (2012b) argues, is based upon and reproduces racist, classist, and gendered stereotypes of Black youth as "immigrants," "troublemakers," "athletes," "underachievers," and "fatherless." Youth neighborhoodism is partly a reaction to the geographical imaginaries of the immigrant, cemented through systematic racism, classism, sexism and territorialized domination in peripheralized areas of the city and partly the internalization of these geographical imaginaries by the youth.

The police are also an influential force in reinforcing youth neighborhoodism. Place-based policing strategies such as the Toronto Anti-Violence Intervention Strategy, which was in practice from 2006 to 2017, used divide-and-rule tactics to gather information and make arrests in priority neighborhoods (see chapter 3). One of the tactics to deal with so-called gangs has been to put youth from different (rival) neighborhoods together in one cell in detention centers or prisons (I3 2014; Powell 2010). Being aware that whatever disputes that take place in those cells would eventually unfold on the street, the police aim to get the rest of the so-called gang members who are out on the street and arrest them (Powell 2010). Youth activists and social workers explained to me how this tactic has added to street violence, criminalization, and deeper neighborhoodism among youth:

> It's kind of well-known in these neighborhoods that, although the police claim to be in these neighborhoods to prevent the violence between youths, it has quite often the opposite effect in which officers directly and indirectly facilitate contradictions between people. . . . When they raided Driftwood [in Jane and Finch] in 2011 . . . a lot of those kids have . . . a little bit of a situation with youths from Rexdale, and police deliberately put a lot of these youth into cell ranges. . . . Let's say they would bring in one kid who was arrested in [Jane and Finch] and put him on a cell range that had all kids from Rexdale. Obviously, these kids would be quite badly assaulted in prison . . . and this was done almost, very, very frequently. The result of that was not just more violence within the prison, but also that played out on the street. (I6 2013)

How is it that such obvious contradictions of neighborhoodism have not made it into policy debates? The scientific appeal of the neighborhood effects literature has justified a localized understanding of complex issues such as racialization and poverty. This form of localism has become the rationale for taking the neighborhood as the ideal scale for identifying, measuring, and dealing with social problems. A major message of *Poverty by Postal Code* was that "neighbourhoods must move to the top of the public policy agenda" (UWT 2004, 15). And so they did. In both the Priority Neighbourhoods Strategy (City of Toronto 2005) and the Toronto Strong Neighbourhoods Strategy 2020 (City of Toronto 2012a), the neighborhood, detached from the broader sociospatial relations of its production, is taken as the unit of analysis and intervention. As we will see in chapter 5, this localized perspective would be reinforced in the Toronto Strong Neighbourhoods Strategy 2020.

The celebratory justification of neighborhood as the territorial unit of analysis and the geography of urban policy intervention rests upon two interrelated forms of logics: one strand appeals to scientism, while the other appeals to a mythic geographical imaginary of Toronto. The former scientific appeal is based on a positivist epistemology that takes for granted the objectivity of quantitative census data. The latter rationality builds upon the geographical imaginary of Toronto as a city of neighborhoods—one that has been propagated in United Way's policy activism. Despite or rather in spite of its resemblances to the raceless, tolerant geographical imaginary of Toronto in the 1960s and 1970s, this mythic geographical imaginary has erased Toronto's White settler-colonial history and the city's history of racial and class segregation and tensions by presenting a picture in which the diversity and distinctiveness of the city's neighborhoods has always been one of harmony. This is the geographical imaginary against which the geography of concentrated non-White poverty is imagined as a security threat to Toronto's political stability. This latter rationality also received an ideological boost from the city's recent cultural policy, which builds upon the creative city discourse and the commodification of culture, diversity, and neighborhood street life (City of Toronto 2003, 2008a, 2011c; Martin Prosperity Institute 2009).[6]

There are qualitative differences between how the youth in poor neighborhoods define the territoriality of their neighborhoods (and thus their geo-political identities) and how the positivist scientism of place-based urban policy defines the neighborhood as a territorial unit of analysis and intervention. While the former is based on violent everyday experiences of the boundaries of public housing developments or within a bundle of rental apartments on a city block, the latter is based upon population density and a cluster of Statistics Canada census tract territorialities. What these different forms of neighborhoodism share, however, is a narrow focus on an arbitrary territoriality of the neighborhood as either the unit of everyday defense or the unit of scientific analysis. In both cases the geographical imaginaries of a locality are taken for granted and the production of poverty and its racial dimension are disassociated from the broader socioeconomic, spatial, and imperial relations of capitalist uneven development and urbanization.

Youth neighborhoodism has had grave political implications when it comes to the question of social justice and activism. It has affected how youth understand their own state of being besieged within the boundaries of poor neighborhoods. According to a youth criminal justice worker I talked to at the time,

> The youth of Toronto view their issues as their own. I don't see many of them seeing outside of themselves or their neighborhood. . . . They view their problems as what's going on in terms of what they can see and what they can feel, and they don't see anything larger than their own community. They don't go beyond their immediate [surroundings], and this gets into how they understand themselves and understand how [broader] issues can affect their community. (I31 2013)

There are, of course, critical voices among youth within these neighborhoods who have been organizing against police brutality and around housing issues. My point here is to highlight how geo-political ideologies have shadowed the lives of youth living in the most marginalized neighborhoods of Toronto. Such dark shadows have political implications for organizing and mobilizing at the grassroots level.

Neighborhoodism has also contributed to the sensibility of the geo-political fear of the immigrant by normalizing the territorialized and racialized security ideology that animates the conception of poverty-as-risk as a threat to Toronto's political stability. In *Poverty by Postal Code,* for example, "the aesthetic quality of the neighbourhood" was perceived as a fundamental characteristic of "strong and healthy neighbourhoods," "the quality of life" and "economic prosperity" of not just the city's neighborhoods, but of Toronto in general (UWT 2004, 6). The concentration of non-White poverty in pockets of the postwar suburbs, in turn, was understood to be the result of the movement of the immigrant in "the search for lower housing costs" presumably into neighborhoods of lower aesthetic quality (UWT 2004, 3). This view is not limited to the United Way's reports. The city councilor I quoted earlier on security issues in priority neighborhoods gave me a very similar explanation, suggesting that immigration policy is one of the reasons for an increasing racial segregation in Toronto:

> You have people who are coming here who have money and start-up businesses. They locate in good neighborhoods. They buy homes and properties that have considerable value. . . . Then, you have some of the poor folks, or especially those that come as refugees, who generally have little with them in terms of value and in terms of wealth. Then they will, more than likely, find themselves in one of the more difficult districts. Because we have high concentration of social housing, poverty, depressed real estate value. . . . So as poverty concentrates, it has that drag on everything and regrettably, or I guess it depends on which way to look at it, un-regrettably, it makes things a little more affordable, so people with reduced means will find themselves located in these types of 'hoods. From that perspective, I guess, our form of immigration concentrates newcomers into these 'hoods. The good thing about it is that, generally, newcomers to the country usually have a tendency to be hardworking and industrious, and while they'll be living in these neighborhoods for few years, they generally have a tendency to sort of plan their way out and move on. It's the people that kind of get stuck that continue to stay, the ones that, for example, aren't very well educated, the ones whose social networks and own families break up, they kind of get stuck and then you have the soft perpetuation of the cycle that takes over. (I2 2013)

At first glance the argument that cheap housing attracts poor people appears logical. But such argument tells us nothing about how this distribution of relatively affordable housing is the logical result of urban uneven development fueled by capitalist economic competitiveness and the reign of private property. Such statements smoothly abstract the questions of housing and poverty from the sociospatial and racial dimensions of uneven urban development (i.e., gentrification, racism, labor-market segmentation, commodification of housing). At the heart of the above statement is an upside-down picture of reality, one that disassociates the production of concentrated non-White poverty from the production of concentrated White wealth in downtown Toronto. The former cannot exist without the latter, and yet it is only the former that is projected as a problem. This ideological argument around "lower housing costs" will be reiterated in years following and will become influential in the formation and consolidation of place-based urban policy in Toronto.

A SPECTACLE IS HAUNTING TORONTO: THE "PARIS PROBLEM"

The 2004 publication of *Poverty by Postal Code* more forcefully brought the territorialized geographical imaginary of concentrated non-White poverty in Toronto to the attention of policymakers. It was, however, a police-induced spike in gun-related violence among non-White youth in the peripheralized neighborhoods of Toronto throughout 2004 and 2005 that brought the territorialized and racialized geographical imaginary of poverty to the public attention (Siciliano 2010; Powell 2010). By mid-February 2004, then mayor David Miller proposed his Community Safety Plan in reaction to the media frenzy around gun violence. The plan was based on a mix of enforcement and prevention measures designed by the City and the Toronto Police Services to target crime in four stigmatized low-income neighborhoods in postwar suburbs: Jamestown in Etobicoke; Jane-Finch in North York; and Malvern and Kingston-Galloway in Scarborough. Despite the fact that "police data showed them to have relatively less violent crime than other areas of the city" (Siciliano 2010, 68), the public discourse around gun violence and the targeting of immigrant neighborhoods gave new life to the warnings of *Poverty by Postal Code*. In April 2004, United Way and the City of Toronto (with the support of the Government of Canada, the Province of Ontario, and the private sector) formed the Strong Neighbourhood Task Force (SNTF) "with the goal of building an action plan for revitalizing Toronto's neighbourhoods"

(SNTF 2005, 8). When the task force published its report in 2005, *Strong Neighbourhoods: A Call to Action,* it provided the first and most explicit call for "targeted investments in specific neighbourhoods" (SNTF 2005, 9). *A Call to Action* became the blueprint for Toronto's first place-based urban policy, the Priority Neighbourhoods strategy.

The SNTF report was a reiteration of *Enough Talk* (TCSA 2003), *Poverty by Postal Code* (UWT 2004), and Miller's Community Safety Plan (City of Toronto 2004). It emphasized the link between concentrated non-White poverty and crime and identified "patterns of social exclusion based on geography" as constituting "a threat to the health, well-being and prosperity of everyone in our city" (SNTF 2005, 13, 4). Emphasizing the "best practices" and "international experiences" of place-based urban policy in the United States, the United Kingdom, and France, the report recommended *prevention* through place-based social development and community participation so as to deconcentrate poverty (SNTF 2005, 16–17). One of the senior City managers explained to me the importance of prevention in the initiative:

> In 2004, we had the increasing incidents of gun violence. We also had a new mayor, and Mayor Miller decided to develop the Community Safety Plan. The mayor was very clear that prevention is of equal importance, if not more so, to enforcement. . . . For him that broke in two primary pieces: one was increasing economic opportunities, and the other was looking at place-based work. (I3 2014)

While the City and United Way were busy crafting Toronto's first place-based urban policy, the number of gun-related homicides among non-White youth spiked in the summer of 2005 as the result of the earlier police raids in 2004 and the police divide-and-rule tactics in the aftermath of those raids. The majority of these deaths and shootings took place across the city's marginalized neighborhoods. From October 26 to 31, 2005, the City Council debated and then adopted the Toronto Strong Neighbourhoods Strategy as "a civic strategy of neighbourhood building" in order "to strengthen priority neighbourhoods through targeted investment" (City of Toronto 2005). Thirteen neighborhoods with a high concentration of non-White, working-class residents in postwar suburbs were designated as priority neighborhoods: Jamestown, Jane and Finch, Weston–Mount Dennis, Lawrence Heights, Westminster-Branson, Crescent Town, Flemingdon Park–Victoria Village, Steels-L'Amoureaux, Dorset Park, Eglinton East–Kennedy Park, Scarborough Village, Kingston-Galloway, and Malvern.

As city councilors began debating Toronto's first place-based urban policy, on the other side of the Atlantic Ocean Zyed Benn and Bouna Traore, two French youths of Malian and Tunisian descent respectively, were electrocuted while being chased by the police in the Parisian *banlieue* of Clichy-sous-Bois on October 27, 2005. Their deaths sparked the largest uprising of non-White youth in France in history. As the media televised the blazing uprising of the French *banlieues* across the world, a new security discourse dominated the framing of gun violence and concentrated non-White poverty in Toronto. The former fear of the American "Black ghetto" in Toronto was quickly replaced by Toronto's "Paris problem." Media pundits aggressively fed the public with comparisons between Toronto's "growing immigrant underclass," which by now had been territorialized in the city's postwar suburbs, and the "ethnic uprising" of the Parisian *banlieues* (Valpy 2005; Jouanneau 2005; Friesen 2005).

Michael Valpy of the *Globe and Mail,* who at the time asked readers "Could it happen here?," was among the vocal voices demonizing the "Jamaican criminal" as "barbarians inside the gates" only a decade before (see chapter 1; Valpy 1994). Joe Friesen of the *Globe and Mail* answered Valpy's anxious question by quoting an eighteen-year-old from the Jane and Finch neighborhood excitingly saying: "There's a possibility of it happening here. . . . That's how we feel about it. It could be a threat" (Friesen 2005). Friesen also quoted Margaret Parson, then executive director of the African-Canadian Legal Clinic, confirming that

> the area [i.e., Jane and Finch] is a tinderbox that could explode in violence, just like the Paris suburbs did over the past few weeks. "It could easily erupt," she said. "We can look at Paris as an example and prevent this from happening . . . I think the sense of despair, I think the sense of hopelessness, the sense of frustration [are all present]." (Friesen 2005)

The comparison between Toronto's postwar suburbs and the *banlieues* of Paris was made easier by the temporal proximity of the two events. In reality, however, it was a territorialized and racialized security ideology focused on peripheralized spaces that brought Toronto and Paris together in 2005 and afterwards.

The geo-political dimension of this comparison became more transparent when on Boxing Day of 2005 a White female bystander was accidentally killed in a gang-related shooting in downtown Toronto. The accidental death of a White woman in the downtown core dispelled the comfort that gun violence can be contained over "There" among "Them" in immigrant neighborhoods. Politicians at all levels quickly shared their compassion and security concerns. "Yesterday's shootings in Toronto," then Canada's prime minister Paul Martin warned, "serve as a painful reminder that we cannot take our peace or our understanding of it for granted" (*Toronto Star* 2005). The death of Jane Creba "stunned and saddened" then Toronto mayor David Miller, "both as a Torontonian and a father" (*Toronto Star* 2005). Dalton McGuinty, then the Liberal premier of Ontario, touched upon the fear of the penetration of gun violence among "us," stating that "with each loss of a young life to the insanity of guns, we are reminded that this could have been our own daughter, or own son or grandchild, and we are sickened and deeply saddened by this family's loss" (*Toronto Star* 2005).

The Boxing Day shooting reconfirmed the still-strong White-settler-colonial legacies of the hierarchal racialized value of humanity in Toronto. While fifty-two gun-related homicides occurred in 2005, almost all of them young non-White youth, it is only the name of Jane Creba—the young White female bystander who was accidentally killed—that has become the name attached to "the year of the gun" in Toronto. Overnight, a neocolonial discourse of Them, the savages, against Us, the civilized, a discourse heavily infused by a geo-political fear of the immigrant, shifted and fixated public attention on marginalized neighborhoods inhabited by non-White, working-class residents in Toronto. Among media pundits, no one articulated this neocolonial geo-political fear of the immigrant with the clarity of *Toronto Star* columnist Rosie DiManno, who a decade before had warned about the "Jamaican criminal" "pillaging" "our city's innocence" (DiManno 1994). Fueled by a racist rage, DiManno reminded Torontonians that the city

> has taken a boot in the gut [in] the last year. While most of us, in fact, have little to fear from the callous disregard for life exhibited by urban savages (except the hug-a-thug crowd won't have us demonize these poor, misbegotten youth, so "victimized" by the root causes of their own misanthropy—Prime Minister Paul Martin, without any supporting evidence at hand, yesterday described

Monday's dreadful incident as a tragedy and "consequence of ex-clusion"), we certainly should worry for distant neighbours, who cannot just shut the door to keep out violence. It follows them inside; it strangles their households. And there is always, as was proven on Boxing Day, the chance—however slim—the gunfire will come to us, in our shared communal spaces, to our innocent children, a parent rushing past with shopping bags in hand, an off-duty police officer. (DiManno 2005)

DiManno's racist rage differs from the above-mentioned state-ments voiced by politicians. Such difference, however, should not dis-tract us from the geo-political fear of the immigrant that animated all these declarations. DiManno and the elite politicians perceived the Boxing Day shooting as a security threat because for them gun vio-lence had unsettled the geographical imaginary of downtown Toronto as the space of peace, civility, and security. For them, the immigrant, who has come from Other geographies, is part of the internal enemy. The immigrant is the foreigner who never integrated into Canadian society, never adapted to so-called Canadian values and way of life, and thus has become the criminal. The difference in their stances is in the way they perceive the fate of the immigrant, hence their solutions to the immigrant problem. For DiManno and many on the Right, the "urban savages" are not civilizable; they are a lost cause. Whereas for the elite liberal and social-democratic politicians, the immigrant has the potential to become civilized, can be rehabilitated, with proper tutelage in the form of integration, empowerment, and policing. That is to say, with proper neocolonial trusteeship the immigrant has the potential to become a resilient liberal subject, one who is no longer a threat to the security and peace of imperialist capitalism. In the fol-lowing chapters, we will see how building on this geo-political fear of the immigrant and liberal humanitarian trusteeship, place-based urban policies of development and policing would become the state solution to prevent the "Paris problem" in Toronto.

3

Policing Immigrant Neighborhoods

FROM MILITARIZED TO PREVENTIVE POLICING

> I was in Paris for a [municipal] dialogue [in 2010], when the federal government brought us forward to talk on two issues: youth violence and immigration. . . . There [in Paris] seems to be racialization, poverty, lack of opportunities, social exclusion, and they are taking to the streets. . . . We've had our moments [in Toronto]. . . . I don't think we're too far from the Paris instability.
>
> —Manager, City of Toronto

PREVENTING THE "PARIS PROBLEM"

In January 2006, less than two weeks after the accidental death of Jane Creba, the Ontario Liberal government of Dalton McGuinty announced a new $51 million Anti-Gun Strategy. The provincial strategy had already been on its way since 2004 with the creation of a Guns and Gangs Crown (i.e., Crown attorney) Task Force and its expansion in October 2005 (Ministry of Community Safety and Correctional Services 2011a). The new Anti-Gun Strategy added funding for a Toronto-specific place-based policing initiative and "a new, state-of-the-art Operation Centre for the Guns and Gangs Task Force" in Toronto (Ontario Attorney General 2009, 4–5). Almost immediately, then Toronto police chief Bill Blair (currently serving as Canada's minister of public safety and as a member of Parliament representing Toronto's Scarborough Southwest) introduced the Toronto Anti-Violence Intervention Strategy (TAVIS). The Toronto Police kicked off TAVIS with an initial budget of $7 million for the first year and a yearly budget of $5 million for the following years until 2016.[1] By June 2007, the McGuinty government had scaled up TAVIS to a regional scale. The Ontario Liberal government established a Provincial Anti-Violence Intervention Strategy (PAVIS) at the cost of $6.3 million in extra investment (Ministry of Community Safety and Correctional Services 2011b).[2] With an allocated budget of $26 million, the "state-of-the-art" Operation Centre was added to a new, 287,000-square-foot Toronto Police College on a sixteen-acre site located in Toronto's southwest end.[3] Opened in the late summer of 2009, the college came at a final cost of $76 million. The College Centre is shared for training purposes between the Toronto Police Service and the Department of National Defense and contains a "Tactical Village" that "simulates a city street complete with stores and offices that have two floors" and a 360-degree "Battle House" that "stimulates an enclosed space where officers can train for high-risk situations in close confines using simulations" (TPS 2009, 4–5).

TAVIS brought militarized policing into the streets of immigrant neighborhoods and intensified police violence. The first spectacular raid by TAVIS took place in the early hours of May 16, 2006, in the Jamestown neighborhood. Six hundred officers in military gear using rams and stun grenades targeted the Jamestown public housing project in the largest raid in the history of Toronto Police at the time. Around one hundred people were arrested, and more than one thousand criminal charges were laid (many of which were later dropped). In a police raid with "military precision," then police chief Blair informed the media, "the leadership of the Jamestown Crew [was] *surgically* removed from the community" (CBC 2006). Similar to the residents' accounts in the 1990s, Jamestown residents described the neighborhood during the raid as "a war zone" that, in their view, was not that different from the televised scenes of Kandahar under the occupation of the Coalition Forces (see Friesen 2006; Jackson 1994). From 2006 to 2014, TAVIS participated in at least one major raid every year. The yearly raids go back to the 2004 Malvern raid and 2005 Jane and Finch one that triggered the "year of the gun" by 2005, which in turn, as we saw, helped rationalize the "Paris problem" in Toronto. With the introduction of PAVIS, these raids increasingly scaled up and intensified in simultaneous regional raids (i.e., ones outside of the City of Toronto proper).

Critics of TAVIS have focused on the naked and spectacular violence of policing. This is understandable partly due to the sudden intensification of militarized policing in Toronto and partly due to the extremely tough task of criticizing the police (see Sewell 2010; I1

2014; I15 2014; I18 2013).[4] There is, of course, an urgent need to stop or at least mitigate the violence that many non-White youths living in working-class neighborhoods have been subjected to on an everyday basis. The very few critical studies on policing strategies in Toronto have only focused on linking policing to the punitive law-and-order turn in Canadian public policy and legislation (see Kishman, Buse, and Steedman 2000; Heroux 2011; Siciliano 2010; Sewell 2010; Gordon 2006). This conception of policing as exclusively a coercive power has resulted in perceiving and analyzing the Priority Neighbourhoods Strategy and TAVIS as separate policies, with the former mobilizing (social) development and the latter injecting coercive policing. Understanding policing as solely a coercive power is a common feature of many critical analyses. While these studies conceive notions of crime, the criminal, and the law as relational and socially constructed, they also conceive of policing as a coercive tool of the state that is central to the repression of the working class. Limiting our understanding of policing to coercion also limits our understanding of state violence to the most visible signs. As Mark Neocleous (2000) has extensively argued, to critically engage with state police power, we should avoid falling into the "repressive hypothesis" of policing and instead critically engage with the productive nature of state police power.

In *Policing Black Lives: State Violence in Canada from Slavery to the Present,* Robyn Maynard underlines that a historicized conception of policing requires an "expansive understanding of state violence," one that would allow us "to examine the seemingly disconnected state and state funded institutions that continue to act, in concert, to cause Black suffering and subjugation" (2017, 7). Scrutinizing the reproduction of anti-Black racism beyond the legal and criminal systems, in immigration, child welfare, social services, and education and medical institutions, Maynard directs us to the importance of the productive dimension of policing in understanding racialization and racism. The productive dimension of police power is essential for the continuation of coercive enforcement (Dubber and Valverde 2006). The productive dimension of policing is about moderating violence, which as Eyal Weizman (2011, 3–4) argues elsewhere, "is part of the very logic of violence"—that is, the continuation of violence necessitates the moderation of violence. As we shall see, by embedding policing in social development and co-opting various agencies in housing, education, and arts, productive policing functions like counterinsurgency strategies, and has become central to both the war on poverty and the recomposition of colonial relations into neocolonial relations of domination in Toronto.

Analyses of policing in Toronto also suffer from what political geographers John Agnew and Stuart Corbridge (1995) called "the territorial trap." More than twenty years ago, Agnew and Corbridge directed our attention to an explicit assumption of the state as a "fixed territorial entity" in political theory, in which the state "operat[es] much the same over time and irrespective of its place within the global geopolitical order" (1995, 78). The privileging of the territorial national state in analysis of security and policing has resulted in a series of geo-political assumptions, including the separation and opposition of the domestic and the foreign dimensions of security (Agnew and Corbridge 1995, 92–95). Maynard's (2017) work on policing Black lives and her emphasis on bringing into our analysis Canada's foreign policy in Africa and the Caribbean is a welcome exception. Engaging with policy mobilities across time, geography, and scale, here I extend Agnew and Corbridge's (1995) critique to examining policing, focusing on how the nexus of racialization-development-security works in making spaces and subjects of policing in Toronto. What policing, counterinsurgency, and humanitarianism have in common is a form of political administration of assumedly problem populations and spaces (Neocleous 2000; Bachmann, Bell, and Holmqvist 2015).

TAVIS was known as the signature brainchild of then Toronto police chief Blair, who by late 2019 became the federal minister of Public Safety in the current prime minister Justin Trudeau's minority Liberal government. According to police and security officials, TAVIS was "an intensive community mobilization strategy," "a multi-pronged approach" intended to "solve community problems" and "reduce crime and increase safety in Toronto neighbourhoods" (PSC 2013a; TPS 2016). The strategy had three components: high visibility; high enforcement; and high suppression (I11 2013). These components were supported by the Neighbourhood TAVIS Initiative, the Divisional TAVIS Callbacks, and the Rapid Response Teams, respectively. Neighbourhood TAVIS officers were responsible for "empower[ing] community" by "engage[ing] with community members" and "partner[ing] with other agencies and community organizations" (PSC 2013a; TPS 2016) through a variety of community activities from planting flowers and cleaning parks to playing basketball with (mostly Black and male) youth.

While TAVIS rationalized their targeting with reference to assumedly scientific police crime statistics (I11 2013), the territorialized and racialized security ideology at the heart of the geo-political fear of the immigrant in Toronto was key to their focus on particular spaces and subjectivities for intelligence gathering. "Troubled," "broken," and "high-risk" were the exchangeable names that the police use to refer to targeted immigrant neighborhoods in our conversations (I11 2013; I12 2013). Key tenets of the neighborhood effects literature are at the heart of the police's perception and conception of these neighborhoods. In 2013, a high-rank TAVIS officer told me that the major issues that affect security in priority neighborhoods are "lack of social cohesion and urban design" (I11 2013). Violence, in this logic, is conceived as the consequence of the breakdown of social cohesion resulting from concentrated poverty in immigrant neighborhoods and the design of particular buildings, public housing projects, and parts of neighborhoods that are both isolating and inaccessible to police. The implicit and explicit environmental determinism in the police conception of so-called troubled neighborhoods is not particular to TAVIS. Such forms of environmental determinism are rooted in the long history of understanding street gangs as territorialized and racialized phenomena, particularly in the influential theories of Robert Park and Fredric Thrasher, major figures of the Chicago School of Urban Sociology in the early twentieth century—which, as mentioned earlier, are also at the core of the neighborhood effects literature.

Fredric Thrasher (1927) had a particular geographical imaginary of gang formation and urban violence, one that was deeply ingrained in the geographical imaginaries of immigrant neighborhoods in Chicago in the early twentieth century. Gangs, for Thrasher, were territorialized and racialized phenomena. It was the high level of "neighborhood social disorganization" in the poor immigrant enclaves and slums of Chicago that, according to him, had turned these areas into breeding grounds for street gangs. In Park's and Thrasher's understanding of street gangs in early twentieth-century Chicago, the de facto racialized figure of the gangster was the immigrant at the time: the Irish, the Italian, and the Polish. In twenty-first-century Toronto, that racialized figure is the immigrant of our time: the Black and other non-White youth living in poverty-ridden areas of the city (Tator and Henry 2006; Smith 2007; Comack 2012; Maynard 2017). A City staff person involved with the City's Youth Development Unit explained to me the Toronto police officers' geographical imaginaries of the criminal:

> When TAVIS first arrived into the city, I was one of the few persons [who] was asked graciously to present to them [information about targeted neighborhoods]. They brought all the options, and we did the presentation and explained [that this is] what you're going to be facing when you enter the neighborhood. And it was actually kind of scary because lots of those guys had already had a pre-conceived notion of what the person they're going after looks like. (I13 2013)

Such perceptions are the outcome of systemic racism ingrained in the geographical imaginaries of crime in Canada; as we saw in the birth of the "Jamaican criminal" in the mid-1990s, these imaginaries were also present in the White Canada Policy. In a manner similar to the legal sanctioning of the "undesirable immigrant" in Canada's immigration policies until 1962, the law has also sanctioned racist perceptions of the criminal in our present time (see Maynard 2017).

By the late 1990s and early 2000s, changes to Canada's criminal code further normalized the territorialized and racialized conception of gang members as a security threat. In Canada, the vaguely defined category of gang was only criminalized in 1997. In 2001, under the Anti-Terrorism Act, Canada's criminal code was amended to decrease the number of members required for the charge of organized crime from five to three individuals. These changes have not only increased the intensity and scale of police surveillance and raids in the name of fighting guns, drugs, and gangs; they have also contributed to the criminalization of entire families and neighborhoods and increasing incarceration of non-White youth, and particularly Black youth. A youth criminal justice worker recounted:

> I had a young person who had older family siblings who were involved in gangs. He was not. . . . He was deemed a gang member and was sent to probation on Guns and Gangs [charges]. I argued at that point, and unfortunately there was no way to take him off that label. . . . This is a huge barrier in marginalized communities

because, just because I'm from this 'hood doesn't mean I'm a gang member, because I'm a young Black male doesn't mean I'm a gangster. . . . these are the things that have been happening on the streets. (I31 2013)

Rather than a rupture in policing, the Toronto Police used the rolling out of TAVIS to systematically intensify many existing policing strategies in Toronto and elsewhere. Place-based policing and the military-style raids, as Heroux (2011) and Siciliano (2010) have mentioned, built upon targeted policing strategies in poor neighborhoods of downtown and postwar suburbs going back to the 1980s. Since 1982, the Metropolitan Toronto Police (which became the Toronto Police Service after the 1998 amalgamation) has been involved in community policing in targeted poor areas, such as Parkdale and Jane and Finch (Murphy 1988). By the end of the 1980s, community policing became an important topic of debate among police forces and policymakers in Canada—as it was in the United States and the United Kingdom. In 1990, the Solicitor General of Canada released a report, *A Vision of the Future of Policing in Canada: Police Challenge 2000,* in which he argued that community policing is an important strategy for strengthening the connections between the police and citizens (Normandeau and Leighton 1990). A year later, the solicitor general of Canada, Barry N. Leighton, declared community policing as "the most progressive approach to contemporary policing" in an article published in the *Canadian Journal of Criminology* (1991, 486).

James Q. Wilson and George L. Kelling's (1982) "broken windows theory" was extremely influential in reviving the debates and strategies of community policing in the United States and soon after in Canada in the 1980s and 1990s (see Leighton 1991; Ungerleider and McGregor 1991; for a critical take, see Harcourt 2001). TAVIS practices of carding and high-visibility policing have their policing rationale in the broken-windows-based community policing strategies such as the stop-question-and-frisk program, which started during Rudy Giuliani's mayoralty in New York City in the 1990s and which continued into the 2000s. In Toronto, in the aftermath of then mayor Mel Lastman's war on squeegees, the city council introduced community policing in 1999. Known as Community Action Policing (CAP), the strategy mandated police officers to target specific "hotspots" and particular behaviors in order to prevent "uncommitted crime" (CSTP

2000, 8).[5] Increased police presence and "stop and chats" were two of the main components of the strategy. Neighborhoods such as Regent Park, Parkdale, the downtown east, Jane and Finch, and Rexdale were the major targets of CAP. Already in 2000, the Committee to Stop Targeted Policing (CSTP) published a report and criticized the disproportionate targeting of homeless people, squeegees, panhandlers, non-White people, Indigenous peoples, psychiatric survivors, street-level drug users, and sex workers (CSTP 2000, 20).

The history of militarized policing in Ontario (and Canada) also goes beyond the introduction of TAVIS in Toronto. Canada's first militarized police unit, the Tactics and Rescue Unit, was established in 1975 by the Ontario Provincial Police in order to help securitize the 1976 Summer Olympics in Montreal in the context of the birth of liberal multiculturalism in Canada and the branding of the country as the peacekeeper and humanitarian. By 2000, there were already sixty-five Emergency Task Force units operating in Canada within the federal, provincial, and municipal jurisdictions (Siciliano 2010, 130). In Toronto, poor neighborhoods with public housing projects, such as Lawrence Heights, Malvern, and Jamestown, were the targets of Emergency Task Force raids during the 1980s, raids that residents at the time described as being similar to occupation "by a foreign army" (Jackson 1994, 226).

RACIALIZATION AND THE VIOLENCE OF ANTIVIOLENCE POLICING

TAVIS was quickly applauded as a success by the Toronto police, the city's mayors (Miller and Ford), mainstream media, Toronto Community Housing (TCH),[6] and some residents. Yet, the spectacular violence of the joint military-style raids of TAVIS Rapid Response Teams and the Guns and Gangs Unit eventually raised eyebrows and criticisms. A few years into its implementation, there was no clear evidence that TAVIS mitigated gun violence in immigrant neighborhoods; on the contrary, increasing numbers of community workers, activists, and academics believed that the combination of intelligence-led policing, raids, and the subsequent detentions and imprisonments had exacerbated evictions, racism (in particular anti-Black and anti-Muslim racism), criminalization, stigmatization, and gang violence in these neighborhoods (Wortley 2013; I6 2013; I16 2013; I22 2013; I31 2013).[7]

As part of intelligence-led policing, TAVIS officers were mandated to "connect" with different partners in targeted neighborhoods. Landlords and particularly Toronto Community Housing were among these partners (I11 2013; I31 2013; I16 2013). Since 1988, Toronto Community Housing and the Toronto Police have had an agreement that allows the police to act as an agent of Toronto Community Housing on their properties to enforce Ontario's Trespass to Property Act (I31 2013). However, neither Toronto Community Housing nor the Toronto Police publicized this agreement until 2013 (I31 2013). The consequence of such opacity was that "a lot of young people in [public housing] communities didn't understand why they were being questioned when they were on those properties, and that resulted in high volumes of cardings and harassment," emphasized a youth justice worker (I31 2013). The often violent and dehumanizing practice of stopping, searching, and questioning non-White youth (particularly Black youth) on Toronto Community Housing properties caused tensions between residents and TAVIS (Winsa and Rankin 2013a). Getting into trouble in these police encounters and being arrested during the raids most often meant collective punishment: the criminalization and eviction of the whole family. Community activists have been vocal about the violence of such practices, even though their voices remain unheard:

> Raids are also an example of how landlords and cops work together to oppress our communities. For example, after the 2005 raids on Jamestown (in Rexdale), which arrested around 100 [people], TCH evicted the families of many of the youth arrested—before the youth were even put on trial! Many tenants have already been kicked out, while others fought and continue to fight the notices. (Joshi-Vijayan 2008)

Another criticism of TAVIS was related to its use of divide-and-rule tactics to gather information. As mentioned in chapter 2, TAVIS officers intentionally put together detained youth from rival neighborhoods in one cell in the hope of getting their followers out on the streets. Another police tactic was to systematically exploit tensions among various racialized groups in order to gain information about the immigrant as the gangster in the targeted neighborhoods (Powell 2010, I16 2013; I31 2013). Here, TAVIS capitalized on already existing deep-seated and hegemonic forms of racism in Toronto, in particular, anti-Black racism and more recently anti-Muslim racism. They also exploited the vulnerability of non-White working-class families who desperately hope for a different future for their children. As a youth activist against police brutality explained to me:

> [TAVIS] community policing is to divide the community, to find people they can work with . . . new immigrant communities that maybe don't have as much experience dealing with police harassment, who can then be used against the more problematized sections of the community, whether that be the Jamaican community, or the Somali community. . . . For example, the South Asian community, or the East Asian, like Vietnamese [and] the Filipino community, I think the police attempt to exploit them because, let's say, their children don't face the same conditions as African children, as not as many of them are pushed out of school. Expulsion and suspension rates are definitely lower for these communities and although they're living in those same buildings and living with the same poverty. The police, I think, feel that they are better able to relate, or better able to convince these communities into endorsing further police occupation. (I16 2013)

The racialized politics of this divide-and-rule has exacerbated antagonisms among various sections of the non-White working-class populations. It has intensified and normalized specific forms of racism such as anti-Black and anti-Muslim racisms as well as racialized forms of horizontal violence among the non-White working class youth.

Criticism of TAVIS was not limited to community workers and activists. Some current and former politicians increasingly became vocal against the violence of TAVIS. The present leader of the federal NDP Party, Jagmeet Singh, has been one of the most vocal and popular critics of racialized policing since his time as the former NDP MPP for Bramalea-Gore-Malton. Among the ten City staff whom I interviewed from 2013 to 2014, from senior managers and directors to community development and youth development officers, all were critical of and at times very disappointed with TAVIS. For some, TAVIS's high visibility in immigrant neighborhoods was the major problem and the cause of tensions between the community and the police (I13 2013). Others saw the racist implementation of policing strategies and the lack of proper informing of and democratic engagement with the community as major issues (I13 2013; I18 2013; I26 2013). The contradiction between the violence of the Rapid Response Teams and the so-called positive and friendly strategies of the TAVIS Neighbourhood Officers was the most common criticism (I13 2013; I18 2013; I19 2013; I26 2013). For policymakers at the City, this contradiction had the exact opposite results in the targeted neighborhoods, producing increasing fear among residents and a pervasive dislike and hatred of the police among non-White youth (I13 2013; I18 2013; I19 2013; I26 2013; I15 2014). In 2013, a City staff person working with at-risk youth shared his frustration about TAVIS:

[What] is challenging . . . is [that] half of the TAVIS division is the Neighborhood Initiative Officers (the ones who are on the bikes). They are smiling. They are happy. . . . The other half is the crash team [the Rapid Response Team]. Those are the guys who come with eighteen black[-dressed] men, dark thing on their faces, and grate through the doors. They put handcuffs on moms. They throw kids in handcuffs. They tear apart the house for drugs and then they leave. And unfortunately for the guys who are doing the good [policing] work, they get to face the aftermath of what happens after these guys [the Rapid Response Team] go into a neighborhood. You have, on the one hand, a neighborhood [which] lacks trust. . . . They don't believe the City has their best interest. Then these guys [TAVIS] come in and prove them right, and then we expect them [people in the neighborhood] to kind of play along when something like a shooting happens. . . . A shooting happens. I want to tell them [the police] that it happened. But those are the same guys who broke into my house and tore down my grandma, or tore down my neighbor's grandma and handcuffed her. You want me to go and talk to them? No way. So now, you have the criminals, the real criminals in the neighborhoods who know these guys will never talk because we all don't trust you [the police]. There is this kind of divide and conquer mentality that comes from this unbalance of policies around. On the one hand, we gonna be nice to them, and on the other hand, we gonna punch them in the mouth. (I13 2013)

Another controversial aspect of TAVIS policing was the practice of carding. Carding is a reference to an increasingly common practice of police officers who, upon stopping a person, fill out "contact cards" to record personal information for intelligence purposes.[8] Since the early 2000s, many community activists and residents have voiced their concerns about the systemic racism embedded in carding and police stops; these criticisms greatly increased after the rolling out of TAVIS in 2006 (Wortley and Owusu-Bempah 2011, 2012). In 2008, after an Ontario court ruling on the case of a Black man, Fitzroy Osbourne, who refused to stop and talk to TAVIS officers, then police chief Blair openly admitted his force has a problem with racial profiling. Much similar to the arguments of the 1970s, Blair saw racism in the Toronto Police force as a problem of "individual bias."[9] It was not until the *Toronto Star*—following a contested freedom-of-information request—obtained information of over 1.7 million civilian contact cards filled out by Toronto police officers between 2003 and 2008 that the racialized dimension of carding practices was publicly criticized as more than the problem of a few bad apples, confirming earlier studies by showing numbers (see Tator and Henry 2006; Smith 2007).[10] In February 2010, the *Toronto Star* published a special series, *Race Matters,*[11] based on obtained police data, in which it argued that "male blacks aged 15–24 are stopped and documented 2.5 times more than white males the same age" (Rankin 2010). In 2012, the *Toronto Star* updated its data analysis and published another series, *Known to Police,* in which it used fresh data of 1.25 million contact cards (involving 788,000 individuals) from 2008 to mid-2011 (Rankin 2012).[12] The updated analysis confirmed the earlier argument of racial profiling and highlighted that "Toronto police stop and document black and brown people far more than whites" (Rankin and Winsa 2012a, 2013).[13]

The issue of racial profiling was also criticized by progressive academics, particularly by criminologists Scot Wortley and Akwasi Owusu-Bempah at the University of Toronto (also see Tator and Henry 2006). Wortley and Owusu-Bempah argue that non-White people in Canada "suffer from racial profiling as well as from relatively harsh treatment with respect to arrest decisions, police use of force, pre-trial decision making and sentencing" (2012, 24; 2011). They concurred with James (1998, 173) that the adversarial nature of these police stops contributes to Black youth's hostility toward the police (Wortley and

Owusu-Bempah 2012, 15). The *Toronto Star*'s investigations pushed the Toronto Police Services Board to call for an independent review of police contacts with citizens (Rankin and Winsa 2012b). The public scrutiny of TAVIS gained additional attention when a few young Black male activists stepped forward and publicized their own experiences with police. In 2013, Kina Singh, a 39-year-old law student and activist at the time, and his friend shared with the *Toronto Star* the results of their freedom-of-information request for contact card data (Rankin 2013). On the same day, Alok Mukherjee, then Toronto Police Services Board chair, stated, "TAVIS [has] lost its way in terms of the community components" and warned, "TAVIS ultimately becomes simply synonymous with an enforcement piece. And that's when it becomes, in my mind, counterproductive" (quoted in Winsa and Rankin 2013b). A couple of days later, the *Toronto Star* (2013) published an editorial call for a "reform [of the] 'carding' system that targets minorities." In early 2014, a group of lawyers and activists (including Kina Singh) moved ahead with a human rights complaint and accused the Toronto Police practice of carding as racially discriminatory (Winsa and Rankin 2014). These public criticisms of and activisms around police racial profiling pushed other mainstream media to pick up the issue (see Cole 2015).

City staff and community workers with whom I talked had similar concerns about TAVIS. In their views, TAVIS was ineffective in building social cohesion in immigrant neighborhoods (I26 2013; I19 2013; I18 2013). As discussed earlier, for many involved with place-based policy in Toronto, the major problem in these low-income neighborhoods is their assumed disconnection from mainstream economy and society in general. Disconnection is seen as the major cause of segregation. The geo-political fear of segregation here is interesting. The alienating experience of marginality, so the argument goes, has resulted in a growing number of youths disassociating themselves from Canadian society and the Canadian state, hence taking their lives into their own hands. Gang formation, these critics contend, is one consequence of this disconnectedness and its quasi-sense of autonomy and belonging (I13 2013; I26 2013; I1 2014). These critics believe that the naked violence of TAVIS adds to the alienation of non-White youth and their distance from Canadian values and society. The violent police raids and the practice of carding, as a City staff member working with the at-risk youth explained to me, ultimately changed the neighborhood opinion in that they [the non-White youth] no longer [consider themselves] Canadian, no longer Torontonian, no longer part of the society that they live in and as a result they create their own subcultures, which in a lot of ways follow that of gang-USA kind of ghetto mentality of Us against Them. [That mentality includes:] we have to create our own trade system, our own economic system, our own way of defending ourselves. And a code that says, if I get hurt or someone victimizes me, I can't go to the police because those are the people who were beating me up the last six weeks. I need to get it done and do it myself, which is where the violence begins to stem from. You have racist policies or policies that were not necessarily racist in intent but in delivery. Racial profiling is of that nature, which led to people being kind of segregated and separated apart, which led to youth being able to be kind of into this system of violence, sex and drugs, and then not being able to return. (I13 2013)

The "ghetto mentality of Us against Them," in this argument, is not simply about (Them) the police, but rather more importantly (Them) the national state via the police. Gangs, for these critics, are not a problem of urban violence per se. They are also a geo-political threat to nation building, which is where the question of social cohesion comes in. These critics are opposed to neither state targeting of concentrated non-White poverty nor community-based policing. Rather, their opposition is limited to opposing naked violence:

I think community policing is an important way for the community to establish a relationship with the police service and for the police service to establish a relationship with the community. When I say "a relationship," I don't mean just knowing the local officers but understanding the system, the services that exist within the police service as a whole. I think it's a very important relationship that for many reasons gets tainted and twisted in all sorts of ways. It's just that the Toronto Police are another service provider that is in the neighborhood. They have a role that potentially could be enforcement. We have to look at how the community accesses that service, to understand how it works and how it navigates and how it responds in some situations. I think community policing is just building that relationship. I also think that it's not an isolated service. If we talk about community policing, versus just policing, *it's about [the question of] how is police service embedded into place-based strategies.* (I26 2013, emphasis added)

The Toronto Police were well aware of these critiques, although they questioned their validity at the time. In my interview with two high-ranking TAVIS officers in 2013, they stated that they did not believe there is any contradiction between the functions of the Rapid Response Team and the TAVIS Neighbourhood Officers. These two arms of TAVIS were complementary, in their view. The real problem, they argued, lay in the gap between the community's perceptions of police work and police work in reality. The pervasive hostility toward the police in immigrant neighborhoods, in their view, was mainly based on "media representation," the "emotional reaction of the community," and "people's ignorance" of what policing is about. Policing, for these officers, is about "protecting life and property," and that was exactly what TAVIS forces were doing through their raids and neighborhood relations (I11 2013). These TAVIS officers also denied any systemic racism in policing and racial profiling. As with then police chief Blair, the officers acknowledged incidents of racism as the result of individual bias, but emphasized that there is no racism in the police system. In response to my question about the *Toronto Star* police data on racial profiling, TAVIS officers argued that what "appears" as racial profiling has to do "with our service delivery and management." It is the result of the "lack of efficiency in service delivery," which, according to them, could be solved by better coordinating various police officers assigned to patrol the same neighborhood (I11 2013).

PREVENTION AND RESILIENCY IN THE RELATIONAL FORMATION OF POLICING AND INTERNATIONAL RELATIONS

The rolling out of TAVIS reignited discussions about and experimentations with embedding community policing in social development strategies (see Russell and Taylor 2014). As mentioned earlier, since the 1980s, community policing has been the dominant form of so-called progressive policing in North America and the United Kingdom

(Murphy 1988; Leighton 1991; Ungerleider and McGregor 1991). Today, the goals of community policing, similar to those of counterinsurgency, are framed through concepts of prevention, resiliency, and intelligence (CACP 2003; Russell and Taylor 2014). Already in 2003, the Crime Prevention Committee of the Canadian Association of Chiefs of Police argued that social-development-based prevention with its core emphasis on community has the benefit of combating "complex social, economic and cultural factors that contribute to crime" and of connecting "criminal justice practices with community-based initiatives" (CACP 2003, 11). In Toronto, social-development-based community policing quickly became a preventive solution to the "Paris problem." The shift to prevention in policing was influenced by the earlier critiques of community policing in Toronto (see CSTP 2000) and the broader popularity of prevention and resiliency in international relations, from the chambers of the World Health Organization (WHO), the World Bank, and the United Nations on to those of the Coalition Forces.

The past two decades have witnessed increasing policy mobilities between police and military forces at various scales (Bachmann, Bell, and Holmqvist 2015). With the return to the fore of counterinsurgency through the War on Terror, the question of what form of policing is best in terms of internal enemies gained a new urgency in Western countries, including in Canada. In 2008, following the recommendation of the Canadian High Commission in London, the Canadian Association of Chiefs of Police conducted and published a discussion paper, *Building Community Resilience to Violent Ideologies* (CACP 2008). The paper focused on Prevent, the (in-)famous radicalization prevention component of the United Kingdom's counterterrorism strategy called CONTEST (for critiques of Prevent, see Kundnani 2009; Qureshi 2018). The paper highlighted the "key lessons" of the United Kingdom's Prevent strategy for Canada. Among such lessons was "the importance of a coherent whole-of-government approach that is highly centralized at the policy level, and highly flexible at the implementation level" (CACP 2008, 9). A whole-of-government approach to community policing, the report explained, "must also involve health authorities, school boards, social and community services, faith-and ethnic-based groups and non-governmental organizations" (CACP 2008, 9). "Non-police, non-security partners," the report argued, "play a significant role" in prevention-focused community policing strategies (CACP 2008, 12). The report also emphasized the importance of the neighborhood scale to the success of the Prevent strategy in the United Kingdom. At the end, the report recommended the adaptation of the Prevent strategy for the Canadian context and only in passing mentioned that the Prevent strategy's focus on "a specific ethno-cultural community [i.e., Arab and South Asian Muslims] is at odds with Canada's long-standing approach to multiculturalism and community engagement" (CACP 2008, 4).

The emphasis on a whole-of-government approach is central to embedding policing in social policy. What it means is that the fight against the internal enemy needs to make use of all relevant policy areas and state apparatuses. The travel history of the concept of whole-of-government is useful for our discussion here. The concept first became popular in international relations in the late twentieth century. It had already been put into practice under a variety of names such as "comprehensive approach," "unity of effort," "joint-up government," and "integrated mission" in a whole array of state warfare and imperialist interventions—from peace operations to international development and humanitarianism and on to counterinsurgency and urban warfare (see Bell 2011b; Friis 2010; Patrick and Brown 2007). In international relations, the ideological premise of the whole-of-government approach is rooted in the geographical imaginaries of underdevelopment, poverty, and inadequate governance in so-called failing states posited as threats to global peace and security (Bell 2011b, 325). Already in 2006, the Canadian government advocated the usefulness of a whole-of-government approach in the war in Afghanistan (Government of Canada 2006; Bell 2011a). By 2008, the whole-of-government approach formed an important pillar of Canada's counterinsurgency strategy (Government of Canada 2008; Bell 2011a)—itself an adaptation of the counterinsurgency strategies of the United Kingdom and United States (see Bell 2011a). Canadian police forces, including the Toronto Police Service, were active participants in Canada's War on Terror in Afghanistan (see TPS 2009, 1); thus the Toronto Police was familiar with the whole-of-government framework in counterinsurgency before bringing its officers back for policing immigrant neighborhoods.

In 2009, the Institute for Strategic International Studies (ISIS), the research institute of the Canadian Association of Chiefs of Police (and later renamed to Executive Global Studies), devoted its annual research report, *The Intervention Zone,* to youth violence, community policing, and prevention (ISIS 2009).[14] The "Paris problem" and the geo-political fear of the immigrant are central to the arguments of *The Intervention Zone* report, which starts from the premise that for a country like Canada that relies on immigration, domestic politics is always connected to international politics. Policing in Canada thus requires, we are told, a new approach:

> Canada is part of a world system and as such, what happens elsewhere can and often will happen here. . . . Canada is a country that relies on immigration as a means to thrive, and new immigrants bring their experience, history, and culture . . . but they can sometimes bring younger new Canadians into conflict with Canadian values and social norms. . . . [A] new approach must be embraced to address emerging trends in youth violence, and that Canada must act before the country is faced with a youth violence problem that is insurmountable. . . . If Canada reaches the point where enforcement is seen as the only option in response to youth violence, as is now the case in some countries studied, police here risk eroding years of community policing efforts and making the re-establishment of important relationship a significant challenge for the future. (ISIS 2009, 5–6)

In its search for best policing practices to prevent "immigrant youth violence," the report's authors looked at community policing strategies across the world, from Latin America (Chile, Colombia) to Africa (Egypt, South Africa), continental Europe (France, the Netherlands), and the United Kingdom. Once again, the UK Prevent strategy was highlighted as one of the best practices. A reiteration of the "Paris problem" is explicit in the way the report cautions about the case of France. "With regard to demographic and social change," stated Debra Frazer, then director general of the Ottawa Police Service, "we are France—that's us (Canada) in a few years—and this could be a disturbing picture of our own future if we don't take this opportunity to act now" (quoted in ISIS 2009, 10). For too long, Canada has been "a reactive country," according to Mike McDonell, the assistant commissioner of the Royal Canadian Mounted Police (quoted in ISIS 2009, 6). Canada needs, he continued, "to change the policing and governance cultures towards preventative measures and earlier interventions" (ISIS 2009, 6).

The report proposed a new vision for social-development-based community policing, summed up in the concept of "intervention zone." The intervention zone, we are told, is "a reconceived field of engagement where police can work with other social system actors in a new service delivery model" (ISIS 2009, 13–14). Police, the report emphasized, "need to actively minimize their involvement in strictly social development issues except for contributing to key areas as identified *by police*" (ISIS 2009, 16, emphasis in the original). This is imperative to the reformed vision of policing, not least because, according to the report,

> both domestic research and global studies tend to reinforce that when police interfere too much in the social development zone, they risk being labelled as an extension of the repressive state, and might even increase perceptions of marginalization among some citizens, which in turn can raise the risk of anti-state motivations for youth. Such unwelcome interference can also lead to public charges of *racially biased policing* or *over-policing*. (ISIS 2009, 13, emphasis in the original)

In 2010, the Ontario Association of Chiefs of Police unveiled *Ontario's New Community Policing Model,* on which they had been working since 2006 (see Russell and Taylor 2014). The new model, framed as "mobilization and engagement model of community policing," categorizes its components in four colors: red is for "enforcement and crime suppression," green for "community engagement and liaison," orange for "community mobilization and crime prevention," and blue for "community safety and consultations" (OACP 2010, 24). "Crime prevention through social development" is the main driver of the "new model" (OACP 2010, 5). This model of community policing, we are told, differs from the previous one in that "past models depicted community policing as a philosophy for the way officers do policing. This model emphasizes roles, responsibilities and philosophies for non-police community members as well."[15]

An important question to ask is whether these internationally mobile policy discussions at the highest levels of policing in Canada and

Ontario on social-development-based policing have affected policing strategies in Toronto. They have. And this is the dimension that is missed when our sole focus is on police as a coercive force. Parallel to TAVIS in 2006, the Toronto Police also kick-started a three-year social development pilot project in targeted immigrant neighborhoods: Youth in Policing Initiative (2006–2009). The goal of the initiative was to "improve the relationship between the police service and the community, build relationships and decrease gang recruitment" (PSC 2013b). In 2012, the initiative turned into an all-year-round program by adding the Youth in Policing Initiative after-school program, which focuses on youth between the ages of fifteen and eighteen years who reside in priority neighborhoods (PSC 2013b). Today, the Youth in Policing Initiative has extended to other jurisdictions across southern Ontario.

In 2007, Jordan Manners, a fifteen-year-old student, was shot dead in his high school in the Jane and Finch neighborhood. In early 2008, then police chief Blair approached the Toronto District School Board and the Toronto Catholic District School Board to implement a new school-based policing project as part of the TAVIS strategy called School Resource Officer Program (PSC 2013c). The McGuinty provincial government allocated a one-year grant of $2.1 million to place up to thirty officers in Toronto schools. The police argued that the school environment is "an excellent opportunity for positive police interaction with young people outside of traditional enforcement activities" (TPS 2011, 5). The overall goals of the School Resource Officer program were to "improve safety and perception of safety in and around schools," "improve perceptions of police," and "improve the relationship between students and police" (TPS 2011, 6). The program was soon extended to forty-five schools across priority neighborhoods. By 2009, the initiative came under harsh criticism, and finally in November 2017, Toronto District School Board trustees, in a hotly publicized debate, voted in favor of cancelling the program.[16]

TAVIS also mobilized popular culture and art in an attempt to connect with youth in priority neighborhoods. In July 2009, TAVIS partnered with the artist-run collective, Mixed Company Theatre, to create theatre for social change with the participation of youth affected by gang violence. The Toronto Police Services Board gave Mixed Company Theatre a $30,000 grant to create *DISS,* a hip-hop-based play (Leong 2010). Written by award-winning playwright Rex Deverell, *DISS* used "hip-hop, choreography and theatre to draw a voice out of [gang-affected youth]" according to Duncan McCallum, the play's director (TPS 2009, 8). Incorporating a mixture of diverse professional actors and community amateur performers with previous gang experience, *DISS* was toured in schools across the priority neighborhoods from 2009 to 2011.[17] Using hip-hop as a prevention tool is not limited to the Toronto Police. In the United States, United Kingdom, and France, "hip-hop is being enlisted in a broad ideological offensive to counter domestic terrorism" (Aidi 2014, 206). In *Rebel Music,* Hisham Aidi (2014) documents the ways in which the U.S. government has mobilized a "hip-hop diplomacy" domestically and internationally since the 2005 uprising in the French *banlieues.* When in 2007 the Home Office introduced the Prevent strategies in the United Kingdom, it made sure that hip-hop figured prominently in it (Aidi 2014, 221–58). Hip-hop intervention, Aidi (2014) underscores, is a kinder, gentler corollary of the U.S. counterinsurgency in Iraq, Somalia, and Afghanistan, one that is directed at the peripheralized spaces of the imperial metropoles.

The criminalization of gangs increased the involvement of the federal ministry of Public Safety Canada in prevention strategies in Toronto's immigrant neighborhoods. In September 2008, Public Safety Canada provided the City of Toronto with a five-year contribution of $4–$5 million per year to kick off a new youth gang prevention project focusing on the three targeted neighborhoods of Jane and Finch, Weston–Mount Dennis, and Rexdale. In December 2009, the City rolled out its Prevention Intervention Toronto (PIT) program. The program continued until March 2013. A City staff member explained to me that

> the program started with the Crisis Response team and two of the Community Development Officers [in 2009], realizing that we had a challenge with gangs in the neighborhoods. . . . There were lots of goals [for PIT]. *But overall, the goal for the program was not to actually save young people. It was to figure out what the City of Toronto could do for that type of youth.* . . . We needed to figure out what strategies should we develop to work with the youth furthest away from opportunities, furthest away from the labor market, furthest away from jobs, furthest away from economic opportunities. How would we work with those young people? Who are they? What kind of things do they need? And how to work with them? (I13 2013, emphasis added)

The program targeted kids who were "at risk of ending up in violence that would end up at jail" (I13 2013). These youth were recruited through schools and community centers, in malls, on the streets and buses, or they were referred to the program by other youth (I13 2013).[18] Part of the rationale behind the program was that without preventive social development strategies implemented by nonpolice agencies, police enforcement would only further alienate the youth. TAVIS officers only cooperated with the program if needed. This was due to the fact that although police "are very good at suppression, they are not so good at prevention: because most of the guys they are intervening [with] already hate the cops" (I13 2013).

It should be emphasized that youth with official immigrant status were not the main target of the program. Second- and third-generation Canadian Black youth (Jamaican and African) composed the clear majority of the youth targeted by the PIT program. According to the abovementioned City staff, most of these youth "did not consider themselves Canadian" (I13 2013). It is this geo-political aspect of the gang problem as the foreign problem, as the internal enemy, that, as mentioned earlier, is perceived as threatening to social cohesion by policymakers. One of the aims of the program was to experience how to undo these forms of political and territorial identification through intensive management intervention. In the words of the same City staff member:

> [For] every kid that came to the program we did a pre- and post-survey with them. We asked them: Where are you from? And they all said, Jamaica, Africa. . . . Number one place was the Caribbean, and two was actually the Middle East, and three was West and East Africa. When we changed the question to where were you born? 100% were Canadian. . . . The problem with the link between the gang problem in Canada and Canadian youth in Toronto is that their parents were never settled . . . as the result of horrible immigration policy. . . . People are told to come to Canada . . . and then there is no support when they get here, no jobs. [They] ended up driving taxis, or did whatever they could to survive. Their kids were the ones who were born here and as the result of poor settlement policies, and again that kind of displacement around justice programs, education programs, their kids are committing crimes. . . . There was a really important lesson for us

to learn that these kids who are newcomers to Canada are doing way better than their Canadian-born counterparts. Because, they have, if you wanna call it, back home, educational standards in their heads that education is good for you. Whereas in Toronto or Canada, many of the kids have seen that [education] doesn't make a difference. Dad has three degrees, he came from Jamaica, and he can't find a job. Why should I get three degrees? Stupid. . . . And then they go to school and they get marginalized and the racism that starts there. Then they leave school and police are giving them a hard time. . . . They don't recognize themselves as Canadian. They are not Canadian in their heads. They are from wherever their parents are from. Even though they have absolutely no idea of where their parents are from. They . . . have no understanding of being Canadian. So actually [they] don't have a culture. Then the culture becomes BET [Black Entertainment Television], or MTV, or Much Music. . . . And what do those things preach? Primarily sex, violence, and drug use. . . . This is why nowadays you see that the guys getting killed and the killers are fifteen years old, because they had fifteen years of nothing but forced television, racism, and now super high access to guns and this kind of I'm-not-Canadian, I-gotta-be-a-tough-guy mentality for the last little while. (I13 2013)

In May 2012, a number of delegates from Toronto went to Prince Albert, Saskatchewan, to examine the usefulness of a new community policing strategy. The delegation was made up of members of the Toronto Police Service, the City of Toronto (Crisis Response Unit), United Way, and Albion Neighbourhood Services (a community center located in Rexdale). The new strategy, Prince Albert Community Mobilization Initiative (known as the Hub Model), was the signature project of then Prince Albert chief of police Dale McFee for fighting crime in one of the highest-ranked crime locations in Canada at the time.[19] The rationale of the model is a shift from "incident-driven" policing to "risk-driven" policing, with an early multisector prevention (McFee and Taylor 2014, I12). In this rationale, risk (i.e., crime, violence) is conceived as predictable and thus preventable through early intervention (McFee and Taylor 2014). Here prevention works through empowering the agencies of those at risk of crime or victimization. According to the Toronto Police delegate, Sgt. Greg Watts:

> The most attractive thing is that it [the Hub Model] talks about a multi-disciplinary approach to community safety. And I think that's what grabs most people, because at the end of the day we have a lot of places and a lot of agencies (Toronto police, City services and community-based organizations) that are out there on a daily basis doing really good work. But, can we imagine what we could accomplish if we started working together on those things? (quoted in Haggen 2012)

The Toronto Police were not alone in finding McFee's signature project attractive. In less than five years, the Hub Model attracted "city delegations from across Canada and the US, from front line practitioners to a Parliamentary Committee and the Governor General of Canada" (McFee and Taylor 2014, 13). The Conservative premier of Saskatchewan, Brad Wall, was so impressed with the model that within a year of its implementation, in 2012, McFee retired from the Prince Albert police force to become Saskatchewan's deputy minister of corrections and policing. In 2015, the Federation of Canadian Municipalities used the example of the Hub Model as a successful preventive policing strategy for Canadian urban centers (FCM 2015, 9).

By the fall of 2012, the Toronto Police Services, the City of Toronto, and United Way designed a new prevention intervention project called Furthering Our Communities, Uniting Services (FOCUS). In January 2013, the city started FOCUS as a pilot project in Rexdale (I26 2013). A fundamental component of FOCUS is the whole-of-government or holistic approach. The project had three co-coordinators—representing the three main forces behind the strategy: Toronto Police,[20] United Way, and City of Toronto. For the City and the Toronto Police, FOCUS was an attempt to experience with a "multi-stakeholder intervention" in crime reduction through prevention by bringing together existing community agencies to provide a targeted, integrated approach to supporting individuals, children, youth, and families who are targeted by one or few agencies as at-risk (I26 2013; I11 2013). According to the Toronto Police, FOCUS "is not a police project" in its conventional sense (I11 2013). As McFee put it back in 2012, "[a] lot of people might think that the police are more about being hard on crime and different agencies and social services could potentially be perceived as soft on crime and this approach is just a smart on community safety approach" (quoted in Haggen 2012).

By the end of June 2016, the City announced that in partnership with the Ontario Government and Public Safety Canada, FOCUS would be extended across Toronto. Introducing the city-wide initiative, Ralph Goodale, then Liberal minister of public safety, stated:

> The Government of Canada is anxious to work with provincial, municipal and community-based partners to build stronger, safer communities. We all need to get beyond jurisdictional stovepipes to ensure seamless collaboration, and we need *holistic approaches* to focus proactively on crime prevention. Federal initiatives are in place to combat gangs, interdict illegal weapons and boost community safety. We will build on these, while also investing in more resilient neighbourhoods through better housing and transit, better access to learning and skills, and better job opportunities for young people. (quoted in City of Toronto 2016, emphasis added)

FOCUS is an interesting case of the relational formation of urban policy and international relations. It is the outcome of policy mobilities across time, geography, and scale. The genealogy of the multistakeholder community mobilization in crime prevention policing has a longer history, however, going back to the late 1990s and the work of criminologist David Kennedy in Boston, Massachusetts (I11 2013; I12 2013).

In 1995, Kennedy, then a researcher at Harvard University, designed Operation Ceasefire to deal with Boston's gang problem, and he soon became a celebrity crime prevention expert nationwide.[21] At the heart of Operation Ceasefire (also known as the Boston Miracle) is the principle of interagency cooperation by engaging gangs and reallocating existing criminal justice, social service, and community resources in targeted neighborhoods. A decade later in Scotland, Karyn McCluskey and John Carnochan at the Strathclyde Police picked up Kennedy's work. In 2005, McCluskey (a trained nurse and police intelligence analyst) and Carnochan (a police detective with three decades of experience in homicide, drugs, and organized crime) initiated the Violence Reduction Unit (VRU) at the Strathclyde Police.[22] Partnership and multisector cooperation are at the heart of the VRU.[23] Similar to Kennedy's initiatives, the VRU also gained much national and international praise, particularly from governments and police forces. Following the 2011 unrests in British cities, then prime minister David Cameron told the House of Commons that initiatives such as Ceasefire in Boston and the VRU in Glasgow should become a "national priority" in combating gangs in the United Kingdom (quoted in Knight 2011).

The Violence Reduction Unit first came to the attention of the police in Canada in 2008 and 2009 through the international case study research of the then Institute for Strategic International Studies (currently Executive Global Studies). In 2008, the main tenets of the institute's annual report were "ongoing alignment of policing resources," "multidisciplinary partnership," and "community-based actions" (ISIS 2008, 2, 28). In 2010, Norm Taylor, who was the CACP-ISIS program director in 2008 and 2009, wrote a consultation report for the Government of Saskatchewan, in which he argued "it would take more than a policing system to reverse the disturbing trend of high crime and violence in Saskatchewan" (quoted in McFee and Taylor 2014, 5). Soon after, then Prince Albert chief of police Dale McFee teamed up with Taylor to design the Community Mobilization Prince Albert initiative. This initiative has been in place since February 2011 with the financial support of the Province of Saskatchewan and Public Safety Canada (PSC 2013d). A couple of years later, Taylor became a consultant for the FOCUS project in Toronto.[24]

Proponents of prevention mobilize the works of Robert Peel, the nineteenth-century British statesman and one of the founders of the modern Conservative Party in England, who established the Metropolitan Police Force for London in 1829. In particular, they appeal to Peel's "ethical policing" and his belief that "the police are the public and the public is the police" (I12 2013). The appeal to Peel, however, is more ideological than historical. The genealogy of the current emphasis on prevention in community policing (in Toronto and elsewhere) goes back to the works of the eighteenth-century Scottish merchant, statistician, and police theorist Patrick Colquhoun, the founder of the Thames River Police in 1800 (see Neocleous 2000, 2006; Rigakos et al. 2009). Let us briefly look at Colquhoun's work in this regard.

Prevention was central to Colquhoun's conception of police (Neocleous 2000; Rigakos et al. 2009, 243–76).[25] In his 1799 text *The State of Indigence,* Colquhoun proposed a strategy of prevention based on a distinction between poverty and indigence. Similar to today's proponents of poverty-as-risk, Colquhoun saw poverty as integral to the production of capitalist wealth and the function of wage labor. The laboring poor are not only "a most necessary and indispensable ingredient of society," without them, "nations and communities could not exist in the state of civilization" (Colquhoun 1806, 7–8). "*Indigence* therefore, and not *poverty*," Colquhoun argued, "is the evil." The problem with indigence was not excessive destitution; rather, for Colquhoun that problem was the refusal to integrate into social relations of wage labor (Neocleous 2000, 55). The indigent's disconnection from capitalist social relations was at the core of Colquhoun's conception of what counts as a threat to the bourgeois society and of that which needed policing in the late eighteenth century.

Historian Peter Linebaugh notes that if a single individual could be said to have been the planner and theorist of class struggle in the late eighteenth- and early nineteenth-century metropole, it would be Colquhoun (Linebaugh 2003, 427). "The key to Colquhoun's science of police," Neocleous underlines, "is that the Criminal Police deals with the criminal 'underclass' (Hegel's 'rabble')," those who have fallen from indigence to crime. The responsibility of the Municipal Police, on the other hand, is "to prevent the class of poverty from falling into indigence" (2000, 54). Colquhoun's Municipal Police and its mandate of "the political management of poverty" (Neocleous 2000, 58) sit at the heart of the concept of prevention in policing. Colquhoun's Municipal Police directs us to an understanding of police beyond the uniformed police officers and the police as an institution. The necessity of the Municipal Police alerts us to the historical link between police, policy, and the urban, and thus for the need to understand police as "social police"—a force in pacifying the perceived threats to the security of bourgeois society. The security of the bourgeois order "involves not just the prevention and detection of crime, but more importantly, the imposition of a form of social police" (Neocleous 2000, 61).

Today's conception of poverty-as-risk is a recomposition of Colquhoun's notion of indigence. The current emphasis on prevention in community policing, I suggest, is a recomposition of Colquhoun's social police. This recomposed mobilization of social police is part of the state strategy to govern racialized ungovernability at the time of the crisis of imperialist capitalism, austerity politics, and imperialist wars. Its aim is to moderate the violence of poverty and coercive policing. Both community policing and counterinsurgency build upon the concept of prevention, which makes the nexus of development, racialization, and security an important pillar of both forms of state interventions.

SOCIAL DETERMINANTS OF HEALTH AND THE RACIALIZED EPIDEMIOLOGICAL IMAGINARIES OF CRIME AND TERROR

Projects like the Scottish VRU and FOCUS in Toronto have a deliberate discursive emphasis on the social causes and dimensions of violence and crime. For police the emphasis on the so-called social determinants of safety and violence is *the* novel dimension in these preventive community-policing strategies, one that is, we are told, scientific and evidence based (Russell and Taylor 2014, 5). At the time of my fieldwork, community workers and activists had increasingly welcomed this apparent social turn in community policing (I22 2013; I31 2013; I1 2014). Today, talking about the social determinants of safety and health has become a new common sense in policy circles and community centers in Toronto. In what follows, I aim to challenge the claims about the scientific and progressive attributes of the current policy focus on the social determinants of safety and health in policing and urban policy. Thinking about social justice seriously requires us to be vigilant about the dangers of taking for granted the lesser evil of social-development-based community policing, particularly in relation to normalizing racism and racialization.

The prevalence of the social determinants of safety is the latest ideological turn in policing (and security) strategies in an attempt to deal with the contradictions of coercive policing and the increasing public reaction to the naked violence of coercive policing. The genealogy of the social determinants of safety/violence in the policing lexicon is complex and deeply intertwined with the genealogy of contagion and international relations. The emphasis on the social determinants of safety is based on a public health framework of crime and violence. Having its roots in the eighteenth- and nineteenth-century debates on public health and disease, this framework is part and a parcel of the broader nexus of development, racialization, and security, and the collusion of imperialist capitalism, militarism, and medicine (O'Malley 2010). By the second decade of the twenty-first century, the public health lens has become central not only to policing and urban policy, but also to international development and humanitarianism.

The Scottish VRU is celebrated for adopting a public health approach to violent crime, drawing inspiration from projects like Cure Violence in the United States, founded by former WHO epidemiologist Gary Slutkin (2012), and adopting the principles of the WHO.[26] In their report on FOCUS, Russell and Taylor (2014) emphasize the usefulness of adapting the WHO social determinants of health perspective for crime prevention in Toronto and Canada. The ascendency of prevention in policing has facilitated the adoption of a public health framework (see CSDH 2008; Akers and Lanier 2009), while the turn to a public health framework has reinforced conceiving violence and crime as *disease.* For McCluskey, the genius of the Scottish VRU was due to understanding that violence works "like an infectious disease" (quoted in Henley 2011), and for Russell and Taylor, "focusing on crime" is like "focusing on disease" (2014, 6). This line of argumentation is fascinated with the new subfield of epidemiological criminology (see Akers and Lanier 2009; Slutkin 2012) that treats violence as an infectious disease. Within the last two decades, epidemiological criminology has become one influential ideological foundation in combating crime, violence, and terrorism through a public health approach in cities in the United States, the United Kingdom, Canada, South America, the Middle East, and Africa.[27]

Geographical imaginaries of crime and violence as disease are not new, however. Environmentally determinist conceptions are central to these geographical imaginaries. The pathologization of crime (as insecurity and disorder) and the criminalization of (what is perceived as) disease were the hallmarks of the growth of capitalism, colonialism, and urbanization, along with the confluence of biology, racism, and politics in the eighteenth and nineteenth centuries. Michel Foucault captured part of this history in his *History of Sexuality* (1978) and *Discipline and Punish* (1995). In the nineteenth century, the bourgeoisie's geographical imaginary of the industrial city was of a space of social contagion, populated by infectious classes, racialized groups, and women. To a great extent, this perception was related to the sudden movement of dispossessed peasants to the booming industrial city for employment and survival. "Migration of any sort," as Neocleous (2016, 62) underlines, "is a recurring theme in the police power: contagion occurs with movement and the City is the site of movement as well as migration." Politics is central to the geographical imaginary of contagion as an ungovernable space. In tracing the genealogy of contagion, Neocleous (2016, 61–65) notes, the concept of contagion is much less a question of microbiology or epidemiology than it is a question of how ideas circulate. . . . With its connotations of "touching together," contagion connotes danger or corruption, in particular the kinds of danger or corruption that occur in "promiscuous" social spaces when ideas can circulate among the crowd. Moreover, implicit in the concept of contagion is the belief that *revolutionary ideas are inherently contagious.* (Neocleous 2016, 63)

Contagion was also a fundamental feature of colonial police power. The colonized (most often perceived as criminal and diseased) embodied the collusion of such pathologization and criminalization, as Frantz Fanon so vividly depicted in *The Wretched of the Earth* (2004) and *Black Skin, White Masks* ([1961] 1967). Colonial genocide was, from the colonizer's perspective, both preventive and curative. Pathologies of immigrant neighborhoods and immigrant families were at the heart of Thrasher's (1927) racialized geographical imaginary of gangs in Chicago. The fascism of National Socialism in twentieth-century Germany built upon the conflation of disease, "race," and crime. Adolf Hitler imagined himself to be the political incarnation of Robert Koch, the famous German bacteriologist (Peckham 2014, 1).

The return of the epidemic imaginary of crime to the table of policymakers and academics has paralleled the return of another epidemiological geographical imaginary: terrorism. In the aftermath of the invasion of Afghanistan, on January 29, 2002, in his State of the Union Address, then U.S. president George W. Bush highlighted the crushing of the "terrorist parasites" lurking in "remote deserts and jungles" and hiding "in the center of large cities." After the invasion of Iraq, in an address to Congress in July 2003, then UK prime minister Tony Blair similarly warned that "a new and deadly virus has emerged. The virus is terrorism, whose intent to inflict destruction is unconstrained by human feelings" (quoted in Lippens 2004, 126). This intertwining of public health with geo-politics is not limited to imperialist counterterrorism strategies in former colonies. In the fall of 2005, the French media were quick to mobilize an epidemiological geographical imaginary to condemn the uprising of the French *banlieues* as "contagious" (see Waddington 2008). In the aftermath of the 2011 urban unrest in the United Kingdom, Gary Slutkin (2011), the first and most influential voice in epidemiological criminology, wrote an article in

The Guardian arguing that "rioting is a disease spread from person to person—the key is to stop the infection." Epidemiological criminology has gained momentum at the time of an increasing emphasis on the social determinants of health; this deserves our attention.

Let us pause on the conjuncture in which the phrase *social determinants of health* became a buzzword in WHO public health policies. This is imperative, as we will see in chapter 5, since in 2012 the City of Toronto also mobilized a social determinants of health discourse (inspired by the WHO Urban HEART project) to reform its place-based urban policy. The recent analyses of the social determinants of health perspective found their way into the WHO corridors in the early 2000s, influenced by the 2000–2001 World Development Report, *Attacking Poverty* (World Bank 2000); the UN Millennium Development Goals (United Nations 2000); the 2002 WHO report on a public health approach to violence, *World Report on Violence and Health* (WHO 2002); and the 2002–2003 SARS outbreak. The 2003 election of Lee Jong-Wook as WHO director-general on a platform of renewed commitment to the social determinants of health perspective was also imperative in this regard (Irwin and Scali 2007). In 2008, the WHO Commission on Social Determinants of Health (CSDH) published an influential report entitled *Closing the Gap in a Generation: Health Equity Through Action on the Social Determinants of Health* (CSDH 2008), which has since become the bible of public health.

The idea of tackling the social determinants of health, however, is hardly novel. Even the current advocates of epidemiological criminology go back to the 1832 cholera epidemic (see Akers and Lanier 2009; Slutkin 2012). What is erased in these accounts, however, is the very sociopolitical and spatial forces that gave birth to these ideas. The genealogy of social determinants of health as a policy concept goes back to the volatile conditions of the rapid yet uneven development of industrial capitalism in the nineteenth century, particularly in its epicenter, England. The occurrence of epidemics, and in particular, the cholera epidemic of 1831 and 1832 pushed sections of the British ruling classes and their organic intellectuals to think about public health and its link to the everyday living conditions of the poor. The focus on the living conditions of the poor was not simply a humanitarian concern. Rather, the birth of that concern was in relation to harsher social relief policies, as exemplified in the Amended Poor Laws of 1834, which aimed to prevent indigence and to quell the increasing revolutionary spirit of the 1830s–1840s. Friedrich Engels's ([1845] 1992) study of the conditions of the working class in the "great towns" of nineteenth-century England uses many official reports that were the outcome of public officials' increasing awareness of the social consequences of public health. Acting upon the sociospatial determinants of health was central to antipoverty laws, policing strategies, and the sanitary and social reform campaigns of the mid-nineteenth century as well as to the birth and evolution of modern public health and urban planning in the late nineteenth and early twentieth centuries. Edwin Chadwick, the driving force behind the first public health legislation, the 1848 Public Health Act for England and Wales, "began inquiries into public health as a means of reducing the costs of public relief," as a means of governing the implementation of the Amended Poor Laws of 1834 (Hamlin and Sheard 1998, 587).

The current policy concept of social determinants of health was born in the conjuncture of decolonization. In 1948, the WHO was constituted, at least on paper, based on a broad definition of health understood as "a state of complete physical, mental and social well-being" (WHO 1948). Three decades later, then WHO director-general Halfdan Mahler made social determinants of health a public health policy issue through his 1976 project of Health for All that was eventually officialized in the 1978 Alma-Ata Declaration (Mahler 1981; CSDH 2008).[28] Mahler's Health for All was a translation and appropriation of the revolutionary community-based health initiatives that flourished in the 1960s and 1970s across the decolonizing world, from Bangladesh, India, China, and the Philippines to Costa Rica, Guatemala, Mexico, and Nicaragua and on to South Africa (Irwin and Scali 2007). The major difference was that the latter community-based health initiatives that sprung from within anti-imperialist and anti-colonial struggles, as Irwin and Scali document, "engaged directly not only with social and environmental determinants of health but also with underlying issues of political-economic structures and power relations" (2007, 238). This was not the case with the Alma-Ata Declaration, which became part of the Western states' attempt to pacify the threat of communism, socialism, and anti-imperialist struggles at the time of imperial geo-political instability (Irwin and Scali 2007).

In his May 2003 speech to the 56th World Health Assembly, Lee Jong-Wook declared the revival of the Alma-Ata Declaration through the renewal of "the fundamental commitment to equity expressed by the notion of 'health for all'" as the new mission of the WHO (Lee 2003). In his speech, Lee squarely situated the WHO "health for all" mission in relation to global geo-political stability.[29] According to him:

> The world leaders who drafted the UN Charter saw that peace and security depended on establishing what they called "conditions under which justice . . . can be maintained." . . . If it is true for global politics, it is equality so for health. (2003)

Lee (2003) justified the WHO's new commitment to the social determinants of health as an essential part of maintaining global peace and achieving the UN Millennium Development Goals.[30] It is precisely through such emphasis on linking health to the nexus of security and development (as defined by the United Nations and the World Bank) that we can trace the reified notion of social determinants of health in the WHO vision. Despite an attempt to situate health in its broader societal context, the CSDH's conceptualization of social determinants of health is deeply de-historicized. As Vicente Navaro (2009) has argued in his critique of the 2008 WHO CSDH report:

> The report's phrase "social inequalities kill" has outraged conservative and liberal forces, which find the narrative and discourse of the report too strong to stomach. And yet, this is where the report falls short. It is not *inequalities* that kill, but *those who benefit from the inequalities* that kill. The [WHO] Commission's studious avoidance of the category of power (class power, as well as gender, race, and national power) and how power is produced and reproduced in political institutions is the greatest weakness of the report. It reproduces a widely held practice in international agencies that speaks of policies without touching on politics. . . . Disease is a social and political category imposed on people within an enormously repressive social and economic capitalist system, one that forces disease and death on the world's people. (Navaro 2009, 440)

The de-historicized conception of social determinants of health and the implicit linking of contagion, health, and security are also evident in the CSDH's emphasis on the United Nations' *Investing in Development: A Practical Plan to Achieve the Millennium Development*

Goals (2005). While the broad scope of the goals—poverty reduction, health improvement, and the promotion of peace, human rights, gender equality, and environmental sustainability—appear to include sociopolitical and ecological dimensions of development, a closer look at how these goals are defined and measured as achieved illuminates that the emphasis on the social takes place at the same time that the concrete sociospatial relations of imperialist-capitalist uneven development are de-historicized and naturalized. *Investing in Development* conceives poverty as risk, as the source and cause of war, conflict, and insecurity. Authors of both *Investing in Development* and *Closing the Gap in a Generation* firmly situate their rationales within the broader liberal nexus of security, racialization, and development, wherein the goal of development is neither the eradication of poverty nor the development of human potentials, but rather the containment of threats to the security of the imperialist-capitalist world order emanating from zones of poverty near and far (see Cowen and Shenton 1996; Neocleous 2008).

This is why recent emphasis on the social determinants of health has paralleled the primacy of prevention and resiliency in security politics both internationally and domestically. In international relations, the shift to prevention was accompanied by a shift in the locus of securing agency from Western actors to the so-called fragile or failing states (perceived to be) in need of capacity building (Bellamy 2009; Chandler 2008). This shift was a reformulation of a bottom-up, so-called empowering approach to human security, which, as mentioned earlier, was born, along with humanitarian wars, in the 1990s (Chandler 2012). Rather than a focus on the economic, political, and sociospatial relations (of the production) of conflict, war, and violence, parallel to the neoliberal ethos in human security and humanitarian interventions, the focus of intervention shifted onto individuals (as decision makers) and the immediate influences on their choices. The goal is not to eradicate the causes of violence; rather, the goal is to *ameliorate the effects* of violence. Amelioration functions through empowering agents and enabling them to overcome their vulnerabilities in order to become resilient in the face of violence. In the reformulated human security ideology of prevention and resiliency, the targeted subject is no more the passive victim in need of protection. Rather, the subject of preventive security politics is a particular active subject:

always the vulnerable subject in need of tutelage to enable their agency and become resilient (Wilson 2012; Chandler 2012).

This is precisely how strategies such as the Hub Model, FOCUS, and Prevention Intervention Toronto approach the problems of crime, gangs, and violence while mobilizing the rhetoric of the social determinants of health and safety. The focus of these strategies is on targeting at-risk individuals or families and their choices. The aim is thus to cure the disease or to prevent the contagion of the infection by means of changing the immediate context and subjectivities of the at-risk subject-targets. In their praise of the Prince Albert Hub Model, Ruddell and Jones observe that "while this collaborative model has yet to be formally evaluated, it represents a step forward toward crime reduction by solving problems in the community one person or family at a time" (2014, 68). Meanwhile, for police in Toronto (and Canada), initiatives like the Hub Model and FOCUS are seen by many as an integrated part of the future of policing (I12 2013; I26 2013; McFee and Taylor 2014; Russell and Taylor 2014).

Parallel to counterinsurgency strategies, the goal of preventive community policing is not the elimination of the enemies of order— whether they are gangsters, or at-risk or radicalized youth. Rather, the goal is to build resiliency among those considered at risk of becoming enemies of order so as to nullify the gang-allure of Us against the State. It is precisely the recognition that the naked violence of enforcement (as much as it is believed to be necessary) is not sustainable for maintaining order. Prevention is thus an ideological concept. The ideology of prevention is about ameliorating the effects of violence, rather than eradicating violence. It is based on this ideology that policy forces have been increasingly framing community policing as social development and with reference to a whole-of-government approach. As we will see in the next chapters, prevention is central to the relational formation of urban policy and international relations.

4

Making Urban Policy

LIBERAL HUMANITARIANISM AND
MAPPING SOCIAL PROBLEMS

> And we [United Way] openly laid a map of our programs
> and services over a map of poverty in Toronto. . . . We also
> overlaid on top of that where [there] was the highest incidents
> of youth violence, and what we said was that we're going to
> deliberately shift our strategy to invest more and more in
> those neighborhoods.
>
> —Executive Team Member, United Way Toronto, 2013

THE RACIALIZED GEOGRAPHICAL IMAGINARIES
OF LIBERAL EMPOWERMENT

The founding rationale of the Priority Neighbourhoods Strategy, as
mentioned in chapter 2, was that the geographical concentration of
non-White poverty is the main cause of insecurity and gun violence
in Toronto's immigrant neighborhoods. Urban policy was thus to emphasize development by directing investment for physical and social
infrastructure improvements in targeted localities. The rolling out of
the Priority Neighbourhoods Strategy facilitated the rapid growth of
a knowledge production industry about urban poverty in Toronto.
This industry and its link to United Way and major academic centers
in Toronto has in turn consolidated place-based urban policy as the
solution to concentrated non-White poverty. Since 2004, the who
questions ("Who are we?," "Who lives here?," "Who works minimum
wage,?" "Who lives in poverty?," "Who are the working poor?"), with
no attention to the how and why questions, have turned into a major
aspect of almost all published research and policy papers. In this thriving knowledge production industry, maps and mapping are used as a
new scientific tool of looking at the city and its residents.

Parallel to the broader discourses in international development, humanitarianism, and counterinsurgency in the global South, in Toronto concepts such as empowerment, participation, economic integration, and the whole-of-government approach became the buzzwords of place-based urban policy. This component of urban policy, with its focus on the agency of residents, became the major rationale for cultivating collaboration and networks across public, nonprofit, and community organizations in targeted localities. The City of Toronto started the implementation of the Priority Neighbourhoods Strategy in targeted neighborhoods by initiatives within its own departments. Within the municipality, the City set up Neighbourhood Action Teams in each of the thirteen neighborhoods designated as a priority to coordinate service delivery across municipal departments. The Priority Neighbourhoods Strategy also facilitated the systematic involvement of the pro-urban bourgeois forces in policy implementation, particularly through the United Way.

The United Way gained an opportunity to extend its political power beyond policy circles and small pilot projects to the so-called priority neighborhoods through funding, building community infrastructure, and organizing capacity. Parallel to the City's Priority Neighbourhoods Strategy, United Way announced its own Strong Neighbourhoods Strategy. A key piece of this strategy was the Action for Neighbourhood Change (ANC) initiative in the priority neighborhoods—much similar to the City's Neighbourhood Action Partnerships. A former United Way policy analyst explained to me that the birth of the Action for Neighbourhood Change was the result of

> a political discussion between the City and United Way about how we are going to work within communities [given] that we recognize that place is as important as other targets—such as specific populations, Black males, or seniors—or as important as targeting social problems, such as focusing on dropouts or new immigrants. . . . The other dimension was to make sure that residents were engaged. . . . We knew about efforts down in the [United] States and in the United Kingdom. . . . It was with those lessons [in mind] and having watched what happened in Boston or [what was done] by the Aspen Institute or other large foundations that have been doing this kind of work. They came up and

talked to us about what was going on. So United Way said, "We've got the community agencies, we're on the ground, we're going to do that." That's how the initiative for the ANC started. (I4 2013)

It would be misleading to understand United Way's seemingly separate yet intertwined and parallel community infrastructure as simply a humanitarian endeavor. The organization's community infrastructure has important political functions for the pro-urban bourgeois forces. First, United Way's seemingly separate place-based strategy and its role as the City's foot soldier have greatly reinforced the illusion that it is not the state but so-called civil society that is involved in community development projects in immigrant neighborhoods. Second, United Way uses initiatives such as the ANC centers and Community Hubs as concrete examples that the organization is "the voice of the community" (I4 2013; I17 2013). Third, the parallel community infrastructure has reinforced United Way's lobbying power *and* the claim that its work is strictly humanitarian and nonpartisan. This latter claim stands in sharp contrast to the organization's actual politics of lobbying the local state behind closed doors. During my fieldwork in 2013, one of United Way's Neighbourhood and Community Investment managers explained to me the organization's "very skillful way" of lobbying the city:

I'll be honest, they [the City] have their strategy and we have our strategy. Our work is often running parallel but *we're not in the same lockstep together, because they have a political agenda.* For us to lobby the City, we have to do it in a very skillful way, we can't just go in there and say, Mayor Ford, what the hell! We actually have to go and sit on the Economic Development Committee and share issues and talk. That's how we operate at United Way. . . . [W]e do a much more subtle lobby[ing]. We can't even call it lobbying, it's more we discuss it and share what we learned from the ground. . . . Our Public Affairs team works with the folks [city councilors] in the [political] middle. They [the Public Affairs team] spend a lot of time keeping them [councilors] up to date on the impacts of their policies. When they come to vote on whatever, they have a knowledge base. Because we know the right wing [councilors], we're not going to change them really and truly. The left[-wing] ones are already on our side. Let's move on to that middle, and that again is through discussions and sitting on committees, and that's how we lobby. (I17 2013, emphasis added)

Finally, the ANC centers and Community Hubs are meant to provide the space and resources for the empowerment and participation of the poor residents (I23 2013). Through the ANC initiative, United Way mainly provided space for other community services, such as tax services, English as Second Language (ESL) classes, immigrant settlement, consultation, and afternoon classes. While such services are needed in many marginalized neighborhoods across Toronto, neither the choice of services nor the form of education that are provided through these services is neutral; United Way has the final say on what should be going on at the ANCs. The idea of empowerment, as a former United Way policy analyst put it, "was around building social capital for people" (I4 2013). According to a former manager of an ANC in the northwest part of Toronto, the goal

> is predominantly looking at how we can engage residents so that they can empower themselves to do the things that they are able to do because they have got all the skills and tools. . . . So really looking at it as an asset-based model versus a deficit model. . . . That is the kind of concept we follow when we are working with residents. (I29 2013)

This emphasis on asset building and empowerment in Toronto's place-based urban policy is heavily indebted to the broader discourses of social capital (Cowen and Parlette 2011) and resiliency that are also central to international development and humanitarian policies and practices (see Mayer 2003; Walker and Cooper 2011; Wilson 2012; Perrons and Skyers 2003).

In this liberal humanitarian discourse, which aims for amelioration, empowerment appears to be a progressive step forward, but in practice the concept of empowerment de-socializes capital as a social relation (Mayer 2003). Rather than aiming for structural change, empowerment aims for amelioration and the recognition of the poverty of the poor (Perrons and Skyers 2003). The goal of liberal empowerment is to involve the poor more actively in the management of their everyday life, while negating any engagement with the social-economic, political, racial, and spatial relations that (re-)produce their marginalization and exploitation. Neither the City nor United Way shies away from this reality. As a senior manager at the City highlighted, policymakers

> were always clear . . . that Strong Neighborhoods or place-based work is not going to achieve the kind of systemic change that is required to address poverty. . . . What place-based work could do is to *mitigate some of the impacts of those systemic issues* and at least not magnify the impacts of those systemic issues so to take away the disadvantage that sometimes comes with place or to mitigate it. The polarization of income, the growing gap, is perhaps the most critical social development issue facing us. . . . Unless we find more effective ways of addressing the growing gap, that challenge would be there. (I3 2013, emphasis added)

The United Way also shares a similar position. A senior executive member of the organization explained to me that

> what brought us [United Way] into this strategy was the concentration of poverty. . . . We knew that it would be virtually impossible for United Way with the resources that we have to come into the neighborhood and move the needle on poverty [*laughter*]. . . . But we knew that some elements in terms of getting to reduce poverty that we had some control over. We can invest in social programs, we can bring residents together and we can advocate and bring other partners at the table and get them to use the same lens that we have to focus investment toward where it is needed the most. *We never set out through the United Way's programs to reduce poverty because we know that's impossible.* (I23 2013, emphasis added)

Similar to international development and humanitarianism, by treating poor people as potential participants in their own economic and spatial rehabilitation, the goal here is not to eradicate or reduce poverty. Rather, in its emphasis on amelioration, there is a tacit recognition that development for the post-colonial poor is about preventing unrest; it entails constituting a low-income individual less threatening to the political stability of the imperialist-capitalist order and more adaptable and resilient to the violence and humiliation of poverty and exploitation (see Walker and Cooper 2011; Wilson 2012; Pithouse 2011). Parallel to policing and international relations, prevention has played a central role in the Priority Neighbourhoods Strategy. The emphasis on prevention is based upon the belief that there is a direct relation between development and security (I23 2013; I3 2014; I19 2013; I16 2013; I25 2013; I11 2013). As mentioned earlier, Johnson's War on Poverty and the birth of urban policy in the United States were based on mobilizing development, participation, and empowerment to pacify the Black urban rebellion of the 1960s. This developmental logic is also at the heart of the emphasis on economic integration, opportunity, and participation in the Priority Neighbourhoods Strategy in Toronto. According to a senior City manager:

> The other focus [of the Priority Neighbourhoods Strategy] was looking at economic opportunities and trying to make sure that we have the right kinds of programmatic support for those youth [who] are most distanced from the labor market, to help them to get engaged in the labor market, to give a productive alternative to becoming involved in guns and gangs. (I3 2014)

For the City's policymakers, prevention requires empowerment, while empowerment means giving opportunities to the poor, the immigrant. In this rationale, opportunity, more than anything else, means economic integration; it means the opportunity to be integrated into imperialist capitalist sociospatial relations. It is important to highlight that many poor residents in immigrant neighborhoods are already integrated into the labor market. Many of these residents are the same workers that today, a year and a half into the Covid-19 pandemic at the time of writing, we call "essential workers," without whose labor long periods of lockdown would have not been possible. It is thus the specific form of their economic integration and systemic racism—as precarious cheap labor for imperialist capitalism—that has resulted in their overexploitation and poverty. The refusal to recognize structural forces is precisely what is overlooked in the ideological concepts of empowerment, participation, and economic integration in urban policy.

The geographical imaginaries of danger, economic integration, and empowerment in Toronto's urban policy parallels those in international relations. Since the 1990s, imperialist geopoliticians such as Robert Kaplan (1994) and Thomas Barnett (2004), along with liberal geopoliticians such as Mary Kaldor (1999), all pointed to poverty in former colonies and their supposed exclusion from the market as danger to the West. They provided political and intellectual backdrops for well-rehearsed neocolonial cartographies of worldwide "ungoverned spaces" of violence, "gaps" in global economy, and "hotbeds" of anarchy, and thus paved the way for humanitarian wars and later the War on Terror (Dalby 2007; Elden 2009). It was in this broader context that the recurrent urban unrest of the racialized excluded in Western cities and urban policies of nullifying such forms of unrest gave materiality to new geographical imaginaries of fear: immigrant neighborhoods. With its emphasis on economic integration, the conception of opportunity in Toronto's place-based urban policy follows Thomas Barnett's logic concerning the need to incorporate the so-called failed states of the global South, the "gaps" in global economy, into the "integrated core" of globalization (see the introduction).

The valorization of empowerment as economic integration reifies the fact that once mobilized by the state and its civil-society apparatuses, "relations of empowerment are relations of power" (Cruikshank 1994, 3). In this preventive project of empowering the immigrant, the state and its civil-society apparatus define the content and form of the empowered liberal subject (I6 2013; I16 2013; I22 2013; Cowen and Parlette 2011). For policymakers, liberal empowerment is essential to security. Many programs that target Toronto youth in the name of empowerment, for example, are required to partner with police, explicitly or implicitly, to the point that some consider it as the unwritten rule for getting funding. As a youth activist explained to me:

> You can't just do your own thing in the neighborhood because the police are the crime prevention. . . . That's what they tell these social service agencies, and I've seen very progressive people who go into these things disliking the police and having to work with them. They have to work with them, and not only is that obviously counterproductive because you're letting in an element that is not concerned with the safety of people, but in fact has a history of abusing and brutalizing youth of the same age that are in this program. (I16 2013)

Here we can see how the ideological allure of empowerment and participation erases the ways the state embeds policing into social development services. Despite its alleged democratic rhetoric, liberal empowerment stays at the boundaries of liberal-colonial recognition that perceives the immigrant as powerless and as potential security threats. Such form of recognition assumes that the powerlessness of the immigrant, not the actions of the powerful and the sociospatial and racial structures of imperialist capitalism, is the root cause of poverty. The object of reform is thus not the sociospatial and neocolonial structures of imperialist capitalist exploitation, which are taken for granted and are understood as a reality to adapt to and to work within its limits. Rather, the object is amelioration by reforming the subjectivities of the immigrant. Participation and empowerment both work to constitute the immigrant into proper liberal, resilient subjects, always ready not just to "bounce back" but also to "bounce forward" upon encountering violence, poverty, and crisis (Cruikshank 1994; Walker and Cooper 2011; Pithouse 2011; Howell 2015). Empowerment gives the post-colonial immigrant limited forms of voice, skills, and resources that would moderate the violence of everyday exploitation and domination. The conception of the targeted subject in preventive urban policy is similar to the one in preventive policing and international security (as seen in chapter 3). This is a far cry from the radical, albeit short, history of popular political empowerment in anti-colonial, anti-imperialist movements and Black radicalism of the mid-twentieth century (see Georgakas and Surkin 1998; Bloom and Martin 2013; Field et al. 2019). In the current state-led valorization of empowerment, the idea of popular empowerment is depoliticized, reduced to capacity and asset building to enhance service delivery.

Many community activists in priority neighborhoods are aware and critical of these contradictions—albeit their voices are marginalized. For some, the United Way and the City have, in the name of empowerment, gained more control over grassroots activism on the ground (I22 2013; I6 2013). This control is implemented through a variety of means, including (1) channeling funds to the community centers, which United Way and the City see as political allies rather than those that actually have roots in neighborhoods and access to the youth who need help the most (I22 2013; I6 2013); (2) getting community elites to become the agents of implementing development policies, hence controlling grassroots activism in the name of the community itself (I6 2013; I16 2013); and (3) the constant micromanaging of community activism and the threat of cutting funds if residents do not comply to the politics of United Way (I6 2013; I29 2013).

THE NGOIZATION OF COMMUNITY ACTIVISM

The uncritical focus on empowerment and asset building through residents' participation also erases the importance of the political economy of empowering the immigrant. As a community activist in Rexdale explained:

> I think what people saw was (a) there's an economic benefit because if you reduce the violence, then we are able to get more businesses coming into the city; and (b) there's a little bit of a self-serving factor because a lot of these are NGOs—so this was going to be a great way for them to marshal even more money for their organizations. United Way raised almost $45 million, in addition to the annual fundraising that they already did; they were able to grow their business on the backs of the violence that happened. (I22 2013)

By the time the City rolled out the Priority Neighbourhoods Strategy in 2006, United Way had already become the major funder of the nonprofit sector in Toronto. By 2012, United Way provided direct investment to its network of about two hundred health and social service agencies across Toronto (Teotonio 2012). According to the ranking of Charity Intelligence Canada (2013), with a donation net worth of $116,900,000, United Way was the sixth largest charity in Canada in 2013. From 2003 to 2006, United Way's revenue jumped from $93,588,500 to $140,243,014, while its expenditures jumped from $91,250,000 to $107,317,000 respectively (Canada Revenue Agency 2016). The organization also had a funding reserve of $116 million in 2013 and $118 million in 2018. From 2005 to 2012, United Way's involvement in Toronto's urban policy greatly facilitated the expansion of the organization across immigrant neighborhoods in the city's postwar suburbs (UWT 2012b, 3). In early 2015, the organization chapter in Toronto scaled up its governance geography to the Toronto region. The boards of United Way Toronto and United Way York Region voted to merge the two organizations under the leadership of the Toronto chapter. The York Region board members celebrated the merger as an "opportunity to leverage our deep understanding of local issues with Toronto's world-leading fundraising capacity" (quoted in Armstrong 2015). In spring 2018, the organization implemented another scaling up maneuver by merging with the United Way Peel Region and renaming the now regional foundation into United Way Greater Toronto.

United Way's fundraising campaign in Toronto is the largest United Way campaign in North America. Susan McIsaac, then CEO and president of the United Way, celebrated the success of the 2012 fundraising campaign by praising how "people care about our city. They take pride and want to . . . build a strong city ensuring we have infrastructure to take care of the most vulnerable" (quoted in Ferenc 2013). In reality, however, United Way relies on the donations of about seven hundred companies and organizations in the private and public sectors (Teotonio 2012). Within the last decade, United Way has developed a sophisticated and professionalized system of fundraising, one that is frequently the topic of mainstream newspapers in Toronto. From hiring high-profile figures such as former Toronto police chief Bill Blair to Gerry McCaughery, president and CEO of the Canadian Imperial Bank of Commerce (Canada's fifth largest bank) as the chairs of its fundraising campaign[1] to having a team of forty sponsored employees ready to go to companies that do not have "fundraising know-how," United Way's yearly fundraising campaign is one competitive spectacle of philanthrocapitalist feel-good politics in Toronto (see Teotonio 2012). The political economy of this spectacular fundraising should not be downplayed. Individual and company donations are not just about care and pride, as McIsaac framed it for the media; the Canada Revenue Agency provides federal and provincial tax credits to individual and company donors for donations to registered charities.

The spectacle of United Way's fundraising reifies the ways in which imperialist capitalist interests and the state use the aura of philanthropy to mask their role in producing and sustaining the sociospatial and racialized relations of domination, exploitation, and accumulation. Take for example the list of major donors to the much celebrated United Way community infrastructures projects such as the ANC program and Community Hubs (see UWT 2012b, 17).[2] Aside from twelve private foundations run by rich, old White families, the top four Canadian banks (BMO Financial Group, RBC Capital Markets

Employees and RBC Foundations, Scotiabank, TD Bank Group) and major national and global companies such as Enbridge Gas Distribution (Canada's largest and oldest gas distribution company), Rogers Communication, and Procter & Gamble are among the donors. Alongside this list of old money and corporate and finance capital, other important donors include eight major regional, national, and North American real estate and financial holding companies and developers: Brookfield Asset Management, Cadillac Fairview Corporation, Calloway Real Estate Investment Trust, First Capital Realty, the Minto Foundation, Retrocom Mid-Market Real Estate Investment, SmartCentres, and the Conservatory Group. These real estate companies have been directly involved in and have greatly benefited from Toronto's real estate boom and the market-led land development, privatization, and intensification projects in and across Toronto. They have been vital forces in the production of Toronto's unevenly developed urban space.

Endowed with political and financial power by the pro-urban bourgeois forces and the City, United Way in Toronto has become one of the major nodes in what Dylan Rodriguez (2007) of the INCITE! Collective coined as "the non-profit industrial complex" and an important force in the "NGOization of politics" (De Souza 2013; Dauvergne and Lebaron 2014, 116, 117–18, 133). In 2008, United Way published a policy paper entitled *Leadership Solutions: Building Leadership in Toronto's Nonprofit and Voluntary Sector* (Gibson and Macklem 2008) to emphasize the opportunities that today's "world of shrinking budgets and expanding social needs" have opened up for the nonprofit sector. Gibson and Macklem write: "Never before has there been such an opportunity for the sector to become more engaged at the decision-making table. Never before has society's need for the sector to play a leadership role been greater. . . . The leadership that is required is the leadership of the highest order" (2008, 11). The policy paper not only called for the centralization of power in the nonprofit sector, but also announced how the United Way intends "to take on a leadership role in leadership development in the philanthropic and community-based sectors" (Gibson and Macklem 2008, 9). The conceptual parallel with the whole-of-government approach in international relations and the new vision of policing in Canada (centralized at the top, but flexible and localized on the ground) should not be dismissed. Of recommended responsibilities raised in this new centralized leadership were, not surprisingly, an emphasis on "single-issue activism" and "partnering" with "private sector partners" and "investors," as well as connecting with "communities of thought leaders" (Gibson and Macklem 2008, 4)—all components of the nonprofit industrial complex. Once seen from within the broader corporatization of activism (see Dauvergne and Lebaron 2014), United Way's politics and actions are neither surprising nor innovative. They are adaptations of the broader NGOization of politics and aid in international development and humanitarianism at the urban level (Wolch 1990; INCITE! 2007; Hearn 2007; Roy 2004).

MAPPING THE IMMIGRANT

The policy goal of empowering the immigrant requires knowing and mapping the geographical imaginaries of the immigrant. As Dikeç (2017) reminds us, urban policy makes its spaces of intervention. The Priority Neighbourhoods Strategy was accompanied by a new wave of knowledge production that soon consolidated the turn to place-based urban policy as the scientific solution to prevent the "Paris problem" in Toronto. While the pro-urban bourgeois forces and their organic intellectuals have remained at the forefront of knowledge production about urban poverty, since 2005 new players have entered the game. Besides United Way and policymakers at the City of Toronto, other influential forces are major academic institutions, urbanists, and for-profit and not-for-profit research institutions in Toronto.[3] The participation of these new players is greatly facilitated by funding opportunities and support from the City, United Way, and other philanthropic organizations (e.g., the Maytree and Metcalf Foundations), all founded and managed by the pro-urban bourgeois factions of the ruling class in Toronto and Canada. The Centre for Urban and Community Studies at the University of Toronto (later incorporated into the now defunct Cities Centre) played an important role in legitimizing and normalizing the geo-political fear of the immigrant and the need for place-based urban policy in Toronto. It was this Centre that published then United Way CEO and president Frances Lankin's warning about "immigrant poverty" and the prospects of "racial tensions" in Toronto back in 2002 (see chapter 2).

Motivated by the federal government's New Deal for Cities, the research papers coming out of this state-funded project strongly advocated place-based urban policy as part of "a new urban and community agenda" in Canada and other OECD countries at the time that the geographical imaginaries of neighborhood have become imperative to capital investment and competitiveness (see Bradford 2005). The emphasis on place was accompanied by linking place-based policy to resiliency (Torjman 2006), underlining the role of United Way as a "community builder" (Leviten-Reid 2006) and suggesting gentrification through the expansion of business improvement areas and social mixity (the buzzwords of gentrification) as strategies to fight the concentration of poverty (Fair and Hulchanski 2008). In 2007, the Centre for Urban and Community Studies merged with then newly established Cities Centre at the University of Toronto.[4] Benefiting from the state-led promotion of university-community joint research initiatives, itself part of the neoliberal turn in academic research funding,[5] Cities Centre started its research activity based on a twofold mandate: "to promote and undertake university-based, interdisciplinary research" and "to work in partnership with governments in all levels, community groups, NGOs, the private sector, etc. to not only disseminate its research but to bring this research into practical application within urban regions at the local, national and international levels."[6] During its short yet influential life from 2007 to 2013, the Cities Centre and its academic research affiliates became important forces in the consolidation of place-based urban policy in Toronto. In 2009, the Cities Centre partnered with United Way, E.R.A. Architects, and planningAlliance (two influential planning and architecture firms in Toronto and Ontario) to found the Centre for Urban Growth and Renewal (CUG+R). We will see, in chapter 6, how through its research on highrise rental apartment buildings in immigrant neighborhoods, CUG+R came to play an important role in designing and incorporating Tower Renewal into Toronto's reformed place-based urban policy: the Toronto Strong Neighbourhoods Strategy 2020.

After the 2005 shootings, then Ontario premier Dalton McGuinty appointed a committee to look into the causes of youth violence. The appointed committee published its report, *The Review of the Roots of Youth Violence* in 2008 (McMurtry and Curling 2008). Many progressives and community activists applauded the report for its emphasis on racism and systematic marginalization as major factors in youth violence. This is understandable given the long history of state denial of institutional racism and discrimination, as we have already seen.

Less attention, however, has been paid to the report's strong endorsement of place-based policy as a solution to youth violence (McMurtry and Curling 2008, 16–17, 34). In the following years, United Way and policymakers at the City of Toronto would use this report to justify the need for urban policy in Toronto's immigrant neighborhoods (I23 2013; I13 2013). The Toronto Board of Trade (TBOT) quickly backed these calls for place-based urban policy and linked its necessity to city–regional economic competitiveness. In 2009 and 2010 in two major reports, *Vote Toronto 2010: Framework for a Better City* (TBOT 2009) and *Lifting All Boats: Promoting Social Cohesion and Economic Inclusion* (TBOT 2010), the TBOT, more explicitly than before, warned about "the economic impact of becoming more spatially polarized by income and segregated by ethnicity" and emphasized the need for more systematic place-based urban policies to "transform the economic and social character" of the city's immigrant neighborhoods (TBOT 2009, 19, 20).

In *Vote Toronto 2010,* the TBOT highlighted that "much of Toronto's immigrant population is concentrated in suburban enclaves that are at risk of becoming permanent poverty traps" and warned about Toronto's "creeping toward the 'Paris problem'—an affluent core surrounded by a 'middle ring' of a marginalized and vulnerable population, encircled in turn by an outer layer of affluent suburbs" (TBOT 2009, 18). In *Lifting All Boats,* the TBOT explicitly linked Toronto's "Paris problem" to "the state of 'middle ring' housing" in the city (TBOT 2010, 12) and called for urban policy in immigrant neighborhoods. Both reports based their warning about Toronto's "Paris problem" on United Way's (UWT 2004) *Poverty by Postal Code* and David Hulchanski's (2007) *The Three Cities within Toronto* published by the Cities Centre. By introducing mapping as part of the scientific techniques of knowing urban problems, both reports were imperative in giving a visual form to the hitherto territorialized, text-based geographical imaginaries of concentrated non-White poverty and the immigrant problem in Toronto. Maps and mapping have also been influential in both reproducing and reifying the territorialized and racialized security ideologies that animated the geo-political fear of the immigrant and the formation of urban policy. It is worth taking a closer look at the recent fascination with mapping in Toronto.

The publication of maps of concentrated poverty at the neighborhood scale by United Way in 2004 was followed by the maps of the thirteen priority neighborhoods in 2005, giving a clear-cut graphic visualization of the spatial boundaries of "hotspots" and "stressed communities" (UWT and City of Toronto 2005). This was followed by another series of maps of the City's Community Safety Neighbourhood Areas in 2006, published by the Tri-Level Committee on Guns and Violence (appointed by the City of Toronto), depicting the thirteen priority neighborhoods this time in relation to gun violence and the spatial boundaries of place-based policing across the city (City of Toronto 2006). In 2007, the Cities Centre published an influential report, *The Three Cities within Toronto: Income Polarization among Toronto's Neighbourhoods, 1970–2000*. In the opening lines of *The Three Cities*, its author David Hulchanski wrote,

> This report provides a new way of looking at Toronto's neighbourhoods—who lives where, based on the socio-economic status of the residents in each neighbourhood, and how the average status of the residents in each neighbourhood has changed over a 30-year period. (2007, 1)

For the first time, the report visualized through maps the "growing gap in income and wealth and greater polarization among Toronto's neighbourhoods" (Hulchanski 2007, 2). Hulchanski argued that this income gap has resulted in "a sharp consolidation of three distinct groupings of neighbourhoods," "even three different cities" (2007, 4). Toronto, he warned, is no longer a "city of neighbourhoods;" rather, it is a "city of disparities" (2007, 4–5). The major contribution of the *Three Cities* report was its documentation of demographic and economic change across Toronto's neighborhoods at the turn of the twenty-first century and, in doing so, it forcefully pushed sociospatial polarization into a major public and policy debate. The report, however, fell short of situating the maps of "three cities" and the production of "three different cities" in Toronto in the broader context of the production of uneven development and racialization in Toronto and beyond. The naming of the maps, "Three Cities," itself conveyed a territorial and geographical separation rather than relationality. In the absence of engaging with the relational formation of wealth and poverty, the *Three Cities* report risked facilitating the rationalization of the already existing environmentally deterministic geographical imaginaries of immigrant neighborhoods.

By December 2010, the Cities Centre published an updated version of Hulchanski's 2007 report, *The Three Cities within Toronto: Income Polarization among Toronto's Neighbourhoods, 1970–2005*. The updated report, based on the 2006 census, reiterated the message of spatial segregation in Toronto while also highlighting the link between crime and poverty, and projected the erasure of the "middle-income" Torontonians from the map of Toronto by 2025 (Hulchanski 2010, 27). As presented in Figure 8, by 2005, "City #1," the (majority White) rich city, included only 17 percent of Toronto's population. It approximately covered downtown Toronto and the areas around the two subway lines along Yonge Street (north) and Bloor (west) and Danforth (east) streets. "City 3," the increasingly non-White poor city, included 43 percent of the city's population. It comprised large pockets of Toronto's postwar suburbs, including the thirteen priority neighborhoods. "City 2," the majority-White, middle-income city, included 38 percent of the city's population and was located in between the other two cities. The major message of the report was the "decline in 'middle-income' neighborhoods and the increase in 'lower- and higher-income areas" from 1970 to 2005 (Hulchanski 2010, 7).

In comparison to the earlier report, the 2010 *Three Cities* report gave a more grounded analysis of the uneven social geography of Toronto by engaging with the various aspects of socioeconomic polarization, including providing trends in employment, housing, mobility, education, and demographic change. At the time of its publication, however, the allure of mapping and maps had already woven its spell on academic and political debates about Toronto's social landscape. Following the 2007 report, maps of Toronto's "three cities" were rapidly reproduced within academic and policy discussions—most often without critical engagement. It was with reference to these maps that the TBOT warned about Toronto's "Paris problem" in its influential reports in 2009 and 2010. By 2010, mapping and maps made their way into the mainstream media. Color-coded maps, based on aggregated data, suddenly turned into the quintessential medium of making visible the apparently invisible social issues, from concentrated poverty to visible minority populations, disorder, violence, and electoral politics in Toronto. When in February 2010 the *Toronto Star* published its special multipart series, *Race Matters,* maps were an integrated part of the series, including maps that looked at the geography and demography of the Toronto Police stop-and-search activities from 2003 to

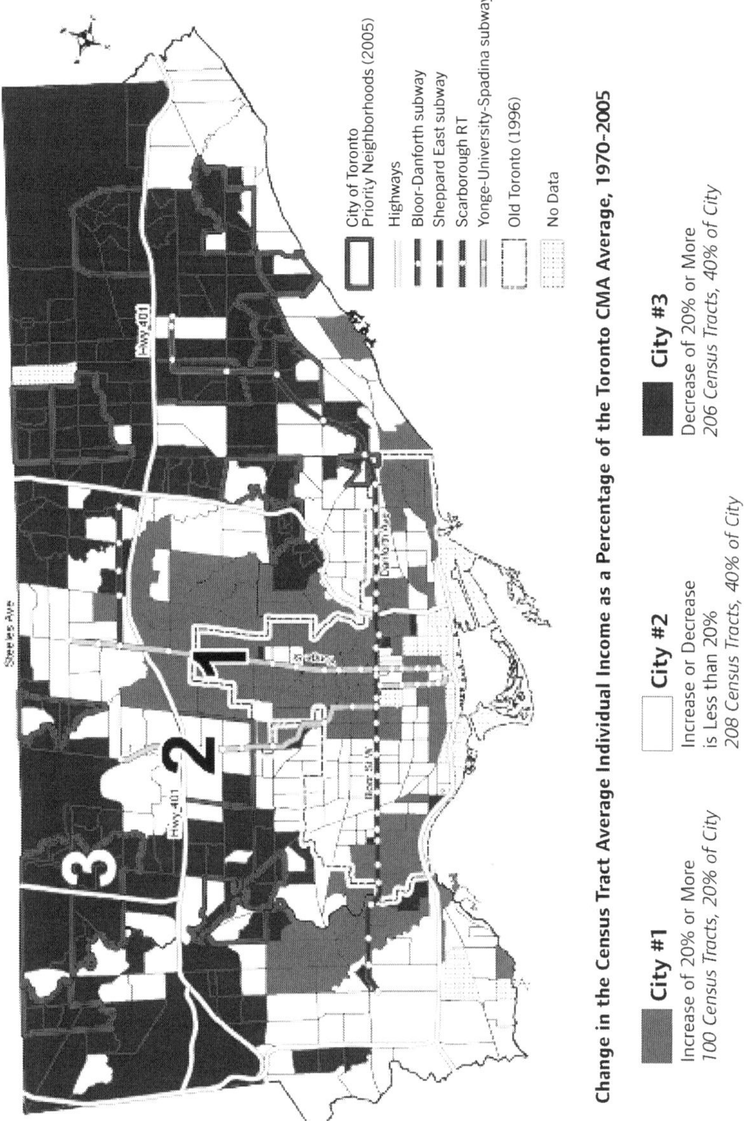

FIGURE 8. The influential mapping of sociospatial polarization in Toronto in the 2010 *Three Cities* report. The uncritical reproduction of this map and similar maps that followed greatly facilitated the making and normalizing of the racialized geographical imaginaries of poverty in Toronto. Source: Hulchanski 2010, 2.

2008. While one of the major aims of the series was to highlight the practice of racial profiling by the Toronto Police, the publication of a series of maps depicting "where Toronto police lay criminal charges" in various shades of red reinforced the racialized geographical imaginary of immigrant neighborhoods as ungovernable (see Bruser 2010; Welsh 2010).

In the aftermath of the 2010 mayoral victory of right-wing populist Rob Ford, maps became the hegemonic medium for grasping politics in Toronto. Color-coded maps, dividing the territories of "Ford voters" (inaccurately depicted as being solidly in postwar suburbs) and "Smitherman voters" (inaccurately depicted as being solidly in downtown) were used as objective evidence for confirming a territorialized political and cultural war between the assumedly two geographical imaginaries of Toronto: the progressive, civilized downtown, and the traditional, uncivilized, anti-urban postwar suburbs. The same media pundits who warned about the "Jamaican criminal" and the "Paris problem" were quick to affiliate the victory of right-wing populism in Toronto to an "immigrant-led working-class uprising" (Valpy and Leblanc 2010), "Toronto's angry (non)-white voters" (National Post Editorial Board 2010), and later, to the "Ford Nation" (see Kipfer and Saberi 2014). Liberal, NDP, and Left forces pointed to immigrant neighborhoods as the electoral territory of Conservatives and as a threat to the assumed urbanity of Toronto. These color-coded maps facilitated the shrinking of the complex social geography of Toronto and that of the ascendency of hard-Right populism into a two-dimensional geographical imaginary that depicted "the suburbs" against "the city." Taking these maps as the representation of reality, political commentators and analysts, in turn, easily blamed the ascendency of hard-Right populism on non-White, working-class populations living in the city's postwar suburbs. The increasing hegemony of reading politics off maps further simplified the historical and spatial complexities of the shift to the Right in politics in Toronto and Canada and normalized territorialized conceptions of politics, urban space, and everyday life (see Kipfer and Saberi 2014).

The publication of the 2010 *Three Cities* report went beyond the usual policy and research circles (mostly affiliated with the pro-urban bourgeois forces in Toronto). Published in the midst of the extremely territorialized political context in the aftermath of the mayoral victory of Rob Ford earlier that year, the 2010 report received a raving attention from the mainstream media. The Neighbourhood Change Research Partnership, the research group affiliated with the project, compiled an eighty-one-page report of the media coverage of the release of the report on December 15, 2010 (Cities Centre 2010). On the morning of the report's release, Matt Galloway, then host of the CBC Radio One *Metro Morning* program, invited Hulchanski to his popular morning talk show to tell Torontonians about the "Tale of Three Cities." Hulchanski highlighted the eventual loss of City #2 and the segregation and concentration of non-White poverty in Toronto's postwar suburbs. As the mainstream media and other research institutions hysterically echoed the report's message of "the loss of the middle class," the author's attempt to point to the causes of such transformations got lost and pushed off the radar. In a frenzy of reprinting the map of the "three cities," the media popularized a geopolitical image of divided and separated "cities" in Toronto. *CBC News* headlined "Toronto's Middle Class Shrinking Rapidly." The *Globe and Mail* allocated its December 15 front page to the geography of income polarization in 1970, 2005, and a projection for 2025 under the title "Toronto a City of Extremes, Losing the Middle Ground." In reference to the findings of the research, Carol Wilding, president of the TBOT, emphasized that this "continuing trend risks creating pockets of the city that become 'no-go zones,'" making "it more challenging for business to want to get in there to invest in those neighbourhoods" (quoted in Paperny 2010).

The second decade of the twenty-first century heralded the beginning of a fetishistic fascination with mapping that has since haunted the fate of urban politics and policy in Toronto. Mapping crime after every shooting is now just as routine a ritual of the mainstream media as it is with mapping politics after every election. Color-coded maps, along with pictures of poor neighbourhoods and their residents, have become part and parcel of an increasing number of research papers that build up the seemingly scientific dimension of place-based policymaking in Toronto. From 2012 to 2015, studies mapped Toronto's immigrant neighbourhoods, focusing on the concentration of non-White poverty in "tower neighbourhoods" (UWT 2012a; CUG+R 2012), "the working poor" (Stapleton, Murphy, and Xing 2012; Stapleton and Kay 2015), unemployment and prosperity "gaps" (TBOT and UWT 2014), neighborhood walkability (Toronto Public Health 2012a), the health effects of poverty (Toronto Public Health

2012b; Urban HEART@Toronto 2014), and diversity (TCF 2010, 2011, 2012, 2013). As map-mediated representations of Toronto's social geography have increasingly become the hegemonic medium to provide a seemingly objective, scientific visual form of social reality, maps themselves, their function as a mode of expression, their production, and the forces behind their production and interpretation are taken for granted.

THE GEO-POLITICS OF MAPPING IMMIGRANT NEIGHBORHOODS

An executive member of the United Way explained to me that the reason *Poverty by Postal Code* (UWT 2004) "made a big splash" was "because it talked about poverty in the same way that the earlier works had, *but this time there were maps. The people could suddenly see themselves in the city*" (I4 2013, emphasis added). In this assertation, maps are neutral images of reality, so realistic that "people could suddenly see" themselves and their city in them. Maps are anything but neutral mirrors, however. Maps are profoundly political constructions. Maps and mapping are as much about technology as they are about politics (Harley 1988; Black 1997; Scott 1998; Wood 2010). With the rediscovery of linear perspective in the midst of the Renaissance and technological advancement in printing in the sixteenth century, the map became central to the production of a new conception of space—what Lefebvre (1991) called the "abstract space," a space disembedded from lived and social relations, the space of capital (also see Jardine 1997). It was through representing this de-historicized and depoliticized conception of space as rational, scientific, empty, and measurable that the map became fundamental to the consolidation of imperialist capitalist sociospatial relations. Historically, the evolutions of mapping and war have been deeply integrated (Black 2016). By assuming a God-like vision, the map represented the state as an already existing thing, having a shape and visual form, thus obscuring the origins of the modern state in history and violence (Wood 2010, 32). Cartography, surveying, and mapping the land were at the heart of (White-settler) colonialism and the establishment of colonial-capitalist property regime, emptying out the colonized land from its hitherto inhabitants and history, erasing the colonial violence of dispossession, and rendering space as an object of calculation and commodification (Blomley 2003; Scott 1998; Harley 1988).

One could argue that the color-coded maps ornamenting policy and research papers on concentrated non-White poverty in Toronto are different from the maps of the seventeenth, eighteenth, and nineteenth centuries. Contemporary proponents of mapping perceive the map as an interpretive frame to understand and study spatial organization and segregation of metropolitan centers. In this argument, interpretation is taken as objective, as being void of politics. Maps based on aggregated census data, we are told, reveal the most neutral visualization of social reality due to technological advances in computerization and data processing of geographical information systems in the last two decades. By focusing on a small scale such as the neighborhood, these maps, we are told, give us a bottom-up tool of observing and depicting the story of poverty and its effects in different neighborhoods. These rationales, however, are neither exclusive to mapping nor entirely new and objective.

Social cartography has been central to urban policies of development, segregation, policing, and public health since the nineteenth century (Vaughan 2018). Geo-political imaginaries of danger have been central to the production of mapping in cities. Charles Booth's mapping of poverty in nineteenth-century London is the classic reference point of the proponents of mapping. What is rarely mentioned is that Booth's mapping took place in the aftermath of the 1886 Trafalgar Square riots, which brought to the attention of the British ruling class the presence of concentrated poverty within shouting distance of London's heartland of the bourgeoisie (Vaughan 2018, 69). By the early twentieth century, the visual impact of social cartography, as Laura Vaughan documents, "was not only on how people viewed urban problems, but also how they conceptualized them" (2018, 11). In the aftermath of World War II, when urbanists and planners started using one of the major technologies of war, aerial photography, they too made similar arguments about the scientific power of aerial photography and its objective use for solving urban problems (see Haffner 2013).

The problem with the above arguments in support of mapping is not that they lack novelty. Rather, the issue is twofold: On the one hand, arguments in favor of the current ascendency of mapping in policy-making are blind to the inherent techno-fetishism of their rationales.

On the other hand, these arguments easily assume the apparent authorless condition of maps and ignore the function of maps as ideology and state apparatus—that is, they ignore the actual social and material relations and institutions that mapping practices help consolidate (see Scott 1998; Neocleous 2003, 118–24; Häkli in Herb et al. 2009; Wood 2010; Haffner 2013). To be clear, the issue is not whether maps are bad or good. Rather, the point is that there is a politics of mapping, because maps are political and ideological (to paraphrase Lefebvre's famous dictum on space). The mobilization of maps as a technique of conceiving and perceiving space always requires bringing into analysis the politics of mapping.

Why should we be cautious about the increasing normality of giving maps the power to *reveal* social reality? Maps are two-dimensional graphic forms that compartmentalize space according to the particular norms, forms, and features of their objects of investigation (poverty, violence, the enemy, etc.). What we see on maps are visualizations of a flattened-compartmentalized space through the cacophony of various colors and shades, reducing social space and socioeconomic issues such as poverty to abstract entities that are quantifiable, measurable, and traceable. The geographical imaginaries that these visual forms reveal flatten the complexity of urban life and its social geography by detaching the production of urban space from the sociospatial relations of neocolonial imperialist capitalism. Think about the very act of mapping poverty. To map poverty, one must first conceive poverty as something mappable, a *thing,* with definitive boundaries—rather than a social relation linked to capital as a world system. To map the territory of neighborhood poverty means to define space along the lines set within a particular epistemological and political experience, a way of knowing and dominating. Maps of concentrated non-White poverty in immigrant neighborhoods, in turn, establish the shape of a bounded space for "the dark side of the nation" (Bannerji 2000) living in poverty. The concept of shading itself, as Denis Cosgrove notes, can carry "powerful moral connotations, especially in the past, when darkness and shadow implied ignorance and decay, both physical and moral" (2012, 1).

Mapping and quasi-ethnographic research focused on the who questions have been influential in making the immigrant and their everyday spaces into objects of investigation, which can be visualized on papers and computer screens, showcased in presentations, studied, analyzed, problematized, and ideally transformed by experts and, of course, through the participation of the objects of intervention—the immigrant. The view from above that the color-coded maps of concentrated non-White poverty or elections in Toronto provide is a metonymy for a more general verticalization and hierarchization of class, racial, and spatial relations of domination and accumulation in the context of an intensified social war in the name of prosperity and competitiveness in the city. Featured through a hierarchy of alarming colors such as red, brown, orange, yellow, green, and so on in various shades of intensity, similar to policing and military visual language, these color-coded maps are graphically designed to attract the viewers' eyes toward the hotspots of social problems, the so-called no-go zones—depicted in dark red, brown, or orange (colors signifying danger), concentrated in immigrant neighborhoods. These growing hotspots and no-go zones are seen simultaneously as Them being out there and yet close to Us (in the downtown). The politics of verticality–hierarchy enmeshed in the politics of mapping contradicts the claims that color-coded maps reveal the bottom-up reality of Toronto. What they do in practice is to visualize a mix of social realities and geographical imaginaries and then abstract them from the reality of their production. It is important to ask certain questions: Why is it that we do not see similar fascination with mapping in academic and policy circles when it comes to the geographies of landlords who illegally discriminate against certain non-White tenants? Why is there no interest in mapping properties of the major real estate companies that donate to the United Way, or where major landlords and donors along with their nannies and housekeepers live? And the list goes on. Rather than decoding the territorialization of wealth, politics, and power in Toronto, uncritical emphasis on mapping has greatly facilitated making territorialized politics into common sense.

Proponents of mapping have been silent on the ways mapping can contribute to the construction of the immigrant as a target of geopolitical fear. Reading the Toronto Board of Trade's mapping of the "Paris problem" in *Vote Toronto 2010* (TBOT 2009) and Thomas Barnett's influential *The Pentagon's New Map* (2004) helps us situate the mapping of the immigrant in relation to the geo-politics of neocolonial imperialist capitalism. There are striking parallels between Barnett's mapping of the "non-integrating gaps" worldwide and the TBOT's mapping of the "Paris problem" in Toronto's "middle rings."

The "non-integrating gaps" for Barnett are a security threat to international peace and imperialism; the "middle rings" for the TBOT pose a threat to Toronto's security, peace, and economic competitiveness. In the logics of both mappings, connectivity is the key, while danger is defined *as* disconnection. Those places that are, assumedly, unconnected to either the Toronto regional economy (the "middle ring") or the global economy (the "non-integrating gaps") are the places where problems will arise, where their problems would affect not just their localities but would be real threats to the security of the whole system—and thus requiring state–civil society intervention.[7] Barnett's argument that globalization in the long run promotes democracy, as Simon Dalby (2007, 298) argues, suggests that the middle classes are key to the stability of liberal democracy. This perception of the middle classes as the cornerstone of political and economic stability is also at the heart of the geo-political fear of the immigrant in Toronto. Recall how the "loss of the middle income" was and remains the main anxiety of the mainstream media, the United Way, and the local state in Toronto. In its depiction of Toronto's "middle ring," the TBOT (2010) underlined the political fragility of these localities as a threat to the city's economic prosperity. We may juxtapose the fragile highrise estates of Toronto's "middle ring" to the so-called fragile states such as Afghanistan, Iraq, and now Libya, Syria, and Yemen. The former is the space of former colonized subjects peripheralized in the badlands of the imperial metropole. The latter is the space of former colonies in the badlands of our imperial world. As we will see in the next two chapters, mapping has greatly influenced the way policymakers conceive immigrant neighborhoods as humanitarian spaces in need of tutelage *and* as danger zones in need of securitization.

5

Reforming Urban Policy

POSITIVISM, SOCIAL DETERMINANTS OF
HEALTH, AND EQUITY

> There is much invested in the fact of naming, in the words
> we use to express our socio-political understandings,
> because they are more than just words, they are ideological
> concepts. . . . To say this is to say explicitly that discourse is
> more than a linguistic manoeuvre. It is a matter of putting in
> words, mediating and organizing social relations of ruling,
> of meanings organized through power.
>
> —Himani Bannerji, *The Dark Side of the Nation: Essays on
> Multiculturalism, Nationalism and Gender* (2000)

THE CONSOLIDATION OF LIBERAL
HUMANITARIANISM IN URBAN POLICY

If mapping rationalized the racialized territorialization of Toronto's
social geography, the territorialized dimension of the Priority Neighbourhoods Strategy exacerbated the policy's contradictions. Five
years into its implementation, Toronto's first place-based urban policy came under (at times fierce) criticism. A great part of this criticism
came from residents and community workers living and working in
targeted immigrant neighborhoods. In their analysis of the implementation of the strategy in Scarborough, Cowen and Parlette (2011, 6)
note that the borders of priority neighborhoods "oversimplif[ied] the
spatial complexity of social networks and everyday life" in these areas.
The constructed borders of priority neighborhoods, as spaces of urban
policy, created particular challenges for social service agencies outside
of priority neighborhoods in accessing resources, even as these agencies may often serve residents from within priority neighborhoods
(Cowen and Parlette 2011, 6). At the same time, the territorialized
and racialized dimensions of the place-based urban policy deepened

the stigmatization of immigrant neighborhoods. "Priority neighbor-hood" became the name for Toronto's so-called no-go zones. Many residents rightly recognized and reacted to the systematic abjection of their subjectivities and living spaces. It became common among youth groups from targeted immigrant neighborhoods, for example, to use spoken word, poetry, theatre, and hip-hop music to debunk the geo-graphical imaginaries of their neighborhoods as bastions of violence, misery, and vice.[1] In my interviews, the problem of stigmatization was a common concern voiced by community activists, community cen-ter staff, and City of Toronto staff working in Neighbourhood Action Teams, Community Crisis Response, and youth programs. Many ar-gued against the designation of priority neighborhood and the media's representations of these neighborhoods, which has added to their stig-matization, marginalization, and alienation (see James 2012a).

By the end of June 2011, the Community Development and Rec-reation Committee under the chairmanship of then Conservative councilor of York-West Giorgio Mammoliti directed the City's Social Development, Finance and Administration Department to review and update the Priority Neighbourhoods Strategy (City of Toronto 2011b). Did the City embark on reforming the Priority Neighbour-hoods Strategy because of the criticisms of residents and commu-nity workers living and working in these neighborhoods? The reality is more complicated than a simple yes or no answer. Parallel to the growing criticisms of the policy by activists and those designated by the policymakers as the community, other (more powerful) political forces questioned the Priority Neighbourhoods Strategy. By 2011, some of the major donors to the Priority Neighbourhoods Strategy pressured the United Way and the City to show evidence of the results of their investments in these neighborhoods (I4 2013). At the same time, homeowners adjacent to designated priority neighborhoods became more vocal and persistent about their opposition to such a designation.

The official demand for review of the policy came from the anti-urban bourgeois forces at the City of Toronto. Then Conservative councilor of Etobicoke North Vincent Crisanti initially sent a letter to Councilor Mammoliti and proposed a review of the place-based policy, emphasizing the need to remove the priority neighborhood label (Crisanti 2011). Between June 2011 and February 2012, the City organized a small-scale community consultation about the Priority

Neighbourhoods Strategy. Rather than involving residents, however, the consultation involved community organization staff members, City staff, councilors and their staff, members of the Toronto Board of Trade, the Toronto Police Service, Toronto Public Health, and representatives from CivicAction (see City of Toronto 2012b). Less than a year later, in the early days of March 2012, the city council adopted a new place-based policy, the Toronto Strong Neighbourhoods Strategy 2020 (hereafter TSNS 2020). It was only then that the news of the City's attempt to reform its urban policy and extend the number of targeted neighborhoods finally made it into the mainstream media.

The most important changes that aimed to differentiate TSNS 2020 from the Priority Neighbourhoods Strategy were: (1) shifting the policy's focus from "community safety" to "the development of the broader opportunities" (City of Toronto 2012a, 7); (2) adopting a new designation terminology for naming the targeted neighborhoods— "Neighbourhood Improvement Areas" (NIA); (3) remapping the territories of the NIAs based on the boundaries of the city's 140 social planning neighborhoods (City of Toronto 2012a, 8–9);[2] (4) approving a monitoring, evaluation, and targeting process based on Urban HEART@Toronto; (5) having an emphasis on equity; (6) adding a place-based housing redevelopment strategy (Tower Renewal) to the City's place-based policy; and (7) officially expanding the involvement of United Way in urban policymaking (City of Toronto 2012a, 12–13).[3] At first glance, TSNS 2020 appears as a progressive turn in the City's urban policy. The new policy claimed to destigmatize priority neighborhoods through positive naming. Bannerji's (2000, 41) sharp critique of the ideological nature of naming in politics, as quoted in the epigraph of this chapter, reminds us that naming in policy is anything but neutral. What appears as a positive turn, I argue, is better understood as a positivist and liberal humanitarian turn, evident in a more intensified fascination with scientism and the incorporation of a public health approach through policy mobilities between the City and the WHO.

According to the City staff members I talked to, the City's change of designation terminology from "priority neighborhoods" to "neighborhood improvement areas" was "a political move to ameliorate" the contradictions of the former policy by distancing place-based urban policy from the stigmatizing aspects of the Priority Neighbourhoods Strategy (I22 2013; I23 2013; I19 2013; I29 2013; see also City of

Toronto 2012a, 8). The goal was to give a "better image" to the City's strategies (I21 2013; I19 2013). As such, TSNS 2020 contradicts some major aspects of Wacquant's (2008) conceptualization of territorial stigmatization. No more "publicly labelled as a 'lawless zone' or outlaw estate,'" the policy represent Toronto's immigrant neighborhoods in a liberal humanitarian language of need, development, empowerment, and resilience. The political move to rename the designation of targeted neighborhoods had partly to do with the contradictions of place-based policy and policymakers' recognition that there is a growing public frustration about the stigmatizing effects of the Priority Neighbourhoods Strategy. A senior City manager explained that the renaming

> was a council decision. . . . There were many residents in priority neighbourhoods that expressed concern with the designation. Actually, a fair number of youths started to raise the issue. So, you know, obviously, I listen to council and I care what council has to say, but I also care when youth in the neighbourhoods are expressing challenges with the designation. We consulted and went back to council and said, "Here are some options," and council chose Neighbourhood Improvement Areas [NIA]. . . . The thing I like about NIA is that we're trying, to a certain extent, to normalize the language, so that it'd be related to BIAs [business improvement areas] or Community Improvement Areas, under planning legislation. It was trying to also kind of align the terminology with the existing City terminology. (I3 2014)

While the City did aim to destigmatize the designation terminology of its place-based policy, it is important to ask what the policy meant by *stigma*. Who is the stigmatized? And who is supposed to benefit from the City's attempt to destigmatize?

The consolidation of the liberal humanitarian turn does not negate the ongoing reproduction of the geo-political fear of the immigrant. As we saw in chapter 2, liberal humanitarianism was already present in the making of the geo-political fear of the immigrant in Toronto in the 1990s. The consolidation of liberal humanitarianism as the dominant ideology of place-based urban policy should concern critical analysts, activists, and residents. Erased in this liberal humanitarian discourse is the politics of the council's "political request to change the name, not to change the designation," as a policy analyst at the City put it (I25 2013). The complex realities of the unevenly developed geographies of postwar suburbs were central to this politics of renaming. In his letter to the Community Development and Recreation Committee, then Councilor Crisanti (2011) argued that the removal of the priority neighborhood terminology "would assist in attracting private investment and contribute to a sense of pride among residents of these neighbourhoods." The City staff report to the city council in February 2012 reiterated this concern and linked the problem of stigmatization to the devaluation of real estate in the priority neighborhoods. The report stated, "There has been a concern that the term sometimes has a stigmatizing effect, making potential business investors or home-buyers apprehensive about locating there" (City of Toronto 2012a, 8). Both then councilors Crisanti and Mammoliti, who were behind the motion to change the designation terminology, were concerned about the complaints of middle-income (majority White) homeowners living adjacent to immigrant neighborhoods in their ridings at the time (I22 2013; I6 2013; I4 2013). A former United Way policy analyst explained to me that

> it was people like Mammoliti who were so appalled that his area was named part of the PN [Priority Neighbourhoods Strategy] or Crisanti as well. They are just responding to that call of stigma. Get the focus off of my neighborhood.... I think in each neighborhood... most of those who push back were from middle-class enclaves, and so they pushed back and came to the city council saying, Why are you calling our neighbourhoods this? The condo owners in Crescent Town absolutely were saying that before anyone else. (I4 2013)

The stigmatized residents living in the priority neighborhoods were the last to hear about the City's benevolent attempt to destigmatize their living spaces. When I was doing fieldwork during the summer and fall of 2013 (more than a year and a half after the City's adoption of the NIA terminology), the new naming terminology was news to many community activists and workers in the priority neighborhoods. This lack of information was partly because the City never had any real community consultations with residents in these areas (I22 2013; I6 2013; I29 2013). At least in the priority neighborhoods of Jane and Finch and Rexdale that fell into the ridings of then councilors

Mammoliti and Crisanti at the time, no genuine community consultation was organized. A community activist in Rexdale highlighted that

> there has been no authentic consultation. Crisanti only scheduled
> one, and there was barely any advertisement. . . . He made sure
> that he had two of his supporters, and they were supposedly at the
> meeting, and supposedly they were the ones saying, "We don't
> want this priority neighborhood labelling." . . . Giorgio Mammo-
> liti has taken that and said, you know, "Priority Neighbourhoods
> gives my neighborhood a bad name," we need to change that,
> and we need to change it to something that's attractive. Strong
> Neighborhoods. . . . I can just picture them all in a room, without
> us, without the others, saying, "This is how we're going to do it."
> (I22 2013)

A senior staff member of United Way Action for Neighbourhood
Change in Jane and Finch also explained to me:

> Even myself as a staff member, I just found out about this maybe
> two or three months ago when we had a meeting [with the City's]
> NAPs [Neighborhoods Action Plans]. . . . We found out from
> our [NAP] community development worker. . . . She said, "We
> don't call it that [priority neighborhood] anymore." It wasn't even
> like, "Here's the change;" it was more like just in passing, "Oh
> yeah, we're not supposed to say priority neighborhoods anymore,
> it's supposed to be called blah blah." I was like, "When did that
> happen?" . . . I didn't get any e-mails of any consultation, because I
> usually get things like that and then I pass them on. (I29 2013)

Normalizing the renaming of targeted neighborhoods was also due
to the City's official claim to broaden the focus of its place-based policy beyond community safety to other aspects of development. Part
of the critique of the Priority Neighbourhoods Strategy was directed
toward its sole focus on security and youth (I3 2014; I19 2013). In
crafting TSNS 2020, policymakers at the City instead chose to mobilize a dominant discourse in international development and public
health politics. Similar to shifts in policing strategies (see chapter 3),
TSNS 2020 focused on social determinants of health and equity in
neighborhood development and incorporated targeted housing re-

development as part of the strategy. I will focus on the housing question in the next chapter. For now, let us see how social determinants of health and equity have made their ways into the corridors of the City of Toronto and what they mean in policy and practice.

WHO IN TORONTO: ON THE GEO-POLITICS OF URBAN HEART

On March 9, 2014, the Sunday edition of the *Toronto Star* ran a front-page article notifying Torontonians that the "City Wants More Areas Added to 'Priority' List" (Doolittle 2014a). It was the first public announcement of TSNS 2020 and an upcoming policy recommendation to City Council to increase the number of designated priority neighborhoods from twenty-three to thirty-one neighborhoods. Announcing the news a week ahead of the city council's vote, the *Toronto Star* anticipated heated debates about the new strategy (Doolittle 2014a). The new strategy, essentially an assessment tool, was said to provide each neighborhood with a "neighbourhood equity score": "a single number designed to capture the total weight of unnecessary, unfair and unjust differences faced by neighbourhood residents" (City of Toronto 2014c). The City analysts calculate "equity scores" by using Urban HEART@Toronto, itself an adaptation of the WHO Urban HEART, which monitors health-related factors in and across the cities in the global South. Like the mesmerizing smell of a rose, the positivist aura of Urban HEART@Toronto washed away the pain of the thorny reality of poverty in the city.

Health researchers involved with crafting Urban HEART@Toronto heralded the new technique as "a quick way to take the pulse of a city," an "objective, user-friendly tool to identify health inequalities and plan actions to reduce them" (quoted in Shepherd 2014). For senior managers at the City, such "an evidence-based standard for measuring the well-being of Toronto's neighbourhoods" (City of Toronto 2014c) was "ground-breaking work" (quoted in Strobel 2014; Doolittle 2014b) in producing data and tracking the impacts of investments. Urban HEART would allow "each neighbourhood to be measured, a little like a blood pressure reading or body temperature taken," explained Sarah Rix (a senior policy development officer at the City) at a consultation session on TSNS 2020 (quoted in Baldwin 2014). The mainstream media reiterated similar messages. The new tool, the *Globe and Mail* confirmed, is a "more sophisticated model" (Church 2014). Urban HEART, according to the *Toronto Star,* is "a solid, evidence-based" strategy that "this city needs to help draft programs improving the lives of the residents at risk" (*Toronto Star* 2014a). In anticipation of the City Council vote on March 17, 2014, the *Toronto Star* ran two editorials reminding the councilors and the public that the "Urban HEART program . . . can point the way to a better Toronto" (*Toronto Star* 2014a); hence, "Let new data guide the way" (*Toronto Star* 2014b). For their part, supportive councilors from different political spectrums publicly declared their trust in the "robust" research method that is able to give Torontonians "the clearest possible picture of where the needs are" (quoted in Church 2014).

On March 17, the city council approved the expansion of designated neighborhoods and the application of Urban HEART@Toronto as the major tool for TSNS 2020.[4] In what appeared as a consensus among social democrat, liberal, and Third-Way neoliberal forces, words such as *scientific, objective,* and *evidence-based* turned into common adjectives describing the new urban policy. The few quick references to the WHO in the media and by researchers and policymakers were all meant to reinforce the assumedly scientific dimension of the new strategy. The public was to believe that if the WHO researchers design a framework, it should be scientific and objective by nature. This positivist fascination with Urban HEART pushed aside more substantial, political questions about the formation of the City's latest urban policy. How did Urban HEART make its way to the City of Toronto? Why did Canada's global city suddenly invest in adapting a strategy drafted for cities in the global South as the framework of urban policy? What are the epistemological pillars of defining and measuring equity? Objectively speaking, how is it possible to deal with a sociopolitical, racial, and spatial phenomenon such as poverty by quantitatively measuring equity like blood pressure, body temperature, and pulse?

Urban HEART stands for Urban Health Equity Assessment and Response Tool. Toronto was the first Western city to mobilize the WHO Urban HEART framework, in the mid-2010s. Today, Urban HEART is also used by the local governments in Detroit and Barcelona (see Prasad 2018). The framework is the outcome of the broader focus on social determinants of health and the emphasis on prevention in the WHO policy and international relations. As we saw in chapter 3, the international focus on the social determinants of health was heavily boosted under the former WHO director-general Lee Jong-Wook in the early 2000s and particularly after the launch of the WHO Commission on Social Determinants of Health (CSDH) in 2005. Soon after, in a joint project the WHO Centre for Health Development in Kobe (Japan) along with the WHO regional offices and city and national officials from the global South developed Urban HEART. In 2008, the WHO introduced Urban HEART as a pilot project to "facilitate the process of proactively addressing health inequities" in major cities in the global South in order to meet the United Nation's Millennium Development Goals (WHO 2010a, 3). After two years of running pilot versions of Urban HEART in seventeen cities in ten countries,[5] the WHO officially launched the Urban HEART framework in 2010. The opening lines of the official document explicitly situate Urban HEART in relation to the 1978 Alma-Ata Declaration of Health for All (WHO 2010a, 4). Two years after its official adoption by the WHO, in 2012, Urban HEART found its way into Toronto's policy circles via the Centre for Research on Inner City Health (CRICH)—a research center affiliated with the University of Toronto and St. Michael's Hospital.

While Urban HEART@Toronto was celebrated for its scientific allure (CRICH 2014, 20, 3; City of Toronto 2013a; 2014a), its arrival in Toronto's policy corridors had less to do with robust, scientific research on best practices than with the increasing hegemony of multisector, multiscale partnerships and policy mobilities around policy buzzwords as well as the broader strategy of the WHO to scale up the application of Urban HEART beyond the global South (see WHO 2010a). One of the City's senior policy development officers described the arrival of Urban HEART in Toronto as the following:

> We were involved in an intersectoral table that was looking at health
> equity and the table didn't have a specific mandate at that point. . . .
> We recognized we were all involved in what could be broadly seen
> as equity or health equity issues that would intersect. . . . The idea
> about trying to adapt the Urban HEART model came up as part
> of that table, and a few of us thought it was a good idea to look
> at adapting this model because it wasn't for urban contexts like
> Toronto. One of the partners, the Centre for Research on Inner City
> Health, had been involved in developing the original tool [with the

> WHO] and they were interested in adapting it to Toronto. . . . We got a research grant. It was sort of one of these opportunity things. The opportunity to partner with people to adapt it arose, and it provided us with, you know, a defensible and reasonable framework for looking at the equities across the city, which is something we wanted to do, as part of [Toronto] Strong Neighborhoods Strategy 2020. We don't have the internal capacity to develop and adapt such a tool ourselves. It was done by others, which is a good thing, I think. So that was basically how it came out. We didn't go searching for all the possible ways to look at the social determinants of health or to see whether the social determinants of health was the framework we wanted to use. (I25 2013)

The above-mentioned intersectoral table was an initiative of CRICH as part of the WHO's attempt to scale up the application of Urban HEART. A senior staff at WoodGreen Community Services, one of the organizations partnering in the development of Urban HEART@ Toronto, explained:

> It was the Centre for Research on Inner City Health (CRICH) who came forward to United Way and the City and said, "Hey, we have this new project, we think it's really important to talk about health equity and [it is] important to remember that it's a health equity tool. . . ." They said, "We want to develop this new tool and spark the policy dialogue of what are the different impacts of community structure that create health problems for people." United Way and the City said, "Yeah, let's do that." The Toronto Public Health, with their health mandate, also came and said, "We would be partners on this." But as the project unfolded, the City recognized that it could be one of the important tools that they can use as part of their measurement for this neighbourhood strategy that they have. (I4 2013)

With the City's partnership research grant and under the directorship of Dr. Pat O'Campo, CRICH initiated and led the process of adapting the WHO Urban HEART framework for Toronto in partnership with United Way, civil-society organizations (e.g., WoodGreen Community Services, the Toronto Local Health Integration Network, the Canadian Institute of Health Research), and the local state institutions (the City of Toronto, Toronto Public Health, Toronto District School Board). The outcome of this partnership was Urban HEART@Toronto, a data-gathering and targeting tool that forms the cornerstone of the neighborhood lens of TSNS 2020.

Conceptually, Urban HEART@Toronto is a replica of the WHO Urban HEART. The Toronto policy document even uses the same logo and color on its cover page and in its page headers. The WHO Urban HEART focuses on social determinants of health through four policy domains: physical environment and infrastructure, social and human development, economics, and governance (CSDH 2008; WHO 2010a). Urban HEART@Toronto "measures neighbourhood-level indicators of local health and well-being in five main domains: economic opportunities; social and human development; civic engagement; physical environment and local infrastructure; and physical and mental health" (CRICH 2014, 5). TSNS 2020, in turn, takes these five domains as the "5 keys to neighbourhood wellbeing" based on which the City will constantly measure, monitor, map, target, and designate the neighborhoods in need of state intervention (City of Toronto 2014c, 3). It is this framework that the City policymakers used for designating the thirty-one neighborhoods as intervention zones in 2014.

At first glance, the City's focus on social determinants of health and equity appears as a move toward more progressive policymaking. After all, in the midst of austerity, the fact that the City and its policymakers showed concern about residents' health, well-being, and neighborhood equity across the city is, in itself, a promising move. There is, however, more to this public-health turn in policy. The reformed urban policy is very vague on the responsibilities of the state regarding residents' well-being. More than the Priority Neighbourhood Strategy, TSNS 2020 builds upon the role of the private and NGO sectors to do place-based policymaking and implementation. This is specifically important given the fact that one of the major critiques of the Priority Neighbourhood Strategy was the issue of funding sustainability and, in particular, the lack of stable government funding for projects, an issue that was mentioned in most of my interviews (I6 2013; I13 2013; I18 2013; I22 2013; I29 2013; I31 2013). It was particularly because of this aspect of TSNS 2020—its silence on the role of the local state—that conservative councilors lined up in support of the City's reformed place-based urban policy (I25 2013).

But the policy's vagueness does not mean a shrinking role of the local state. According to a community activist in the Jane and Finch neighborhood, by having United Way and the private sector on the frontline of funding and policy implementation, the City has deepened the corporatization and co-optation of community activism (I6 2013). To have a better understanding of the politics of TSNS 2020, let us go back to the conjuncture in which social determinants of health became prevalent in policy discourse and continue our discussion from chapter 3. The travelogue of social determinants of health as a policy concept is an interesting aspect of the relational formation of urban policy and international relations.

SOCIAL DETERMINANTS OF HEALTH: A TRAVELOGUE

As mentioned earlier, the ascendency of prevention in international relations was imperative to the popularity of the concept of social determinants of health in international health policy and beyond. The by-now popularized emphasis on the social determinants of health emerged in a global conjuncture at the turn of the twenty-first century characterized by a few interrelated conditions that are important to our discussion: (1) a growing awareness of deepening world poverty and the resultant local and social turns in development and the emergence of neocolonial trusteeship in the global South (Hart 2009); (2) a deepening of the nexus of security, racialization, and development, with poverty being increasingly associated with violence, unrest, and terrorism (Duffield 2007; Kaldor 1999; Barnett 2004); (3) the intensification of imperialist aggressions and wars in the global South; (4) the normalization of racism as the result of a politicized xenophobic obsession with migration flows; and (5) a growing awareness of worldwide urbanization. We have already seen how the concept of the social in the influential 2005 report of the CSDH sidesteps the very power relations that produce disease and inequality in health (see chapter 3). The links among poverty, disease, and security are central to the WHO emphasis on the social determinants of health. We can trace such links to the way the WHO situated Urban HEART and social determinants of health in relation to achieving the UN Millennium Development Goals as articulated in *Investing in Development* (United Nations 2005). The main objective of the Millennium Development Goals is said to be facilitating "the means to a productive life" for the poor (United Nations 2005, 4). How to define and actualize "a productive life" is of course an extremely ideological and political struggle. One could say that actualizing a productive life has been *the* ideological and political struggle since the dawn of capitalism.

Marx's ([1844] 1992) critique of the political economy of capitalism in *Capital, Volume I* and in the *1844 Manuscripts* is based on a defense of a humanist conception of productive life, one that would facilitate the development of human potentials that are denied under capitalism. This denial of a humanist productive life is precisely because of the alienated nature of humans' relation to their productive activity, to their labor. Productive activity in capitalism is, for Marx, "active alienation, the alienation of activity, the activity of alienation" ([1844] 1992, 326). Rather than an affirmation of human capacity, capitalist productive activity diminishes the qualities that mark a person as a human being, denying the fulfillment of human's productive activity. From the very beginning pages of the UN's *Investing in Development*, it is clear that the adjective *productive* in the project of building "a productive life" for the poor refers not to human capacity, but to capitalist productivity:

> A healthier worker is a more productive worker. A better-educated worker is a more productive worker. Improved water and sanitation infrastructure raised output per capita through various channels, such as reduced illness. So, many of the [Millennium Development] Goals are part of capital accumulation, defined broadly, as well as desirable objectives in their own right. (United Nations 2005, 4)

In this logic, the goals of poverty reduction, health improvement, the promotion of peace, gender equity, and so on are set to facilitate and secure capital accumulation. The amelioration of poverty is only possible through the integration of the poor into the market economy.

Those subject positionalities (the poor, the working class, the formerly colonized, the indigenous, the racialized excluded, the immigrant, the refugee, etc.) that are constantly reproduced by sociospatial relations of imperialist capitalism are also the ones that constantly need to be contained and kept under domination since they are conceived as security threats to the system that feeds upon their exploitation. Here too, poverty is conceptualized as risk and vulnerability, an unfortunate result of disconnection from or lack of proper integration into the market. In *Investing in Development,* poverty reduction is declared as being "a linchpin of global security," because

> poor and hungry societies are much more likely than high-income societies to fall into conflict over scarce vital resources. . . . Many world leaders in recent years have rightly stressed the powerful relationship between poverty reduction and global security. Achieving the Millennium Development Goals should therefore be placed centrally in international efforts to end violence, conflict, instability and terrorism. (United Nations 2005, 6)[6]

The link between poverty and global security is central to the ascendency of prevention in the politics of international development and security; it breathes at the heart of the geo-politics of the empire of capital (Wood 2005) and its War on Terror (Klassen and Albo 2013).

The geographical imaginaries of the UN's mapping of poverty-as-risk parallels those of Barnett's mapping of "gaps" in the global imperial order. The focus on social determinants of health has turned into another way of integrating the "gaps" into the "core." The UN *Investing in Development* report (similar to the earlier one, *Attacking Poverty* [World Bank 2000]) erases the ways that poverty and violence have been historically produced as the result of capitalist uneven development, colonization, imperialist wars, and exploitation. The report is firmly situated within the broader liberal discourse on development and security, wherein the goal of development is neither the eradication of poverty nor the development of human potentials, but rather prevention—the containment of potential threats to the imperialist-capitalist world order that could emanate from the zones of poverty (see Wilson 2012; Immerwahr 2015). The obsession with worldwide poverty has also resulted in compelling geo-political imaginaries of poverty and insecurity, from Africa and the Middle East to the so-called failed states and the slums of global South. The focus on slums has accompanied the increasing attention to worldwide urbanization and the urban dimensions of uneven development.

The 2008 CSDH report initiated the organization's renewed focus on urbanization after the modernization era of the 1950s and the 1960s. It is important to mention that the WHO focus on urbanization is a focus on rates of urban poverty and population growth rather than on the relational formation of poverty and wealth through processes of capitalist urbanization, displacement, and dispossession. The goal, we are told, is to manage and contain urban poverty through "participatory urban governance" and "urban planning and design" (CSDH 2008, ix, xi, 21, 30, 33, 39, 53, 55). In 2008, the Knowledge Network on Urban Settings, a research body established by the CSDH, published its report *Our Cities, Our Health, Our Future: Acting on Social Determinants for Health Equity in Urban Settings.* The report emphasized "urban development and town planning" as "key to creating supportive social and physical environments for health and health equity" (Kjellstrom, Mercado, and Barten 2008, iii). *Our Cities* further linked poverty, health, and security by highlighting urban poverty not only as the source of "unhealthy living" (Kjellstrom, Mercado, and Barten 2008, viii), but also as the source of "urban violence and crime" (Kjellstrom, Mercado, and Barten 2008, ix) and the breakdown of social cohesion (Kjellstrom, Mercado, and Barten 2008, x). None of these reports question the very principles of capitalist urbanization. Rather, here too the goal is to empower the poor, to integrate them into the market economy through supposedly more efficient urban planning and governance; in other words, the goal is to ameliorate the conditions of poverty through the political administration of poverty.

WHO Urban HEART was produced in this broader context. In 2010, when the WHO officially rolled out Urban HEART, the organization also sponsored the Global Forum on Urbanization and Health in Kobe, Japan, with Canada as one of the participants. The forum emphasized the role of cities in concentrating "opportunities and risks to health" and the need for "particular attention" "to the urban poor and disadvantaged:"

> City planners and policy-makers must have a clear picture of the social and economic health determinants—information broken by neighborhood, gender, age, employment—and use the data to guide effective health actions. (WHO 2010b, 4)

The forum also gave its collective support to "scal[ing]-up Urban HEART implementation to new countries and cities through WHO Regional Officers" (WHO 2010b, 5). The University of Toronto Centre for Inner City Health was one of the participants of the WHO Global Forum in 2010, and its interest in adapting Urban HEART for

Toronto came out of this venue and the WHO strategy of scaling up Urban HEART implementations.

When seen from this broader perspective, it becomes clear that the emphasis on the social determinants of health is anchored neither in a genuine concern about the well-being of human beings *as* human beings nor in a concrete grasping of the role of sociospatial and racial relations in the production of urban poverty. The emphasis on social determinants of health—whether in policing or urban policy—is about ameliorating the violence of poverty, smoothing the hard edges of capitalist development, extending the geographical depth of the markets, facilitating capital accumulation, and producing a resilient labor force in order to secure the hegemony of the imperialist-capitalist order.

THE FETISH OF EQUITY

What about the recent emphasis on equity in Toronto's urban policy? One comes across the term a few times on every page of TSNS 2020 (City of Toronto 2014b). Outflanking *creativity, equity* is now the new buzzword that can be added to anything and everything. We have "neighbourhood equity score," "neighbourhood equity benchmarks," "equity across all neighbourhoods," "Toronto Youth equity strategy," "neighbourhood equity measurement," "equity area," "equity-focused," "place-based equity work," "population-focused equity efforts," "equity issues," "equity-building," "equity lens," "equity indicator," and "equity index." What is the definition of equity? Why such an obsessive emphasis on equity rather than equality at our current conjuncture? Equity and policy are no strangers to each other, of course. The history of their institutional marriage goes back to the conjuncture of decolonization and particularly the Black urban rebellions in the late 1960s in the United States. In 1971, H. George Frederickson (1971) introduced the term *social equity* into the canon of public administration theory (Guy and McCandless 2012). Since the 1990s, equity policies (e.g., affirmative action, positive discrimination), with the official goal of diversifying the workforce and challenging institutional racism and sexism, have increasingly become part of the strategies of public institutions in the Anglophone world and, to a lesser degree, in parts of Europe. Sarah Ahmed (2012) has brilliantly documented how these equity strategies have become an important part of diversity management, rather than tackling institutional discrimination, in public institutions in countries such as the United States, Canada, and the United Kingdom.

Since the mid-2000s, through the international development policies of the World Bank and the WHO, the rhetoric of equity as fairness has also made its way into international relations. The current emphasis on equity in Toronto's urban policy has its immediate roots in this latter trend. It was under the leadership of Paul Wolfowitz, one of the main architects of the Iraq War, that the World Bank first popularized the concept of equity in relation to development with reference to fairness and justice. As deadly counterinsurgency operations were taking place in Iraq and Afghanistan, the World Bank (2005) *World Development Report 2006: Equity and Development* announced equity as a fundamental dimension of poverty reduction and market prosperity. In the same year, equity also became the focus of the Human Development Report of the UN Development Programme. Heavily indebted to John Rawls's (1971) theory of justice (World Bank 2005, 19, 77), the 2006 World Bank report defined a liberal conception of equity based on two basic principles: "equal opportunities" and "avoidance of deprivation in outcome" (Wolfowitz 2005, xi). Equity, defined as such, we are told, is not antagonist to "the major emphasis in development thinking of the past 10 to 20 years—on markets, on human development, on governance, and on empowerment" (World Bank 2005, 17). Rather, equity as such "builds and integrates" and "extends existing approaches" (World Bank 2005, 226).

The World Bank's two principles of equity are translations of Rawls's second principle of justice as fairness, wherein social and economic inequalities are not to block "fair equality of opportunity" and "are to be to the greatest benefit of the least-advantaged members of society (the *difference principle*)" (1971, 42–43). Writing from the chambers of Harvard University, Rawls published his theory of justice in the same year (1971) that Frederickson released his theory of social equity. But unlike the latter, which remained limited to mainstream debates on public administration, Rawls's (1971) theory of justice, which he later linked to international relations and foreign policy (see Rawls 1999), was influential to the development of liberal thought in the late twentieth century. The influence of Rawls's theory has less to do with the depth of his thought than with the way his theory of justice functions as a political and philosophical legitimization of an unjust liberal capitalist society.

With the idea of justice as fairness, Rawls (1971) attempted to re-define the social contract for late twentieth-century liberal society. His two principles of justice as fairness aim to provide a just design for political constitution (first principle) and to regulate fair economic institutions (second principle). Rawls, however, takes the capitalist market, private property, and the racial and sociospatial relations of imperialist capitalism for granted. This is why for Rawls inequality is a problem of distribution. He thus constructs justice not against, but rather from within existing legal, economic, and political relations and practices of imperialist capitalism. As a result, he erases the injustice that is embedded in and integral to capitalist relations, private property, and the market economy (see Wolff 1977). Rawls's (1971, 1999) conception of liberal society is extremely de-historicized and blind to sociopolitical and racial relations of domination and exploitation. Yet, if his theory of justice is abstract and detached from history, his attempt to legitimize injustice in the name of fairness was a concrete outcome of the conjuncture of decolonization and its specific vibrations in the United States. Confronted with the surge of Black radicalism and a crisis of the entire social formation, both its economic content and political form, the White liberal American establishment of the 1960s witnessed one of its most volatile periods of hegemony. It was in this conjuncture, when place-based urban policy emerged as a strategy to nullify Black radicalism in the cities in the United States, that Frederickson (1971) put forward his theory of social equity in public administration and Rawls (1971) proposed his theory of justice with an emphasis on equal opportunity.

Thirty years later the World Bank policymakers found political utility in Rawls's theory of justice to frame their imperialist strategies embedded in international development with reference to equity. Similar to the discourse of human security and the "new wars" (see Kaldor 1999), this Rawlsian equity discourse understands inequality not as a barbaric feature of our human civilization under imperialist capitalism, but as an unfortunate reality, one that without intervention would turn into a major cause of civil conflict and an imminent threat to the security of imperialist capitalism (see World Bank 2005, 118, 129, 161). Equity as such is imperative for the efficiency of the market and the stability of market growth (World Bank 2005, 89, 129). Equity as fairness is about "achieving more equal access to markets" (World Bank 2005, 178), facilitating the integration of the poor and the wretched of the earth into the sociospatial and racial relations of imperialist capitalism, as if they are not already the products of those same relations.

How have urban policymakers translated equity and social determinants of health in urban policy in Toronto? In a similar way to the WHO initiatives, the emphasis on social determinants of health in TSNS 2020 and Urban HEART@Toronto is concerned with the symptoms of urban poverty and uneven development rather than their causes. The "5 keys of neighbourhood wellbeing"—economic opportunities, social and human development, civic engagement, physical environment and local infrastructure, and physical and mental health—are all the outcomes of the sociospatial, economic, and racial relations of capitalist urbanization in the Toronto region and beyond. The policy, at its best, can only ameliorate symptoms of poverty, rather than tackling the root causes of poverty production. The very quantification of equity (as in "neighbourhood equity score" or "equity index") is only possible by flattening, abstracting, and fragmenting the racialized sociospatial relations of inequality and poverty. Equity thus works as an ideological tool for the political management of urban poverty, for governing racialized ungovernability.

Despite, or rather in spite of, the emphasis on social determinants of health and equity, neither Urban HEART@Toronto nor TSNS 2020 considered racism as a relevant factor in well-being and equity. In their positivist framework, racism, racial exploitation, and domination are not key to people's well-being. Racism, as Fanon ([1961] 1967) forcefully reminded us, is a lived ideology and an alienating social relation that is mediated through everyday life. We have already seen the deep-seated historical roots of the erasure of systemic racism in Toronto and Canada. The absence of systemic racism as a factor in TSNS 2020 took place at a time when an increasing number of progressive reports on the immigrant problem in Toronto had focused on the impacts of systemic racism in labor and housing markets (see Block and Galabuzi 2011; Stapleton, Murphy, and Xing 2012; Block 2013). In answering my question as to why racism is not a factor in the City's focus on equity, a senior City staff explained to me that the policy

doesn't address the issues of racism or sexism directly. . . . Those [five] keys are based on a modified social determinants of health framework that came to us from the Urban HEART tool. That tool specifically focuses on things that are actionable, and then looks at the populations afterwards, who are affected; and the reason for that [lack of focus on racism] is that race is not actionable. (I25 2013)

The erasure of racism is the result of a politically conscious decision to not wrestle with power relations. The consequence is an ideological conflation of causes and symptoms of systemic racism. It is only since the second half of 2020, as the naked violence of the Covid-19 pandemic has most severely and visibly devasted Toronto's immigrant neighborhoods, where many "frontline workers" live, and in the context of the popularity of the Black Lives Matter movement, that the link between racism and social determinants of health has slowly become a topic of debate in public discourse.

The ideological mobilization of equity and the social determinants of health in Toronto's urban policy were also evident in the processes of community consultation after the City adopted TSNS 2020 in 2012. From October 3 to November 5, 2013, the City organized nine (first eight and later another) community consultations on "the key issues facing Toronto's neighbourhoods." Given that "participation in decision making" is one of the five "keys of neighbourhood well-being," one would think that the City would have facilitated the participation of residents from priority neighbourhoods. Alas, they did not. Out of the initial eight community consultations, only three were located in the priority neighbourhoods—two in Scarborough and one in north Etobicoke. There was, for example, no consultation in Jane and Finch, and the residents did not take it lightly. On October 8, 2013, the resident-based antipoverty group Jane-Finch Action Against Poverty (JFAAP) wrote an open letter to the City of Toronto "denouncing the City's phony 'consultation'":

Those who have limited access to private and public means of transportation or internet and who live in "priority" neighbourhoods, such as our area, have clearly been excluded from the process. We are dismayed that there will be no consultation in the Jane and Finch community and for that matter the whole North West North York. . . . The persistence of a very high level of poverty, unemployment as well as targeted policing and a wide-range of other socio-economic barriers in racialized neighbourhoods like Jane and Finch means that we need to have stronger voices in order to achieve real social and economic justice. . . . We are therefore calling on the City of Toronto and those in charge to expand these consultations in order to ensure that community residents will have easy access to these meetings. (JFAAP 2013)

Confronted with an unexpected resident-based backlash, the City announced on October 23 the addition of a "community conversation" in the Jane and Finch neighborhood to take place on November 5. As opposed to other community consultations in which City staff members and (out-of-the-area) professionals outnumbered residents, more than two hundred residents attended the meeting at Oakdale Community Centre. Residents and activists were concerned about the content of consultation, and in particular, the City's sole emphasis on the "key" social determinants of health. In a follow-up statement, JFAAP argued:

Those attending were presented with a set of meaningless "keys" instead of addressing true needs of our communities. These were crudely adapted from a model used by the World Health Organization which deals with global poverty (i.e., access to clean drinking water, education, sanitation, etc.). This excluded the issues of local concerns such as access to housing, low minimum wages, transit city, City cutbacks, over policing, etc. All of these were brought up by community residents in the follow-up meeting, but none of these issues were addressed. (JFAAP 2014).

JFAAP and local residents were not the only ones who criticized the abstractness of the City's "key" areas of action. This concern was also voiced loudly at other consultations in Scarborough, downtown east, and midtown at which I was present in the fall of 2013. The City also failed to provide residents with the results of community consultations. More importantly, none of the concerns voiced during the consultation meetings were included in the final drafting of the policy, which came out in 2014 (City of Toronto 2014d). The policy that advocated equity as fairness easily undermined fairness in the process of its own so-called participatory decision-making.

THE GEO-POLITICAL FEAR OF THE IMMIGRANT: FROM PARIS TO TOTTENHAM TO TORONTO

When in 2011 the City of Toronto staff embarked on reviewing and updating the Priority Neighbourhoods Strategy, once again the specter of so-called race riots emanating from Toronto's immigrant neighborhoods haunted the public imagination in the city. On August 4, 2011, on the other side of the Atlantic Ocean, the London Metropolitan Police Service fatally shot a Black youth, Mark Duggan, in the Tottenham Hale district of London. Following the death of Duggan, Tottenham and several other London boroughs quickly turned into the sites of youth unrest between August 6 and 11. As the unrest in London spread to other towns and cities in England between August 8 and 11, their geo-political vibrations were also felt in Toronto. Hume (2011) was quick to remind the *Toronto Star* readers that "it's a long way from Tottenham to Toronto, but not as long as we might like," since here in Toronto "many of the same conditions prevail." Hume's (2011) comparison is evidenced: "To begin with, there is a growing number of young men, aged roughly 15 to 20, largely immigrant, who feel little connection to the larger community. This sense of disenfranchisement, mixed with growing inner-suburban decay, perceived police hostility, overcrowding and lack of decent jobs, do not bode well for the future of Toronto." Hume (2011) highlighted how the middle-income residents "ha[ve] moved out of the inner suburbs" to Brampton, Vaughan, and Markham. The concentration of non-White poverty in postwar suburbs, he reminded the readers, is not just a threat to these areas; rather, it is also a threat to downtown Toronto:

> In the British experience, rioting is neighbourhood-focused and occurs on the nearest high street. The communities most at risk in Toronto—priority neighbourhoods such as Jane/Finch, Rexdale and Eglinton/Kennedy—have no equivalent district. There are malls, highways and subdivisions, none particularly conducive to a riot. This means that the violence here would probably unfold downtown, where context and opportunities abound. (Hume 2011)

John Michael McGrath (2010) reprinted Hume's article in the trendy *Toronto Life* magazine the next day, stating, "Hume has a point. There is some evidence that . . . periods of government austerity lead to riots and civil unrest." A day after, on August 11, the popular media-outlet *Torontoist* published a brief history and video of the Yonge Street unrest in 1992, portrayed as Toronto's first so-called race riot and entitled, "There's a Riot Goin' on Down Yonge Street" (Bradburn 2011). On the same day, Haroon Siddiqui, *Toronto Star*'s editorial emeritus, wrote another warning article about "The Lessons of Britain's Rainbow Riots." He brought together the unrest in Britain since the 1980s with those in the Parisian *banlieues* in 2005 and 2007, and the conditions of Toronto's immigrant neighborhoods. Siddiqui, too, reminded Torontonians of the supposedly first so-called race riot in the city (the Yonge Street Riot) and warned readers:

> Canada has not been immune. In 1992 we had the mini-riot on Yonge St. Stephen Lewis wrote an eloquent report on the need to be inclusive. In 2008, Roy McMurtry, former chief justice, wrote a report on youth crimes: "The sense of nothing to lose and no way out that roils within such youth creates an ever-present danger." He, too, called for tutoring the young to keep them in school, recreational programs to keep them off the streets, mentoring to guide them into a career, etc. Reached yesterday about the events in Britain, he said: "They should serve as a wake-up call." (Siddiqui 2011)

Both Siddiqui and Hume took the youth unrest in England as an opportunity to reinforce the geo-political fear of the immigrant in Toronto. This geo-political fear also had echoes within policymaking circles. In 2013 and early 2014, interviews with senior City managers, City staff involved with place-based urban policy, and United Way personnel involved with different aspects of TSNS 2020 all pointed out that the reference to the "Paris problem" in policy circles speaks to the fear of urban unrest in Toronto. While they had different interpretations of Toronto's "Paris problem," they all pointed out to the fear of the unrest of the racialized excluded as a force behind the urgency of the urban policy. It is worth hearing in their words the working of the nexus of security, racialization, and development:

> We've already seen the riots. We had the Yonge St. riot. We've seen elements of it and given the demographics of our population, we

can't afford not to have those people in the labor market, which otherwise will cause us trouble, similar to what we've seen as the Paris problem. (I3 2014)

I think it [Toronto's "Paris problem"] is a bit of fear-mongering; like we better do something or those Black people will start causing us problems. . . . I think there's some well-intentioned warnings [that] if we don't address inequities now and how they're manifested, these things are not going to go away on their own, and one of the consequences could be violence. So, yeah, I think it probably comes from both sides. (I25 2013)

In terms of riots, I think there is always the potential. We just had this unfortunate [fatal] shooting of Sami Yatim [by a Toronto Police officer] and people mobilized that day. There were marches through downtown. I think people have discovered that [taking to the streets]. . . . And I think there is an interesting opportunity that we have, so we don't get to the place of riots. If left unattended to and not thinking of the city as a whole, I think we could potentially end up there, which [happens] often in politics. Because it's more based on downtown versus suburbs. (I26 2013)

We have many of the same dynamics around social and economic exclusion of young people from racialized and newcomer backgrounds, living on the outside, literally geographically separated from the downtown core. And we have seen expressions of the dissatisfaction with this situation that have been a little bit indirect . . . and it reminds us that what's happening in the inner suburbs is not just a contained challenge of those people, it's actually something that concerns all of us. . . . Has that exploded into the kind of social upheaval that we saw in Paris? Not just this time around. . . . Thankfully it's never manifested itself that way in Toronto. But that doesn't mean that we don't have many of the same issues here, it's just that it's manifesting itself in different ways. . . . So just because things are not literally on fire, doesn't mean that there are not some serious issues. . . . I'd say it [the prospects of riots] is an immediate concern. (I23 2013)

The comparison between Toronto and Paris is because
we're having increasingly suburbanized poverty and ethnic
overconcentration . . . and to be honest with you, the postwar
suburbs aren't the only ones that people should be thinking about.
The inner suburbs are decreasingly the site of new arrival and
new settlement; the outer suburbs are increasingly the site of new
arrival and new settlement. The fastest growth, if you look at a
map of the pace of growth in settlement, what you see is the outer
suburbs trumping the inner suburbs by a country mile. (I27 2013)

The "Paris problem" was a concern for those at the senior levels of
policymaking, whether at the City or at the United Way. Junior City
staff, those working on the ground in the priority neighborhoods and
those working at community centers and organizations, had not heard
about the comparison between Paris and Toronto or the phrase "Paris
problem." Interestingly, however, almost all the above-mentioned
interviewees quickly differentiated Toronto from Paris with reference
to the powerful role of liberal multiculturalism in Canada. It was argued repeatedly that Canada's multiculturalism has made the inclusion of immigrants easier in Canada, and, hence, the sense of exclusion
and alienation is less in Toronto than in Paris. The premise of such an
argument is that Canada's multiculturalism is itself a state strategy for
preventing racial tensions.

TSNS 2020 was above all about injecting a liberal humanitarian
ideology in urban policy. The emphasis on equity and social determinants of health took place not only in relation to the prominence
of both concepts in international relation but also within the limits
of Canadian multiculturalism and its liberal-colonial recognitions of
"the dark side of the nation" (Bannerji 2000). Similar to the efforts of
liberal humanitarianism and counterinsurgency on the international
scene, the proposed remedies on the part of TSNS 2020 did not attempt to disturb the sociospatial and racial relations of domination and
exploitation that produce poverty, inequality, and violence. The goal is
amelioration; that is, to reconstruct the immigrant as resilient liberal
subjects who take responsibility not only for their wretched poverty,
but also for their becoming empowered, smart, creative, entrepreneur-
ial, peaceful, and civilized. The post-colonial resilient liberal subject
is destined to internalize violence and bounce back stronger than

before—to reform themselves in tune with the exploitative requirements of the market and to integrate despite being besieged within the walls of exclusion, discrimination, and dispossession. In the next chapter, we will see how urbanists and the local state mobilized liberal humanitarian ideology and the geo-political fear of the immigrant to rationalize the need for the most pervasive place-based housing redevelopment project in Canadian history, Tower Renewal.

6

Urbanizing Concrete Towers

LIBERAL HUMANITARIANISM AND DESIGN SOLUTIONS

> In Toronto, an unusually large number of high-rise apartments
> poke above the flat landscape many miles from downtown. . . .
> This is a type of high-density suburban development far more
> progressive and able to deal with the future than the sprawl of
> the U.S.
>
> —Richard Buckminster Fuller, American architect, 1968

> The picture that emerges from our examination is troubling:
> It not only shows that poverty in Toronto has continued
> to intensify *geographically,* in Toronto's inner suburban
> neighbourhoods, it also shows that poverty is becoming
> increasingly concentrated *vertically* in the high-rise towers
> that dot the city's skyline.
>
> —Susan McIsaac, United Way Toronto, 2011

MAKING AND MAPPING TORONTO'S HIGHRISE TOWERS

The "high-rise towers that dot the city's skyline," in the words of then United Way president and CEO Susan McIsaac in the above epigraph, are not a reference to the highrise towers that one sees in any tourism image of Toronto's skyline, towers that feature Canada's biggest and most diverse city by Lake Ontario. The latter highrise towers with their shiny glass facades and luxury residential apartments, as presented in Figure 9, dot Toronto's downtown and midtown skylines. For the United Way, policymakers, and urbanists, these phallic concentrations of real estate capital are neither troubling nor are they called *highrise towers*; rather, they are called *condominiums.* They are the residential spaces of Richard Florida's (2002) cherished "creative class"—(relatively) mixed groups of young and old (petty-) bourgeoisie and a minority of the superrich. These glass towers are conceived of

FIGURE 9. A view of Toronto's celebrated downtown and its highrise skyline from Lake Ontario, featuring headquarters of banks and luxury highrise apartments. Photograph credit: Parastou Saberi, August 2014.

as Toronto's vertical prosperity, a sign of the city's booming (or rather ballooning) real estate economy facilitated by gentrification and the reign of big developers along with a footloose international capital coming from a diversity of geographies worldwide.

Toronto's so-called troubling highrise towers, those that also troubled Hume (2015a) as "degraded" and "dangerous," are from a different era, located in different yet connected territories. Built during the postwar decades of economic and urban growth, these residential highrise concrete towers were the products of Metropolitan Toronto's experimentation with regional planning, modernist design, mass housing, and top-down regulation. Perhaps the main similarity between these highrise concrete towers and today's highrise glass towers is that they too were financed by the state, constructed by private developers, and quickly turned into profitable real estate ventures. Inspired by Le Corbusier's tower-in-the-park concept, modernist planners and private developers envisioned and built these highrise concrete towers across Toronto's growing urban landscape. At the time, planners considered the blocks of highrise concrete towers as "complete communities" for the rising White middle-income families of the postwar era. The highrise concrete tower soon became a significant feature of Toronto's postwar urbanization. Across Toronto's postwar suburbs, the verticality of 1,189 residential highrise concrete towers frequently disrupts the horizontality of Fordist bungalow urbanism, as Figure 10 shows. Morphologically, these selective interpretations of modernist planning and architecture have brought Toronto closer to European cities such as Paris and London than to the sprawling horizontality that has typified North American postwar urbanization. It was this particular feature of Toronto's regional landscape that, as mentioned in the epigraph of this chapter, fascinated American futurist architect Buckminster Fuller as "progressive" in 1968.

With the rise of Toronto's urban reform movement in the 1970s, however, the highrise concrete towers lost their progressive appeal. For close to forty years, the Jane Jacobsian pro-urban bourgeois forces harshly lamented these residential urban spaces as *sub*-urban and oppressively lifeless and hence relegated them to the margins of urban politics. The marginality of the highrise concrete tower as an urban form went hand in hand with the systematic marginalization of its new inhabitants. As mentioned in chapter 1, with the gradual opening up of Canada's immigration system to non-White populations from 1962, the demography of the inhabitants of Toronto's postwar suburbs changed in the late 1970s and dramatically so in the following

FIGURE 10. An aerial view of part of Rexdale, showing highrise rental apartment buildings in the midst of the bungalow and green landscape of Toronto's northwest end. It is this particular form of highrise residential building and its geographical imaginaries that Susan McIsaac referred to as "troubling" in her introduction to the 2011 United Way report, *Vertical Poverty.* Photograph credit: Parastou Saberi, August 2021.

decades. The blocks of highrise concrete towers, the major rental housing market in postwar suburbs, quickly became the geography of this demographic change. In contrast to its majority White European and middle-income demography of the 1960s and early 1970s, today the majority of the more than half a million inhabitants of these highrise concrete towers are non-White working-class populations, many struggling with poverty, systemic exploitation, racism, and police brutality. The vertical urban form of these legacies of Le Corbusier, as depicted in Figure 11, along with their majority non-White inhabitants, have been central to the comparison between Toronto's postwar suburbs and the *banlieues* of Paris and to the rationalization of the geo-political fear of these spaces as bastions of violence, insecurity, and threat. Similar to the development of urban policy in France, in Toronto, this geo-political fear has, in turn, played a crucial role in the introduction of the most pervasive place-based housing redevelopment program, Tower Renewal, a policy that is being expanded to the Greater Toronto Area (GTA) and southern Ontario more generally (CUG+ R 2018).

FIGURE 11. An aerial view of Jane and Falstaff in the northwest end of Toronto, featuring public housing apartment buildings cutting through the bungalow landscape. Public housing composed 23% of Toronto's highrise concrete towers. The public housing component of Tower Renewal has its own structure and programs, namely, Social Housing Apartment Improvement Program (SHAIP) and Social Housing Apartment Retrofit Program (SHARP). Since 2017, the City of Toronto has slowly implemented some aspects of these programs, particularly work on envelope rehabilitation, recladding, and window replacement in public housing apartments. Here, the front building in white has gone through some steps of SHAIP and SHARP. Photograph credit: Parastou Saberi, August 2021.

While major public housing redevelopment projects in downtown, such as the Regent Park Revitalization, had already started even before 2005, these projects were not officially part of the Priority Neighbourhoods Strategy. The developmental dimension of the Priority Neighbourhoods Strategy was mostly focused on social development projects and the construction of seven neighborhood hubs within already existing spaces owned by the City of Toronto. The introduction of Tower Renewal into Toronto Strong Neighbourhoods Strategy 2020 brought place-based urban policy in Toronto closer to those policies in France and the United Kingdom, where urban redevelopment has been in the forefront of targeting the perceived problem areas. Yet, major differences have made Tower Renewal unique in its scope, form, and duration. As opposed to the emphasis on demolishing the old public housing stock in French place-based policy (Dikeç 2007; Kipfer 2015), for example, Tower Renewal is an ambitious long-term (twenty- to thirty-year-long) multiphase project of housing and urban redevelopment *without* demolition that targets both public housing and privately owned rental buildings.[1]

How did such a shift in Toronto's place-based policy take place? By the late 2000s, the fate of Toronto's highrise concrete towers and their residents took another turn. In January 2011, United Way published a new report, *Poverty by Postal Code 2: Vertical Poverty: Declining Income, Housing Quality and Community Life in Toronto's Inner Suburban High-rise Apartments.* Confident of the organization's role in fostering the urban agenda for the Toronto region, the report's authors underlined the importance of the report's finding for place-based policy, the "new economy," and Toronto's competitiveness (UWT 2011, 9). Loyal to the gurus of urban competitiveness, *Vertical Poverty* opened with Richard Florida's (2007) observations of how economic polarization can threaten Toronto's competitiveness (UWT 2011, 16). The publication of *Vertical Poverty* brought the highrise concrete tower once again into the forefront of urban debates in Toronto. This time, however, it was neither cherished as progressive nor explicitly demonized as oppressive. Rather, from urbanists and policymakers to United Way researchers, all carefully presented the highrise concrete tower as a securitized object of liberal humanitarian intervention: a "troubling" space of "vertical poverty" and violence, one that is not just a threat to the health and well-being of its inhabitants, but to the prosperity of Toronto. At the same time, these towers of "vertical poverty," we are told, have a great deal of "potential"; they are "urban assets" that only need to be empowered, urbanized, and integrated in partnership (UWT 2011, iv–x).

Vertical Poverty reiterated the previous emphasis on Toronto's neighborhoods as the city's greatest strength (UWT 2011, 7), the conception of poverty-as-risk, and the obsession with mapping non-White poverty. In mobilizing mapping, the report narrowed down its focus on "the role of highrise housing" in the trends of the growth of concentrated non-White poverty in postwar suburbs. The "apartment towers," as the report referred to them, and in particular, to the privately owned rental apartment towers, became the new object of investigation and intervention.[2]

Color-coded maps highlighting in dark red and orange the increasing concentration of non-White poverty from 1981 to 2006 in pockets of postwar suburbs, as shown in Figure 12, draw attention to immigrant neighborhoods, this time, however, with a focus on highrise rental concrete towers. The report used mapping and a survey of 2,803 inhabitants of rental apartment buildings to highlight the concentration of "vertical poverty" (UWT 2011, ii). The report also looked at six aspects of the housing conditions in these buildings: affordability, physical structure, building environment, the protective and safe place dimension, social environment, and building infrastructure (UWT 2011, 7). While mapping shrank the scale of analysis to buildings, the tautological logic of the neighborhood effects literature remained central to the report's argument in a fashion in keeping with previous reports. In 2013, an executive member of United Way explained to me that

> One of the explanations for why there is such a high concentration of poverty in some neighborhoods is because there is such a high concentration of affordable rental housing in those neighborhoods. . . . It's a really essential part of the city that we've built, and those towers were built in a completely different time. . . . Of course, over time situations changed, and those towers . . . have now become the sites or settlements for, essentially, access to affordable housing. (I23 2013)

In the absence of any concrete analysis of the production of concentrated non-White poverty, the fact that "highrise apartment buildings have increasingly become sites of concentrated poverty within

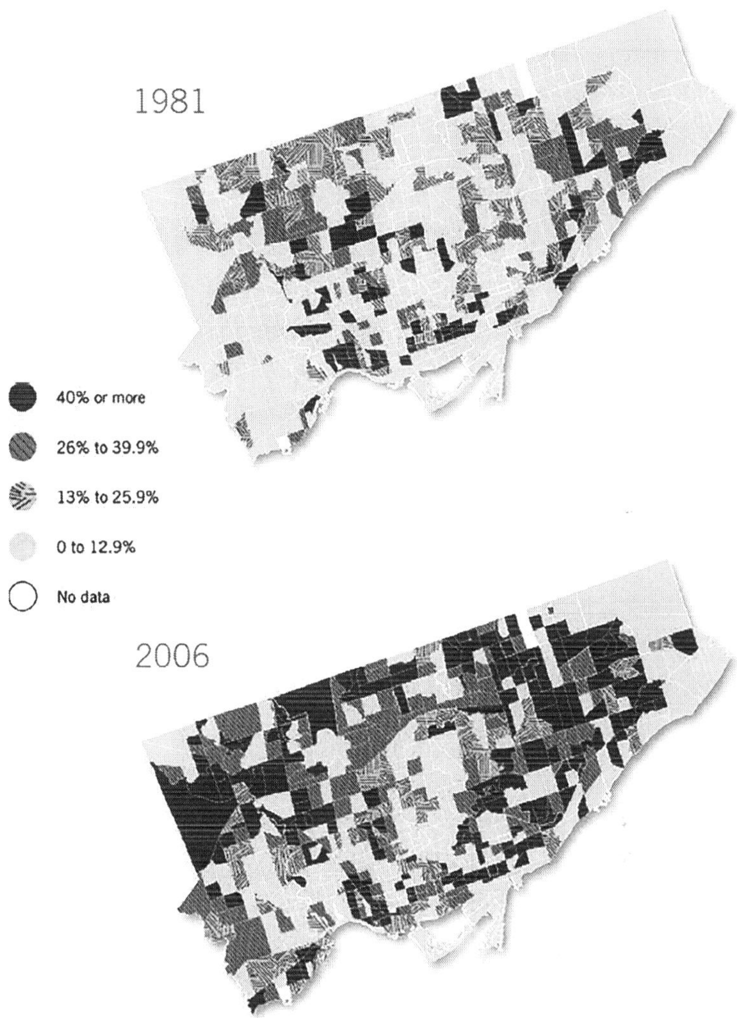

FIGURE 12. United Way's mapping of the concentration of poverty in highrise apartment buildings in 1981 and 2006 in the *Vertical Poverty* report. Based on the 1981 and 2006 census data and the census tract boundaries, the maps depict the percentage of low-income family renters in "apartment towers" (5 stories or more), showing the increasing concentration of poverty in highrise rental apartments in immigrant neighborhoods. Here, the darker the shade of an area indicates the higher level of poverty. Source: UWT 2011, 39. Courtesy of United Way Greater Toronto.

neighbourhoods" (UWT 2011, v) was used to conclude that highrise concrete towers are the cause of the concentration of non-White poverty.

Why did United Way, a philanthropic organization, suddenly become interested in Toronto's housing issues and particularly in those highrise rental apartments that are privately owned? According to the executive member just quoted:

> It's just a fact that the vast majority of the affordable housing stock in Toronto is privately owned. And the vast majority of low-income people live in privately owned rental apartments. We had—just by virtue of working in neighborhoods and doing engagement—it just stares at you in the face that the people with whom you've been working live in highrise apartments—and that when you begin to engage people in a conversation about what's wrong and begin to ask, "What is it that we can fix?" . . . people inevitably turn to places [where] they live. . . . They inevitably pointed us to towers. We thought it was really important for us to actually get a sense of what was happening in those towers. That's why we got out [there] and we have data . . . And it just so happened that in our sample we really prioritized the private rental market, because we felt that was an area that was really missing in the policy debate. . . . We felt that the private sector conversation was missing something and we really want to put our focus on. So we did *Vertical Poverty*. (I23 2013)

This is an arresting statement that touches upon all the official mandates of United Way, its humanitarian mission to care for the people, to work with the people and to ameliorate their sufferings. Recall Susan McIsaac's appeal to the people in reference to the organization's sources of fundraising in 2012 (see chapter 2). And yet, as was the case with the organization's fundraising politics, the reality on the ground is always less flowery than such public-relations statements imply. The reason that United Way became involved with highrise rental apartments had less to do with residents' voices, needs, and sufferings and more to do with already unfolding plans for a place-based housing redevelopment policy at the City of Toronto, namely, Tower Renewal. *Vertical Poverty* explicitly tied itself to the Priority Neighbourhoods Strategy and the Tower Renewal program (UWT 2011, 3–4).

Similar to *Poverty by Postal Code* (UWT 2004), *Vertical Poverty* (UWT 2011) quickly became an influential report on the rental housing situation in the postwar suburbs. The report gave the City the opportunity to justify Tower Renewal as a scientific antipoverty strategy (I3 2014). United Way, in turn, gained an official role in place-based urban policymaking by 2012. Why did *Vertical Poverty* become so influential in policymaking? Was it because of the report's findings about the crisis of affordable housing? The answer is more than a simple yes or no. When the *Vertical Poverty* report was published in 2011, there was nothing fundamentally new about the crisis of affordable housing in Toronto or the notorious housing situation that most often affects non-White working-class tenants. Already by 2000 researchers involved with the Centre for Equality Rights in Accommodation (CERA) had highlighted the increasing number of illegal evictions and the complicity of the Ontario Rental Housing Tribunal and the Tenant Protection Act in the eviction of low-income tenants (CERA 2000). Other studies pointed to the consequences of withdrawing subsidies for new rental housing (Skaburskis and Mok 2000). In the early and mid-2000s, more studies by an array of politically diverse institutions—from the Canada Mortgage and Housing Corporation and the Centre for Urban and Community Studies at the University of Toronto to the Canadian Centre for Policy Alternatives and the Advocacy Centre for Tenants Ontario—warned about a crisis of affordable housing in Toronto (and Ontario). These studies zeroed in on the dehousing consequences of the neoliberal housing policies of the Conservative Harris provincial government and the impact of racial discrimination against non-White populations in terms of access to proper rental housing in the city (Deacon et al. 2002; Murdie 2002; Paradis et al. 2008; CERA 2009). By 2003, the crisis of affordable housing even became a topic of discussion and caution for sections of the representatives of capital such as the Toronto Board of Trade (2003) and TD Economics (2003).

If the crisis of affordable housing was not new, neither was the crisis of overcrowded housing, or what *Vertical Poverty* framed as "densely populated" housing. Overcrowded housing or hidden homelessness[3] is an increasingly common situation wherein two or more families live in a space designed for one family. It is easy to point to the lack of affordable housing for such a phenomenon, as many policymakers do. No attention has been paid, however, to how this lack of affordability takes place on the ground and what role landlords play in exacerbating this situation. One of the major reasons for hidden homelessness among low-income, non-White populations in Toronto's immigrant neighborhoods is an increasing class and racial discrimination that occurs through landlords' illegal demands on particular racialized groups for extra rent deposits in advance (sometimes called a key fee or a security deposit), which push some families to come together to raise the money and share the apartment.[4] A senior staff member at the Scarborough Housing Help Centre (SHHC) explained to me:

> It is common knowledge that in order to get rental housing you have to pass a three-part test. You need proof of income, you need credit checks, and then you need references. Since newcomers don't have any of these things, landlords will make them an offer, saying, like: "If you pay me six months' rent up front, as a deposit, then I'll allow you to move into a rental unit." And that is where the problem starts because the newcomer is probably not informed that this is illegal. . . . There are multiple ways in which racism intersects with the issue of housing. I know certainly of landlords who are very uncomfortable with renting to newcomers. I mean, newcomers, not due to the fact that they probably can't pay, or [because] you have lost the ability to continue paying rent, but because of the way they [newcomers] look, the way they talk. There is an issue with strong smells, that's always an issue that comes up. . . . [In Peel Region] they actually put up posters saying: "No strong smells or children." . . . That kind of racism is still seen and sometimes it is subtle, sometimes it kinda just confronts you in the face. (I9 2013)

This illegal practice of landlords "has been going on for at least the last twenty years, if not longer" (I9 2013).

In my interviews with City staff members at the Social Development, Finance and Administration Department and at the Newcomer Office, they all mentioned that the City is aware of the growing phenomenon of hidden homelessness in rental units *and* the illegal discriminatory practice of landlords. They also acknowledged that this has been the situation for at least the last two decades (I30 2013, I3 2014). A City staff member at the Newcomers Office told me:

> It has been there when . . . I worked for the Red Cross; we, the
> Red Cross [at the time], were very much aware of people being
> underhoused, and hidden homelessness was an issue in the
> late 1990s and early 2000s too. . . . It may be that the impact on
> newcomers is now more prominent than before, or on some other
> populations, I'm not certain. And there's definitely the fact that
> the rents have increased hugely in Toronto. (I30 2013)

The City staff members I talked to all justified the silence and inaction of the City regarding the illegal practices of landlords based on the fact that rental agreements are under the jurisdiction of the Province of Ontario. For its part, *Vertical Poverty* was absolutely silent on racism, racial discrimination, and the illegal practices of landlords in its two-hundred-plus pages. Instead, the report, strategically and implicitly, took the side of the landlords. As opposed to previous reports, the report also downplayed the racial dimension of the highrise concrete towers by breaking down the demography of the poor inhabitants into the categories of female, single parent, families with children living at home, low income, reliance on social assistance, older immigrants, racialized communities, and less educated, without any engagement with the intersections of these categories (UWT 2011, viii).

What attracted the attention of policymakers and urbanists to *Vertical Poverty* was the mapping of highrise concrete towers, its appeal to residents' surveys,[5] and its linking the state of highrise concrete towers to the urban agenda in the Toronto region. Most importantly, it was the report's call for the revitalization of highrise concrete towers and the injection of social mixity into these neighborhoods. The authors of *Vertical Poverty* explicitly identified zoning by-laws as an obstacle to the economic prosperity of these neighborhoods. Echoing the logic of ongoing housing redevelopment policies in France, the report applauded the public housing redevelopment projects in the public housing neighborhoods of Regent Park and Lawrence Heights as successful practices of integrating segregated areas into "Toronto's neighbourhoods." Lost in this celebration of social mixity in downtown public housing developments was the increasing critique in academic research and the media of the gentrifying effects of these urban interventions and the displacement of many public housing residents from the core of downtown (see August 2014; McKnight 2014;

Fiorito 2014; August and Walks 2012; Kipfer and Petrunia 2009). In the process, the report sanctioned the systemic downtown gentrification and the erosion of affordable housing (UWT 2011, 156). Sponsored by the Social Housing Services Corporation,[6] Toronto Public Health, Toronto Community Housing, and the Ontario Ministry of Municipal Affairs and Housing, the *Vertical Poverty* report came out after an intensified multisector, multilevel interest in the idea of Tower Renewal in Toronto.

The geo-political fear of the immigrant was also central to *Vertical Poverty*'s urgent call for the revitalization of rental highrise buildings in immigrant neighborhoods. While heavily loaded with the neoliberal, neocolonial development and humanitarian buzzwords of *need, asset, potential, empowerment,* and *social cohesion, Vertical Poverty* did not shy away from implicitly bringing to the fore the comparison between Toronto's postwar suburbs and the *banlieues* of Paris. As the report warned about the "deteriorating housing condition, crime and social disorder" (McIsaac 2011) in so-called tower neighborhoods, both its

FIGURE 13. The image of this particular form of highrise concrete tower has come to define the geographical imaginary of immigrant neighborhoods in Toronto and to make sensible the comparison between Paris and Toronto. The image on the left is the cover page of the *Vertical Poverty* report, and the image on the right is the opening page of the report's sixth chapter. Source: UWT 2011. Courtesy of United Way Greater Toronto.

cover page and the opening pages of its chapters were decorated with grim pictures of highrise concrete towers in Toronto's postwar suburbs. Figure 13 illustrates how, aesthetically and symbolically, *Vertical Poverty* reproduced the abjection of immigrant neighborhoods. The geographical imaginary of the postwar highrise concrete tower has become the image of immigrant neighborhoods, replicated in reports on the condition of the working poor by other philanthropy organizationssuch as Metcalf (see Stapleton, Murphy, and Xing 2012). As rental highrise concrete towers became the space and cause of concentrated non-White poverty, increasingly, Tower Renewal became the one bold solution to the deepening of "vertical poverty."

TOWER RENEWAL: THE POWER OF URBANISTS

The idea of Tower Renewal was born long before the publication of *Vertical Poverty* in 2011. The idea goes back to studies undertaken between 2004 and 2006 by academics at the University of Toronto and architects at E.R.A. Architects. Initially, building engineer Ted Kesik and architect Ivan Saleff (2005) at the University of Toronto's John H. Daniels Faculty of Architecture, Landscape, and Design studied the cost-effectiveness of retrofitting the highrise concrete towers in Toronto. Graeme Stewart, then a graduate student in architecture at the University of Toronto and an architect at E.R.A., expanded on this idea in his master's thesis. Stewart looked into the revitalization of similar buildings in cities such as Amsterdam, London, and Moscow. Immediately after his graduation in May 2007, Stewart was introduced to then mayor David Miller (by his colleagues at the University of Toronto and E.R.A.) to present his big idea for Toronto's "troubling" towers. At the time, the issues of greenhouse gas emissions and sustainability were hot political topics at the City, and Mayor Miller in particular was keen to coin his name as an environmentalist mayor. Stewart, in turn, had what appeared to be the most revolutionary idea. Writing in the *Toronto Star,* Stewart argued that,

> regrettably, Toronto's aging towers remain off the radar. Recent financial support for "greening" of the city, such as the federal government's commitment to infuse hundreds of millions of dollars into sustainable growth, is welcome news. Yet, in a missed opportunity, tower restoration is not part of these plans, nor is it

in the city's official green strategy. Overlooked, these buildings are underutilized, blighted, and extremely inefficient. Programs are needed to encourage public and private investment that will allow them to reach their potential. With international precedent, broad awareness of the climate, and a growing number of "at risk" neighbourhoods associated with apartment towers, greening and investment in these projects have moved beyond an interesting speculative exercise to an issue fundamental to the ecological and social sustainability of the GTA. It's time to get on with it. (Stewart 2007)

If the City was serious about a significant reduction in greenhouse gas emissions, then it could not ignore "the opportunity inherent in Toronto's extensive stock of hundreds of bulky concrete residential 'slab' (i.e., big) high-rise apartment houses" (Stewart 2007). If Toronto wants to keep its image as a progressive city in North America, Stewart pointed out, it only has to look east, to Europe, since

for many years, the European Union has been actively restoring its enormous stock of tower blocks as a key component of its environmental strategy. Across both Eastern and Western Europe, the carbon-saving potential of aging Welfare State and Soviet-era towers has been exploited to achieve greenhouse gas reduction targets. In my own tour of European tower districts last fall, the abundant examples of regeneration, "greening," intensification and retrofitting were truly eye-opening. (Stewart 2007)

From the beginning, Stewart (and his E.R.A colleagues) envisioned Tower Renewal not just as an environmental project, but also as an urban renewal project (I10 2013). In sharp contrast to other urban redevelopment projects in France and the United Kingdom, Stewart rejected the idea of *demolition* in favor of *retrofitting* the existing structures alongside infilling in the vast open spaces around the towers in the parks. Tower Renewal, according to Stewart (2007), was a win-win project for all—the City, the developers, landlords, and immigrant neighborhoods. Fascinated by the bold idea, Mayor Miller soon established a working group on the topic. On September 24 and 25, 2007, the city council approved the mayor's Tower Renewal

Project and Opportunities Book. The council also approved the establishment of the Tower Renewal Office at the City of Toronto. Mayor Miller argued that Tower Renewal is

> an opportunity to make tremendous progress on the major themes of city-building contained in my mandate. By dramatically improving the energy efficiency of the more than 1,000 high rise residential concrete frame buildings located throughout Toronto, Mayor's Tower Renewal will reduce greenhouse gas emissions by between three and five per cent for the urban area. Mayor's Tower Renewal will also generate social, economic and cultural benefits by creating local green jobs, increasing on-site small-scale retail and markets, upgrading green space around the buildings, providing more space for neighbourhood meetings and interactions, installing solar, wind and geothermal energy solutions, and green roofs where appropriate, increasing water conservation and on-site management of waste, increasing the demand of locally-produced green and clean technology, and fostering community and urban agriculture at the sites. (quoted in City of Toronto 2008b)

With the support of E.R.A., the University of Toronto, and the City of Toronto, Graeme Stewart soon became not just the major architect behind the project but also the public urbanist face of the project. A confident, friendly, and energetic public speaker, Stewart developed his mission, which soon became rationalizing the idea of Tower Renewal not only for the City and regional bureaucrats and politicians, but also for the larger urbanist and architectural community, the pro-urban bourgeois forces, and the residents of the "faulty towers" in Toronto as well as urbanists and policymakers on the other side of the Atlantic Ocean, particularly in the United Kingdom. In accomplishing this mission, he has also established himself as a savvy strategist. Stewart, who in 2014 won the Jane Jacobs Prize on account of his work on Tower Renewal, began his mission-cum-vision by voicing a critique of Toronto's urban reform guru, Jane Jacob, and her ethos of urbanity that demonized postwar suburbs. He revived the legacy of modernist planning in Metro Toronto as progressive, even reminding his audiences and readers in the *Toronto Star* of how Metro Toronto was the refuge of communist and socialist European planners:

> Much of the mythology surrounding Toronto is focused on the image of a "city of neighbourhoods," enabled by the city's early rejection of modernism through citizen groups and the Reform Council. Yet, what is perhaps of equal interest is the thoroughness and completeness with which Toronto accepted the modern project prior to this point. . . . In the wake of the formation of Metro, Toronto became an attractor for international, particularly European trained, modern planners. . . . Among the leaders of international planners at work in Toronto were Englishman Gordon Stevenson and German émigré and card-carrying Communist Hans Blumenfeld, both of whom left the United States for Canada during the turbulent years of McCarthy politics. (Stewart 2008, 23–25)

But as much as the Tower Renewal project begins from a critique of the Jane Jacobsian demonization of tower neighborhoods, its geographical imaginary and discourse about highrise concrete towers are not fundamentally different from the former. Although Stewart came out in defense of the postwar highrise concrete towers, for him and for the advocates of Tower Renewal, the problem with these spaces is precisely their *lack* of urbanity; the conception of urbanity for Stewart (and in the Tower Renewal program) is not much different from Jacobs's celebrated conception of urbanity. In both cases, urbanity is perceived as a way of life and a Western, bourgeois way of life, leaving aside the sociospatial and racial relations in the production of urban space and everyday life. In both cases, urbanity is conceived through an environmentally deterministic lens. Tower Renewal differs from Jacobsian ideology in that its architects believe these abjected towers have the *potential* to become urbanized through design interventions. If for Jacobsians environmental determinism is too strong to save these sub-urban highrise towers, for Stewart and Tower Renewal advocates, environmental determinism can bring the necessary transformation into these so-called troubling towers. This latter environmental determinism is one that is infused with liberal humanitarianism.

Despite (or because) of its positive view of highrise concrete towers, Tower Renewal builds upon the geo-political fear of the immigrant in Toronto. Part of Stewart's argument is that urbanizing and integrating these towers is the best way to prevent the "Paris problem" in Toronto. Reminding other planners and architects of the 2007 unrest in the French *banlieues,* Stewart cautioned,

> While the historic centre [of Toronto] is becoming increasingly
> wealthy, areas of the city considered "Priority Neighbourhoods"
> of acute poverty and lacking services are all examples of the post-
> war communities in question. The recent Paris riots reinforce the
> inequality and social tensions that may arise if this trend is to con-
> tinue. As issues of climate change and social inequality become
> central political concerns, reengaging this aging and significant
> housing stock is becoming a key priority. (Stewart 2008, 28)

Stewart was not the only force behind making Tower Renewal sensible. The rationalization of Tower Renewal as the remedy for the assumed malaise of immigrant neighborhoods involved an orchestrated production of knowledge by the City of Toronto and its old and new civil society partners. The 2007 establishment of the Tower Renewal Office at the City kick-started a systematic knowledge production about highrise concrete towers and their renewal in Toronto. The City itself published the first report, *Tower Renewal Guidelines: Projects Brief,* in August 2008. Written by Ted Kesik, Ivan Saleff, Robert Wright, Graeme Stewart, Nick Swerdfeger, and Jan Kroman, the report was financed by the City of Toronto, the Toronto Atmosphere Fund, and the Canada Mortgage and Housing Corporation. It framed Tower Renewal as

> a social, economic and environmental imperative of the City of
> Toronto. It is a timely initiative that aims to preserve affordable
> housing stock, protect the investments and assets of property
> owners, and reduce energy use, water consumption and green-
> house gas emissions. It also promotes the creative redevelopment
> of lower building sites to accommodate much needed social ser-
> vices and amenities that strengthen the vitality of diverse commu-
> nities and improve our quality of life. (Kesik et al. 2008, iii)

The economic crisis of 2007–2008 turned beneficial for this knowledge production industry. Following the Canadian federal government stimulus package in 2009, the Province of Ontario and the City of Toronto allocated part of the federal government's Infrastructure Stimulus Fund to boost research on highrise concrete towers for two consecutive years (2009–2010) (I23 2013). The money was crucial for United Way to start a series of foundational research projects that took place on the topic (I23 2013). Not surprisingly, between 2010 and 2012 ten major research and report papers on highrise concrete towers were published, while between 2012 and 2014, at least ten public professional events were organized—all with the aim of making Tower Renewal sensible. The chief concern of the City and the Tower Renewal Office was how to make the project attractive for major rental property-owner companies (I21 2013). This is not surprising given that in the era of neoliberal austerity, investing in any large-scale urban renewal project requires extensive financial justification. Tower Renewal's financing was even more complex given that 77 percent of highrise concrete towers in Toronto (about 915 buildings) are privately owned. The problem of financing was thus framed as a question of how to engage private owners and how to sell Tower Renewal to them. In May 2010, Morrison Park Advisors published a study (commissioned by the City) on *Tower Renewal Financial Options*. In order to convince private owners to participate in the project, the report recommended that the City providing a form of financing that is "both low cost from an interest rate perspective, and not consume high value of building owners' equity" (Morrison Park Advisors 2010, 2). It went on to argue:

> The solution . . . is believed to be a credit-enhanced capital tool, backed not by mortgage security but rather property tax-based security. In this scenario, private sector funds would be raised by a dedicated Tower Renewal Corporation in order to finance projects. (Morrison Park Advisors 2010, 2)

In October 2012, the Ontario Liberal provincial government amended the City of Toronto Act to permit the City to offer financing to a property (rather than to an individual). Later in 2013, the City initiated a three-year pilot program, the Highrise Retrofit Improvement Support Program, or Hi-RIS, to help residential property owners to pursue energy and water efficiency and conservation improvements. The promise that credit financing would not affect the real estate value of the properties and that future redevelopment and infilling would add to property values has gradually helped sell Tower Renewal to building owners. In 2010, the Cities Centre tried to inject Tower Renewal into the 2010 mayoral election debates on public transit expansion (proposed by then outgoing mayor Miller). In July 2010, André

Sorenson at the University of Toronto Scarborough Department of Human Geography argued that the Transit City expansion "also promises to accelerate the rate of investment in the Tower Renewal projects by promising more attractive neighborhoods, increased property values, greater opportunities for intensification and mixed-use projects and making reinvestment in aging building more attractive" (2010, 5). Sorenson's intervention exposed and justified the gentrifying ambitions of the project in advocating for broader revitalizing potential of Tower Renewal without any attention to affordable housing.

The most important event in the production of expert knowledge was the founding of a new nonprofit research institute dedicated explicitly to place-based urban redevelopment. In 2009, the E.R.A, planningAlliance, and regionalArchitects (later renamed SvN), in collaboration with then Cities Centre at the University of Toronto and the United Way, founded the Centre for Urban Growth and Renewal (CUG+R). CUG+R's mission is "to engage in cross-disciplinary research initiatives fundamental to achieving livable and sustainable urban, suburban and rural environments."[7] Capitalizing on the ideological appeal of nonprofit organizations as part and parcel of neoliberal mantras of civil-society partnership, CUG+R was meant to formalize the role of E.R.A and SvN in the formation of the Tower Renewal project. Both E.R.A. and SvN are private, for-profit architecture and planning firms involved in major urban (re-)development projects across Canada and outside of Canada, in the case of SvN. By 2014, E.R.A., for example, was involved in the heritage revitalization project in downtown Peterborough, Ontario. SvN has been pushing for urbanizing the mid-Canada corridor, where major resource extraction sites and disputed Indigenous lands are located (see Van Nostrand 2014). One of the founders of CUG+R explained to me why there was a need to have a nonprofit organization at the forefront of research and activism around Tower Renewal, which is worth quoting at length:

> They [E.R.A.] have invested a lot into this [Tower Renewal] project, in terms of funding and continued research, or engagements or whatever that is not funded, they financed it themselves. We have a close working relationship with planningAlliance [SvN], and they also wanted to work on this. We realized that [CUG+R] is the vehicle for both of us together. . . . And we thought if we

> start a nonprofit we would be able to officially liaise with other
> types of entities, like academic institutions, which would be a lot
> more difficult as a private company. Also the work we've done
> with United Way has been through our research nonprofit. The
> idea is that they fund the research for us. . . . We are able to create
> MOUs [memorandums of understanding] about sharing data
> and research . . . [W]e need to get this message [of the need for
> Tower Renewal] across. Even though there is a lot of proof for
> the concept—still the everyday Torontonian doesn't think about
> these things. So how can we have a culture shift, so that people
> realize the importance of this [Tower Renewal]. And by having a
> Centre for Urban Growth and Renewal, we can sort of say, "I rep-
> resent that" and speak to an audience. It's not a private company
> trying to sell them something. (I10 2013)

CUG+R published its first major research report, one commissioned by the Ontario Ministry of Infrastructure, in November 2010,
entitled, *Tower Neighbourhood Renewal in the Greater Golden Horseshoe: An Analysis of High-Rise Apartment Tower Neighbourhoods Developed in the Postwar Boom (1945–1984)* (Stewart and Thorne 2010).
Decorated with gloomy images of the aging highrise concrete towers
across southern Ontario and shiny examples of revitalized towers in
Europe, the report had a twofold goal: it mapped and analyzed 1,925
apartment towers at a regional scale across southern Ontario, and it
examined the potential for expanding the Tower Renewal project to
support Ontario's development policy objectives. In a language very
similar to the neoliberal discourse of international development, the
report rendered the aging highrise concrete towers as an "opportunity" and "urban asset" (Stewart and Thorne 2010, 45).[8] It argued that
renewing this vast housing stock, which compromises one-third of
the Greater Golden Horseshoe's rental housing stock, is completely
aligned with the broader project of growth and development in Ontario (Stewart and Thorne 2010, 25). The report particularly underlined the compatibility of Tower Renewal with Ontario's then current
transportation plan (the Big Move), its poverty and crime reduction
strategy (Breaking the Cycle) and environmental strategy (Go Green
Action Plan on Climate Change), and its Places to Grow, the growth
plan for the Greater Golden Horseshoe (Stewart and Thorne 2010,
iv–viii).

CUG+R's report underlined three major challenges in implementing the Tower Renewal project: (1) the private ownership of almost 80 percent of this housing stock and the fragmented nature of this private ownership divided among multiple owners; (2) the planning policy framework and zoning restrictions (i.e., single-use, residential zone); and (3) "ensuring equity" and maintaining housing affordability once Tower Renewal is implemented (Stewart and Thorne 2010, 29–31). The report reiterated Morrison Park Advisors' suggestion on financing the project in an attractive way for private owners and strongly proposed the need for new zoning by-laws, while only mentioning the housing affordability challenge in passing (Stewart and Thorne 2010, 28–31). Most importantly, the report turned the urban design and the built environment of immigrant neighborhoods into a new object of investigation in Toronto. Following its publication, the Cities Centre and Jane's Walk published *Walkability in Toronto's High-Rise Neighbourhoods* (Hess and Farrow 2010). It was within and in relation to this broader context that United Way shifted its research focus on privately owned highrise concrete towers and published *Vertical Poverty* in January 2011. A few months after its publication, in September 2011, the City of Toronto (2011a) published *Tower Renewal: Implementation Book.*

DESIGNING HEALTHY IMMIGRANT NEIGHBORHOODS

The sudden interest in highrise concrete towers went beyond players such as urbanists, the City of Toronto, and United Way. By 2017, a whole array of local government institutions and nonprofit sector organizations had already become involved in the growing knowledge production industry around Tower Renewal, extending the geography of the project beyond Toronto to southern Ontario. Building on the momentum of the policy popularity of social determinants of health and mapping (see chapters 3 and 5), public health authorities in Toronto were first to take the geography of immigrant neighborhoods as their object of investigation. Following the publication of *Vertical Poverty,* the Board of Health directed Toronto Public Health to develop strategies to improve the health and well-being of residents of highrise concrete towers in immigrant neighborhoods by identifying policy barriers (Toronto Public Health 2012b, 3). Toronto Public Health published three important reports, namely: *Healthy Toronto by Design*

(2011), *The Walkable City: Neighbourhood Design and Preferences, Travel Choices and Health* (2012a), and *Toward Healthier Apartment Neighbourhoods* (2012b). All three reports were based on mapping the concentration of particular health problems (for example, diabetes) and walkability across Toronto's postwar suburbs.

Similar to the mapping of the "Paris problem," the analysis of the reports were based on overlaying the maps of concentration of diabetes onto the maps of concentrated poverty in immigrant neighborhoods to delineate the geographical imaginaries of highrise concrete towers. The reports were important in making visible the extremely uneven geographies of health in Toronto. The major message of these reports, however, was "how public health objectives can be achieved through design interventions directed at apartment neighbourhoods" (Toronto Public Health 2012b, 7). Urban design and public health, of course, have been longtime bedfellows in both the metropole and the colony since the mid-nineteenth century. Environmentally determinist conceptions of disease and urban fabric, particularly in working-class neighborhoods of the metropole and the colony, have been central to the marriage of urban design and public health, as briefly mentioned in the Beginnings chapter of this volume. In Toronto, since the early 2010s, the emphasis on design solutions for public health problems in immigrant neighborhoods has become a recurrent reference point in justifying the urgency of Tower Renewal in the media and among urbanists and public health authorities. When in June 2017, the disastrous Grenfell Tower fire in London brought the plight of the wretched of London's council housing into the flashlight of the media, on the other side of the Atlantic Ocean, commentators in the *Globe and Mail* and the *Toronto Star* pointed to the real and assumed similarities between Toronto's highrise concrete towers and the Grenfell Tower in London (Micallef 2017; Bozikovic 2017). Graeme Stewart, who at the time of the fire was in London to speak at a forum on Estate Regeneration organized by Urban Design London, also commented on the issue and highlighted the urgency of the Tower Renewal project in Toronto and southern Ontario (see Micallef 2017).

In addition to emphasizing design solutions, the 2012 final report of Toronto Public Health (2012b) also advocated for changes in zoning restrictions and diversifying tenure options as part of design interventions that would in theory enhance public health in these neighborhoods. If this message resonated well with the particular goals of Tower Renewal, it was not accidental. Graeme Stewart, Jason Thorne, Michael McClelland, and George Martin, all members of E.R.A., were among the eight coauthors of *Toward Healthier Apartment Neighbourhoods* (Toronto Public Health 2012b). In May 2012, a few months before the publication of *Toward Healthier Apartment Neighbourhoods,* CUG+R had already published another major report, *Strong Neighbourhoods and Complete Communities: A New Approach to Zoning for Apartment Neighbourhoods* (Stewart et al. 2012). Reiterating the main messages of *Vertical Poverty* and the need to revitalize highrise concrete towers, the major focus of *A New Approach* was on zoning by-law barriers in these tower neighborhoods. Almost all highrise towers are located within single-use, residential zones. The residential zoning by-law, a legacy of postwar functionalist urban planning, is undoubtedly problematic in its simplistic separation of different spheres of life into neatly delimited territories of residence, commerce, recreation, and industry. What is also important for our discussion is the relation between zoning by-laws, property values, and gentrification in the absence of any progressive rent regulation aiming to preserve housing affordability.

Since the Harris government's vacancy decontrol in 1998, which allows landlords to raise rents after a previous tenant vacates to whatever the market will bear, the increasing shift to mixed-use zoning in Toronto has become one of the first steps of a gentrification process. *A New Approach,* however, was not concerned with gentrification and its devastating effects on housing affordability in downtown Toronto; quite to the contrary, in its critique of the functionalist single-use, residential zoning of tower neighborhoods, *A New Approach* underlined the "benefits" of zoning changes in the gentrified downtown core:

> While our city's avenues, transit corridors, downtown "Kings" neighbourhoods and central waterfront are benefiting from policy shifts in support of revitalization, many apartment neighbourhoods continue to face complex and rigorous zoning barriers to positive interventions both small and large. (Stewart et al. 2012, 2)

Without any discussion of how rezoning has been part of the systematic gentrification and a force behind the concentration of (predominantly White) wealth in the above-mentioned areas in Toronto, *A New Approach* proposed a similar treatment for tower neighborhoods, starting with the liberalization of zoning restrictions. The report envisioned the implementation of Tower Renewal in three long-term phases:

> The first tier focuses on broadening land use permission to enable a wide range of community, commercial and institutional activities. . . . The second tier would expand on this permit as-of-right changes to the physical form of the building or property in order to accommodate modest additions or small buildings to house new uses. Tier 3 is intended to support more significant changes, such as new mixed-used infill development, and is therefore envisioned to apply only to select apartment neighbourhoods in the city. (Stewart et al. 2012, 3)

To facilitate renewal and investment in immigrant neighborhoods, the report further proposed a new "Apartment Residential Commercial" zone for Tiers 1 and 2 (Stewart et al. 2012, 41) and an "Apartment Neighbourhood Reinvestment" zone for Tier 3 (Stewart et al. 2012, 42). These recommendations did not land on deaf ears. On April 3 and 4, 2013, the city council adopted a new city-wide zoning bylaw that included the creation of the new Residential Apartment Commercial (RAC) zone. By the end of January 2014, the City's then chief planner, Jennifer Kessmaat, proposed selected areas for implementing the RAC zoning (City of Toronto 2014b). In early May 2014, the council approved the finalized list of five hundred apartment properties across the city (City of Toronto 2014b). The questions of rent control and the possibility of displacement still remain unclear, even though in the City's 2014 approval residents' concern over rent increase was acknowledged and there were questions as to whether the new permission might result in increased rents (City of Toronto 2014b).

While policymakers and urbanists have relegated the question of housing affordability to the dustbin of planning bureaucracy, they have facilitated the mushrooming of organizations involved with knowledge production around Tower Renewal. In April 2016, another new entity was formed in the growing network around Tower Renewal: the Tower Renewal Partnership. The initiative started as a collaboration between CUG+R (the project lead), the nonprofit Maytree Foundation (whose current director, at the time of writing, is the former United Way president and CEO, Susan McIsaac), and the newly formed housing and finance consultancy, DKGI Inc.

(linked to the Canada Mortgage and Housing Corporation).[9] In October 2017, Tower Renewal Partnership organized the Tower Renewal Action Forum, which turned into a significant space for expanding the partnership network and the scope of the Tower Renewal project to southern Ontario. By 2018, Tower Renewal Partnership, under the leadership of CUG+R, had three core partners (United Way, Maytree Evergreen, DKGI Inc.) as well as thirty-one governmental, nonprofit, and private institutions, organizations, and companies as its advisory network, along with six universities as its academic partners.[10] Since 2016, Tower Renewal Partnership has also published a series of reports and discussion papers on the financing of the Tower Renewal project and the regional expansion of the intervention to all apartment buildings in the Greater Golden Horseshoe (see Tower Renewal Partnership 2018, 2016a, 2016b). None of these reports have addressed the important questions of rent control for and the possible displacement of current tenants of the highrise concrete towers in immigrant neighborhoods.

ARRIVAL CITIES AND THE GEO-POLITICAL FEAR OF THE IMMIGRANT

In justifying the need for rezoning in immigrant neighborhoods, *A New Approach* (Stewart et al. 2012) referred to an increasingly popular concept in the Toronto urban lexicon: "arrival city." Canadian journalist Doug Saunders, a foreign correspondent of the *Globe and Mail,* coined the term in his celebrated 2010 book entitled *Arrival City: How the Largest Migration in History Is Shaping Our World.* Referring to immigrant neighborhoods as "arrival city," *A New Approach,* following Saunders, identified "the key attribute of a successful Arrival City" as "the ability to support and nurture small enterprises that directly service the community" (Stewart et al. 2012, 21). One of the architects involved with Tower Renewal explained to me:

> The main thrust with [rezoning] is actually about social investment to make sure the quality of life and economic and entrepreneurial potentials [of these neighborhoods]—kind of like Doug Saunders's arrival cities. These communities are where newcomers live, and they don't have the tools of the arrival cities to invest and start businesses, to collaborate and to do all those things. (I10 2013)

Saunders's concept of arrival city and its popularity deserves our attention as it directs us to another moment in the relational formation of urban policy and international relations. In *Arrival City,* Saunders painted a picture of the last civilizational transformation of human history fueled by "the final great human migration . . . from village to city" (2011, 21). The arrival city is both populated with people in transition and is itself a place in transition (2011,10). For Saunders, arrival city is an all-encompassing, homogenized concept across time and space; it includes "the slums, *favelas, bustess, bidonvilles, ashwaiyyat,* shantytowns, *kampongs,* urban villages, *gecekondular,* and barrios of the developing world, but also the immigrant neighbourhoods, ethnic districts, *banlieues difficiles, Plattenbau* development, Chinatowns, Little Indias, Hispanic quarters, urban slums and migrant suburbs of wealthy countries" (2011, 19). *Arrival City* received national and international recognition following its publication in 2010. From conservatives to liberals and social democrats, all applauded the book for its attentiveness to public policy and foreign affairs.[11] In the United Kingdom, Gordon Brown, the former British prime minister, called it "a remarkable achievement." *The Guardian* praised it as the twenty-first century version of Jane Jacobs's *The Death and Life of Great American Cities.* In Toronto, it was not just CUG+R that linked the Tower Renewal project to arrival city. Saunders himself turned into an advocate of Tower Renewal. Saunders took Stewart's celebration of Toronto's highrise concrete buildings to the national level and argued that suburban apartment-dwelling is part of Canadian identity (Saunders 2013). Two years before Hume's 2015 advocacy for "transforming" Toronto's immigrant neighborhoods by Tower Renewal, Saunders already had applauded Tower Renewal as influential for "transforming [Toronto's] postwar slab *farms* into thriving urban-style neighbourhoods" (Saunders 2013, emphasis added). The fact that Saunders, a seasoned journalist, chose the word "farm" to refer to residential apartments, wherein more than half a million Torontonians live, should not be missed here; such naming carries in itself colonial imaginaries of animality and contagion, historically associated with the assumed "uncivilized" nature of colonies. His juxtaposition of "slab farms" and "thriving urban-style neighbourhoods" also builds upon the liberal-colonial separation of urbanity and rurality, to which I will come back to shortly. Five years later, in 2018, he called Tower Renewal "an architectural revolution" (Saunders 2018), a revolution that presumably will simultaneously civilize and urbanize the immigrant and immigrant neighborhoods.

Saunders's book and its concept quickly gained popularity among urbanists, academics, and the City of Toronto's planners and policymakers, as well as community organizations in immigrant neighborhoods. In October 2013, Toronto's Chief Planner Roundtable focused on arrival city as part of the City's effort to have "a better understanding of what's going on in our suburbs" (Keesmaat 2013).[12] In May 2014, Architecture for Humanity Toronto organized a lecture series on "Incremental Strategies for Vertical Neighbourhoods" and a design charrette inspired by the City's Tower Renewal program at Ryerson University. Part of the aim of the design charrette was to use opportunities in the new RAC zone to redesign "vertical neighbourhoods" as successful arrival cities. Graeme Stewart and Eleanor McAteer (then the project director of the Tower Renewal Office at the City) attended the charrette as jurists. In December 2014, Cities of Migration (an initiative of the Maytree Foundation and Ryerson University) organized a public talk on Arrival Cities: Global Framework + Local Discourse.[13] In 2015, four major events were organized around arrival city. In January 2015, the Cities of Migration's City Book Club launched an online reading of *Arrival Cities,* inviting urbanists, migration experts, practitioners, and advocates from across the world to join a guided reading and global discussion of the book. In March, Cities of Migration organized a webinar on "Tower Renewal in the Arrival City," featuring Graeme Stewart and Gerben Helleman (from Rotterdam, Netherlands) discussing the relationship between Tower Renewal and arrival cities.[14] In April, as part of its *Cities of Arrival* program, the Toronto Ismaili Centre in collaboration with the York University City Institute organized an event, Arrival Cities: How Immigration Succeeds and Fails on the Edge of the City. In July, Heritage Toronto organized another public event, Thorncliffe Park: Canada's Arrival City, focusing on the history and current situation of that neighborhood, which Saunders had identified as a successful arrival city in his book. In October 2017, Saunders gave the closing public lecture at the above-mentioned Tower Renewal Action Forum that initiated the expansion of the Tower Renewal projects and partnership.

Why did the narrative of a journalist who has mostly written on international affairs suddenly become such an important topic in the urban visions of redevelopment in Toronto's postwar suburbs? *Arrival*

City is neither a revelation nor does it have any scientific and analytical depth. There is nothing new to its argument of an increasingly urbanized world. Already in 2007, the United Nations had announced that more than half of the human population would be living in urban areas soon. By conflating different historical periods, geographies, scales, and forces of migration and immigration, Saunders homogenizes the complexities of migration in our conjuncture. Rather than its analytical and scientific value, it is, I suggest, the epistemology and political message of *Arrival City* that were both attractive and useful for popularizing the Tower Renewal program and normalizing the geo-political fear of the immigrant in Toronto (and perhaps elsewhere).

The immigrant has an important place in Saunders's account of arrival cities; what he calls "the villager." The villager is the agent of "the final great human migration . . . from village to city" (2011, 21). Taking for granted the sociospatial relations of imperialist capitalism,[15] Saunders provides his readers with a liberal humanitarian vision-cum-mission: If we want to save "our urban" world from the threats of the poor "villagers," who have come from "out there" to live amongst "us," "we" need to empower the poor villagers to urbanize themselves. Spatial form plays an important role in Saunders's liberal-colonial recognition of the villager/the immigrant. "The arrival city" he writes, "is often barely urban, in form and culture" (2011, 23). Not surprisingly in writing about Toronto's immigrant neighborhoods in the *Globe and Mail,* he mobilized a colonial imaginary of animality and contagion and referred to these residential spaces as "farms," as mentioned earlier (Saunders 2013). Calling himself an environmental determinist (Saunders 2010), Saunders strongly argues that "a good part of the success or failure of an arrival city has to do with its physical form" (Saunders 2011, 32–33). The social-Darwinist force of this environmental determinism is such that "it serves as a sorting and selection mechanism" (Saunders 2011, 39). Eventually, we are told, what arrival cities "produce, through this cycle of selection, are among the most inventive and resilient population groups in the world" (Saunders 2011, 47).

The epistemology of this liberal humanitarian vision infused with environmental determinism, social Darwinism, and colonial imaginaries builds upon the geo-political imaginaries of colonial-imperialist capitalist progress and development. These geo-political imaginaries are key to Saunders's differentiation between the "urbanites" of the global North and the "villagers" of the global South. The culturalized and hierarchical separation between urbanity and rurality, urbanites and villagers, builds upon the historical geo-political imaginaries of the civilized and the uncivilized, the colonizer and the colonized, the modern and the traditional, the developed and the underdeveloped, the liberal democratic and the terrorist. Such civilizational separation, differentiation, hierarchization, and abstraction are at the heart of the conception of arrival city. Arrival city, in the words of Saunders, is

> a place of transition. Almost all of its important activities, beyond mere survival, exist to bring villagers, and entire villages, into the urban sphere, into the centre of social and economic life, into education and acculturation and belonging, into sustainable prosperity. (2011, 10)

Saunders's civilizational logic is nicely glossed in a liberal humanitarian discourse. One of the celebratory aspects of Saunders's account is to provide a liberal humanitarian geographical imaginary of "the villagers" as having the potential to become "urbanites," of joining the "urban civilization." Similar to the conceptions of the immigrant and highrise concrete towers in urban policy, Saunders's villagers have assets and potentials that only need to be unleashed through the tutelage of experts. Thus, his call for facilitating access to entrepreneurship, property ownership, and citizenship for "the villagers" in order to transform them into liberal subjects that are nonthreatening to the state, as well as his call for the redevelopment of arrival cities. Saunders's recognition of "the villagers" is deeply rooted in the colonial-liberal form of recognizing the colonized and the subaltern, a recognition that aims to construct colonial-liberal subjects whose "inferiority complex"—to quote Frantz Fanon ([1961] 1967)—would lead them to identify with the oppressor and the state.

For the advocates of Tower Renewal, Saunders's liberal humanitarian narrations of environmental determinism and the immigrant are most attractive for advocating redevelopment in immigrant neighborhoods. "Going back to Doug Saunders," one of the architects of Tower Renewal explained,

> I think this [Tower Renewal] is more of an idea of how do you create agency in people and provide the tools for individual

agency in these neighborhoods. The way I look at it is that [these towers] were designed and planned as though they were state-owned. . . . They were designed for middle-income people who drove cars. And now they need to function as a village where people are walking, do things locally. . . . It's been groups like myself and United Way and other people who have been fighting and working with the City . . . to sort of challenge the status quo to liberalize these spaces and to allow these things from sort of a regime that would be happy to see them just frozen in time, which is something totally inhuman. (I10 2013)

Such colonial-liberal recognition of the immigrant has deep-seated roots in Toronto, even among the non-White population. A member of the Scarborough Housing Help Centre, whom I mentioned earlier on overcrowded housing in immigrant neighborhoods, explained to me how in their view the lack of agency of the immigrant living in highrise concrete towers is one of the reasons behind the lack of any class-action lawsuit against the illegal practices of landlords:

Much of the immigration that we see to Canada is from developing countries. I think in many of the developing countries what happens is the old concept of challenging the law is something that is usually not encouraged. . . . They bring that mentality with them here. . . . To bring a class-action lawsuit you need somebody who is brave enough to step forward and say, "Yes, I will take this to court." But you will not find anyone who has this kind of courage, because of their own experiences in their own native countries. . . . The lack of information, the lack of will to make these kinds of things happens from within the community— and that has affected them the most. And since they will not do anything, there is very little incentive for the other side to do anything. Right? (I9 2013)

Saunders's *Arrival City* is also important for our discussion for the ways he frames the geo-political fear of the immigrant, the importance he gives to the prospect of so-called race riots and terrorism in arrival city, and the solutions he provides for nullifying those threats. The geo-political fear of the immigrant goes hand in hand with Saunders's liberal-colonial recognition of the villager/the immigrant, one that opens space for their potential. The "Paris problem" haunts the fate of the arrival city, according to Saunders. Left to itself, the arrival city could transform into a "place of failed arrival," reminiscent to the fate of so-called failed and failing states in the international geographical imaginary of imperialism. Recalling the "Paris . . . riots in 2005, London in the 1980s, Amsterdam . . . in the first decade of this century" (Saunders 2011, 19), those in the "African-American ghetto" (25), and the "Islamist terror plot" designed in Mississauga (Toronto) in 2006 (318), Saunders ends his book by reminding his readers that if the villagers of arrival cities "are driven out or trapped on the margins or denied citizenship or an ownership stake in the larger city, they will turn into a far more expensive threat" (323). This specter of an urban subaltern uprising threatening the peace and security of so-called urbanites parallels the racialized and territorialized security ideology at the heart of the geo-political fear of the immigrant in Toronto. "The new arrival cities of Europe and North America," Saunders reminds his readers, "have plumbing, sewage and internet access, but they are sometimes as alien and threatening to their native populations as the slums of Asia are to their cities' established residents" (31).

Saunders's particular liberal humanitarian ideology is another reason for the praise the book received. *Arrival City* is a celebration of liberal imperialism via liberal humanitarianism par excellence. Saunders's conception of "resilient villagers" parallels Bernard Lewis's (2002) conception of the "good Muslim" (see Mamdani 2004), which has been fundamental to the formulation of the U.S. imperialist war policy in the Middle East. Both conceptions are based on the philanthropy of the West. Not much different from Lewis, who emphasized the need to support the "good Muslims," one of the major messages of *Arrival City* is to push the state (and its civil society apparatuses) to cultivate a loyal constituency among the subaltern villagers by using the opportunity to appropriate their aspirations so as to transform them into securitized and urbanized liberal subjects. Saunders's conception of failed arrival cities parallels Thomas Barnett's (2004) conception of "non-integrated gaps," which, as discussed earlier, has been influential in the War on Terror. For both Saunders and Barnett, threats are perceived in the disconnection from imperialist-capitalist relations. Thus, for Saunders, making villagers into small entrepreneurs and homeowners, giving them "paths into the 'core city,'" and increasing the real estate value of arrival cities through redevelopment are among the most strategic ways to pacify the threat of subaltern uprisings (2011, 20–21).

In this sense, Saunders's narrative affirms the conception of immigrant neighborhoods as securitized spaces of liberal humanitarian interventions. *Arrival City* confirms and justifies the geo-political fear of the non-White working class in Toronto. Saunders's silence on the concrete forces of imperialist-capitalism, his environmental determinism and liberal humanitarianism, his celebration of neoliberal ideology, his fetishization of the informal economy, and his promotion of home ownership all resonate well with policymakers in Toronto; the latter, too, have shown a deep-seated reluctance to deal with the concrete causes of the production of non-White poverty and the crisis of affordable housing in the city. Ideologically and epistemologically, Saunders provides a civil narrative reminiscent of those of the gurus of American counterinsurgency such as David Kilcullen (2013) and John Nagl (2014), in particular in the way they locate the enemy of the West in the peripheralized urban spaces of metropolitan centers, as mentioned earlier. Saunders, Kilcullen, and Nagl all build upon a Malthusian conception of a surplus population that has nowhere to go except to urban centers, a Darwinist politics of the survival of the fittest, in which the fit one is the resilient liberal subject, and a Hobbesian notion of war of all against all that manifests itself in the specter of the subaltern revolt. Hume's fearmongering about Toronto's immigrant neighborhoods and his call for Tower Renewal was born out of this broader history of making Toronto's immigrant neighborhoods as spaces of racialized ungovernability. And that is precisely why it was not simply sensational journalism. After all, neither sensational journalism nor sensational politics functions in a void; their sensationality is grounded in common-sense ideologies.

By Way of Conclusion

In its ongoing efforts to keep Canadians safe, the Government of Canada is expanding how it responds to violent extremism. Specifically, the federal government is investing in the prevention of radicalization to violence as articulated through the *National Strategy on Countering Radicalization to Violence.* . . . Prevention and countering violent extremism is an effective complement to security agencies' traditional methods of safeguarding national security.

—Government of Canada, *National Strategy on Countering Radicalization to Violence,* 2018

The attacks that shook European cities from 2014 to 2017 made the vague category of radicalization and its prevention the major security concerns of Western states, nationally and internationally. The locationality and positionality of these attackers, as mentioned in the Beginnings chapter of this book, shifted the racialized geographical imaginaries of the enemy in the War on Terror onto the uneven geographies of Western cities. In Europe, alongside the racialized figure of the Muslim as the public enemy number one (Kundnani 2009; Mondon and Winter 2017; Fadil, Ragazzi, and de Koning 2019), immigrant neighborhoods have increasingly become the target of state investigation and intervention (Saberi 2019). This preventive turn in national security is facilitated and rationalized by a growing knowledge production industry on radicalization prevention, the Muslim, and immigrant neighborhoods. Politically and financially supported by the European Union and European national and regional governments, this booming knowledge production industry has become influential in deepening the convergence of security politics, racialization, and urban governance (Saberi 2019; also see Kundnani and Hayes, 2018; de Goede and Simon 2013).

In Canada, media commentators like Hume were not the only ones concerned with radicalization and the need for place-based urban policy to prevent it. A few weeks after the attack on the *Charlie Hebdo* office in Paris, on January 30, 2015, then prime minister Stephen Harper publicly introduced Bill C-51 in an election-style rally in Richmond Hill—a suburb north of Toronto and a federal election battleground for his Conservative Party at the time—emphasizing that "violent jihadism . . . seeks to harm us here in Canada—in our cities and in our neighborhoods" (quoted in McGregor and O'Malley 2015). Bill C-51 brought the most drastic changes to Canada's national security apparatus since the National Security Act of 2001: it expanded the powers of the police and security agencies as well as the vague category of the radicalized/the terrorist in criminal law. Civil liberty organizations, legal experts, and analysts denounced and challenged Bill C-51 as unconstitutional (see CCLA 2015; Forcese and Roach 2015). As a response to the critiques of Bill C-51, in June 2017, the Trudeau Liberal government introduced Bill C-59, officially known as the National Security Act, 2017. The 2017 National Security Act, however, only softens some coercive edges of Bill C-51 by adding new review and oversight bodies while keeping intact the expansion of state security powers (Roach and Carvin 2017; Parsons et al. 2017; Ahmad 2019). What differentiated the Trudeau Liberal government's national security strategy from that of the Harper Conservative government was the former's explicit emphasis on prevention in counterterrorism.

Parallel to developments in Europe, shortly after the introduction of Bill C-51, Public Safety Canada (PSC) launched a new knowledge production center on radicalization in 2017: the Canada Centre for Community Engagement and Prevention of Violence (Canada Centre). Then public safety minister Ralph Goodale introduced the Canada Center as one that

> will engage with stakeholders and the public to develop a national strategy to countering radicalization to violence. Through the Community Resilience Fund, the Canada Centre will support local-level prevention and intervention initiatives by providing funding and expertise in efforts to combat terrorist use of the Internet, action-oriented research and youth-focused initiatives. (PSC 2018a, 3)

In less than a year, Canada's first *National Strategy on Countering Radicalization to Violence* (Government of Canada 2018) was officially published. The *National Strategy* identified prevention as the cornerstone of dealing with "home-grown radicalization," as mentioned in the above epigraph, and elevated the role of Canada Centre as "a centre of excellence" that "provides national leadership on Canada's efforts to counter radicalization to violence" (Government of Canada 2018, 5).

The Toronto Police was one of the first recipients of the Canada Centre funds. In September 2018, the Canada Centre gave Toronto Police Services $1,048,000 over three years from its Community Resilience Fund to help expand and adapt FOCUS Toronto (Furthering Our Communities, Uniting Services) as a radicalization prevention strategy (PSC 2018b). Marco Mendicino, the parliamentary secretary to then minister of infrastructure and communities, announced the funding and collaboration:

> This investment in FOCUS Toronto will advance the important work of the Toronto Police Service in implementing a collaborative program that draws on the support, expertise and advice of practitioners and civil society to prevent this phenomenon. The Government of Canada is proud to support locally-driven initiatives such as this. (quoted in PSC 2018b, emphasis added)

Mark Saunders, then Toronto Police chief, backed up Mendicino, underlining that "the most beneficial aspect of this funding is that it will enhance the ability of multiple agencies to identify individuals of elevated risk of offending and allow for referral to existing multidisciplinary collaborative agencies city-wide in order to prevent and counter radicalization as early as possible" (quoted in PSC 2018b).

My intention is not to examine the formation and politics of the Canada Centre here. That requires its own study, one that is urgently needed and is out of the scope of this book. Rather, I think the expansion and adaptation of FOCUS Toronto for radicalization prevention in Canada is an appropriate open ending to the story of this book. In chapter 3, we saw how FOCUS was born and developed through the collaboration of the City of Toronto, the Toronto Police, and United Way through policy mobilities at a multiplicity of scales, geographies, and temporalities, from the 1990s to the 2010s, from Boston (United

States) and Glasgow (Scotland) to Prince Albert (Canada). Rather than a "locally-driven initiative," FOCUS, as we saw, is the product of the ascendency of prevention in international relations, urban policy, and policing in the second decade of the twenty-first century. With its emphasis on whole-of-government, epidemiological criminology, social development, and social determinants of health, FOCUS rearticulates some major pillars of Western counterinsurgency, international public health, and international development in Toronto's immigrant neighborhoods.

This brings me back to the starting lines of *Fearing the Immigrant* and my goal to write about the relational formation of urban policy and international relations by historicizing the formation of place-based urban policy in Toronto's immigrant neighborhoods. Limiting our understanding of the rapid mushrooming of place-based policy to the sole force of neoliberalization severely constrains our conception of the politics of place-based urban policy. Erased are the ways the nexus of security, racialization, and development has historically affected visions and missions of place-based urban policy. The nexus of security, racialization, and development, as we saw, has been imperative to the ascendency of prevention and the continuous reconstruction of the racialized geographical imaginaries of the Other as danger, which, in turn, are central to the relational formation of urban policy and international relations. Focusing on the geo-politics of danger—that is, on the constitution of the geographical imaginaries and boundaries of inside and outside, domestic and foreign, the enemy within and the enemy without—throughout the book, I engaged with the force of geo-political fear in the construction of the figure of the immigrant and immigrant neighborhoods in Toronto and Canada. In the Beginnings chapter and chapter 1, we saw that the history of this geo-political fear in the making of the immigrant goes back to the constitution of Canada as a White settler colony of the British Empire (the White Canada Policy) and the relational formation of immigration policy and foreign policy in the conjuncture of decolonization and its aftermath. Canada's national and foreign policy ideologies, namely, liberal multiculturalism and liberal humanitarianism, have played fundamental roles in the making of the immigrant as a security subject. We saw, in chapter 2, how this history has played out alongside the uneven urban development of Toronto in the late twentieth and early twenty-first centuries as the local state and philanthrocapitalist forces zoomed in on the geographical concertation of non-White poverty in Toronto's immigrant neighborhoods as a threat to Toronto's prosperity and competitiveness.

The hegemony of liberal multiculturalism in Canada and the specificities of its immigration processes have necessitated the articulation of the geo-political fear of the immigrant in Toronto within the boundaries of a liberal humanitarian ideology (chapters 1 to 6). With roots in the eighteenth- and nineteenth-century liberal humanitarian thought about the wretched and the colonized of the world, today's liberal humanitarian ideology has an intrinsic neocolonial dimension to it. Tutelage and trusteeship are central to this neocolonial dimension. In a manner similar to eighteenth-century humanitarianism, in today's liberal humanitarian ideology the spaces of humanitarian intervention—in our case, immigrant neighborhoods—are simultaneously conceived as spaces of securitization and tutelage. Recall how those sociopolitical forces that have lived the farthest from the misery and violence of poverty aimed at addressing the problem of concentrated non-White poverty in Toronto, or how United Way has become the so-called voice of Toronto's marginalized populations and has taken on the trusteeship role of empowering the immigrant. The emphasis on the tutelage of the immigrant and the need to ameliorate violence in this humanitarian logic has made prevention through development a major policy concept.

Throughout chapters 3 to 6, I followed the ascendency of the concept of prevention and its function as an ideology in place-based policies of policing, social development, and housing redevelopment. In chapter 3, I traced the history of prevention in policing to the ideas of Patrick Colquhoun (1806) and his concept of social police in the late eighteenth century. Starting from the premise that poverty is integral to social relations of capitalism, Colquhoun proposed prevention as a productive strategy for the political management of poverty and of the working class, along with that of the reproduction of capitalist social relations. Colquhoun's conception of prevention has powerful echoes in today's policy frenzy around this topic. The mandate of the Canada Centre is the latest reverberation of such echoes in Canada. By the time the Canadian government elevated prevention as a major national security strategy, the concept had already become hegemonic in urban policy and policing in Toronto. As we saw, the current popularity of the concept of prevention in Toronto's policy circles is also related to the centrality of prevention in international relations, from Western counterinsurgency to international development and international public health policies of the International Monetary Fund, the World Bank, and the World Health Organization (WHO) in the global South.

While the liberal humanitarian concepts of trusteeship and tutelage are central to the neocolonial dimensions of place-based urban policy in Toronto, I also engaged with the role of ideologies of space in this neocolonial dimension, particularly focusing on the geographical imaginaries of racialized ungovernability at the urban and international scales. Territorialized, homogenized, hierarchized, racialized, and fragmented conceptions of space are predominant in the conceptions of so-called troubled neighborhoods, hotspots, and no-go zones of crime and violence in the neighborhood effects literature, which as we saw has formed the assumedly scientific pillar of urban policy in Toronto and other places. We saw how similar ideologies of space works in the conceptions of so-called ungoverned spaces, hotspots, and failing states in international relations, in the narratives of new wars, human security, humanitarian intervention, and the War on Terror. These ideologies of space in the geographical imaginaries of racialized ungovernability owe their validity to an ideology of order that has been historically linked to the insecurity of private property and imperialist capitalist social relations and has been imperative for the reification of the liberal ideology of security, policing, and the construction of the geo-political fear of the immigrant.

The popularity of the ideology of poverty-as-risk was born out of this context. Poverty-as-risk came to international prominence through the policy activism of supranational, imperial institutions such as the World Bank and the International Monetary Fund in the early 1990s. In this articulation, while poverty is understood as integral to capitalist growth and development, unmanaged concentrations of poverty are also seen as a threat to the smooth functioning of imperialist capitalism. We saw how poverty is understood as simply the result of a disconnection from the market, rather than the result of particular forms of exploitative integration into the sociospatial relations of uneven development under imperialist capitalism. By the late 1990s, the conception of poverty-as-risk entered Toronto's policy lexicon through the policy activism of United Way. For policymakers, the problem with immigrant neighborhoods is that they are not connected to Toronto's economy. Their solution is thus to integrate these localities into Toronto's economy and urbanity. The ideology of poverty-as-risk has also helped revive the ideology of contagion in state policy. From the discussions on reforming community policing to reforming social development and housing redevelopment policies in Toronto, we traced the revival of the nineteenth-century ideology of danger and poverty as disease. Epidemiological criminology, with its conceptualization of crime as disease, has been imperative to normalizing the conceptions of poverty and crime as disease. Epidemiological criminology is central to the logic of FOCUS, which the Canadian government attempts to mobilize for radicalization prevention. The popularity of epidemiological criminology, I argued, is in relation to the recent policy popularity of a de-historicized concept of social determinants of health and its emphasis on prevention. Following policy mobilities concerning the concept of social determinants of health, I pointed to the role of the WHO and to the predominance of similar ideologies in war and policing strategies.

Appeals to science and objectivity have been fundamental to making these ideologies seemingly innocent and invisible, which is why it is important to scrutinize knowledge production institutions such as Canada Centre. I have particularly focused on quantification and visualization as two major techniques mobilized by policymakers, academics, and urbanists in Toronto. We saw how policymakers have mobilized seemingly progressive concepts such as social determinants of health and equity as quantitative tools to give a positive aura to place-based policies of community policing, social development, and housing redevelopment (chapters 3, 5, and 6). Borrowed from the chambers of the Work Bank and the WHO, such appeals to equity and social determinants of health have greatly reified the violent contradictions and consequences of structural uneven development and racialization in Toronto, and indeed worldwide. While such appeals are quite recent in Toronto and implementation outcomes are not yet clear, so far the state has used these appeals as a way to pacify more radical bottom-up claims. We saw, for example, how policymakers were reluctant to address racism as a factor in equity and social determinants of health, because, we were told, racism is not measurable. By 2020, ironically the year that Toronto's reformed urban policy was supposed to come to fruition, the hollow promises of equity and social determinants of health shattered under the weight of the ongoing devastating effects of the Covid-19 pandemic in Toronto's immigrant neighborhoods. While the naked violence of the pandemic has, to some extent, pushed the questions of racism, uneven development, and social determinants of health into public and official debates, *Fearing the Immigrant* is a cautionary tale concerning the ease with which the state mobilizes de-historicized and abstracted versions of these concepts and realities, and highlights the importance of critically engaging with the ways these concepts are mobilized in policy.

If quantification has turned into a scientific alibi for policymakers to comfortably shy away from engaging with questions of systemic racism and uneven development, visualization in the form of maps and mapping is another way of claiming objectivity. The ascendency of visualization as a scientific way of comprehending reality has brought a new level of abstraction in urban and international strategies of intervention. I have problematized the production and mobilization of mapping as an instance of the ascendency of the visual not just in perceiving and conceiving immigrant neighborhoods, but also in understanding urban politics. Mapping is not a problem in itself; mapping is a visualization technique and an important one for understanding social space. Rather, it is the politics of mapping that is the concern of *Fearing the Immigrant,* because maps are political. We saw the logical-political overlaps between the maps of Toronto's "Paris problem" and Thomas Barnett's (2004) geopolitical mapping of the dangerous "gaps" in the imperial world. Uncritical endorsements of mapping as an objective technique that reveals reality have ignored these parallels and resulted in normalizing the violence involved in the production of immigrant neighborhoods as spaces of racialized ungovernability, here and there, near and far. At the same time, an aura of scientificity, produced by academics and professionals and popularized by the media, has normalized mapping's erasure of violence. Uncritical engagement with mapping non-White poverty and violence has solidified territorialized and racialized geographical imageries of poverty and violence in Toronto.

The ascendency of quantification and visualization has also resulted in the simultaneous prevalence and normalization of environmental determinism in state-led strategies of intervention. The current popularity of design solutions has gained part of its justification from the normalization of environmental deterministic visions. We saw this in community policing, social development, and even more so in Tower

Renewal. With its emphasis on solving social problems through urban design interventions, liberal humanitarian conceptions of poverty and the immigrant as security problem and asset, neocolonial conception of empowerment and community participation, and a neoliberal conception of economic integration, Tower Renewal is the most condensed embodiment of the penetration of this environmentally determinist thought in Toronto's urban policy. The point here is not to negate housing redevelopment in itself. Redevelopment is needed for keeping our urban spaces livable. As a trained architect, I can relate to the excitement of architects and urbanists involved with grand-scale projects such as Tower Renewal. Rather, here too my point is about the politics ingrained in redevelopment policies. Tower Renewal is not a stand-alone project in its emphasis on design solutions for urban problems. This logic is part of the broader trend in urbanist thought that has gained momentum in the second decade of the twenty-first century, and which is variously referred to as "social architecture" (Feireiss 2011) "tactical urbanism" (Lydon and Garcia 2015), "acupuncture urbanism" (Lerner 2014), and "incremental urbanism" (Balestra and Göransson 2009). When, in May 2014, Tower Renewal and Architecture for Humanity organized a design charrette on highrise concrete towers in Toronto's immigrant neighborhoods at Ryerson University School of Architecture, they named the event Incremental Strategies for Vertical Neighborhoods. Filipe Balestra, an influential advocate of incremental urbanism, was one of the major advisors of the design charrette, who also gave a talk on the topic at Ryerson School of Architecture a day earlier. This urbanist thought celebrates informality and advocates local intervention and participation for tackling the hard-to-avoid reality of sociospatial and racial polarization and poverty across and within metropolitan centers worldwide.

The production of the aura of scientificity has not been a simple, transparent affair. As we saw, a whole array of diverse sociopolitical forces has been involved in the knowledge production industry surrounding urban policy in Toronto. These sociopolitical forces go beyond policymakers within the institutions of the state and include a good portion of civil society actors, from charity organizations such as the United Way and nonprofit and for-profit research institutions to major banks and academic institutions and on to urbanists and architects. The social and political diversity of this large web of forces involved in the production of knowledge on the immigrant and urban policy directs us to the importance of Gramsci's concept of the integral state (1971) and crystallizes Lefebvre's point about the ways in which state-like thinking and symbolism penetrate everyday life and turn into common sense (1976, 1991, 2009).

Some readers would argue that the very diversity of these sociopolitical forces could turn into an opening for democratizing knowledge production about the immigrant. Perhaps. But I am less optimistic, not because I believe in the total hegemony of state ideology, but because of two other crucial pillars in the relational formation of urban policy and international relations. The first pillar is the phenomenon of whole-of-government approach. As we saw in previous pages, the state has been actively intensifying ideological dominance over policymaking and implementation. The whole-of-government approach is about the political management of this vast knowledge of the production and policymaking industry as well as that of policy implementation through community centers and selected grassroots groups. An increasingly popular approach in military and civil governance, the whole-of-government approach can be seen as the latest strategy to sustain the balance of forces in favor of the ruling classes. Is it a coincidence that Canada's *National Strategy on Countering Radicalization to Violence* also emphasizes the whole-of-government approach? (see Government of Canada 2018, 16).

The second pillar is the conception of the subject of security in state intervention. The ideology of prevention, as we saw, is anchored upon a particular neocolonial conception of the subject of security, whether in policing-security strategies or in social development or housing redevelopment strategies. Born out of human security discourses that came to international prominence in the 1990s, the subject of preventive intervention is not a passive subject. Rather, it is a particular form of an active subject: the vulnerable subject in need of tutelage to become resilient. In international relations, the shift to prevention in security politics was accompanied by a shift in the locus of securing agency from Western actors to the fragile or failing states (perceived to be) in need of capacity building and humanitarian intervention. The revival of counterinsurgency in the War on Terror came out of this context. In place-based urban policy, we can trace this shift in targeting so-called at-risk individuals or families and their choices or immigrant neighborhoods and their physical characteristics. The conception of crime and violence as infectious disease and the logic of design solutions build upon this conception of the subject of security. FOCUS also mobilizes a similar conception of the subject of state security and intervention. Such a conception of the subject of security directs us to the powerful force of dominant ideologies and their deep penetration into everyday life and common sense.

As we saw, even the progressive fractions of the sociopolitical forces involved in the production and implementation of place-based policy in Toronto have deeply internalized such ideologies. This is not to say, and should not be taken as a declaration, that the state has total domination. As I have emphasized throughout this book, urban policy and particularly place-based urban policy have been the products of the contradictions of the sociospatial and (neo-)colonial relations of imperialist capitalism. The geo-political fear of the revolt of the racialized excluded, of the subaltern, is central to both urban policy and international relations. This is why the specters of so-called race riots and anti-colonial and anti-imperialist revolutions have been imperative to the formation of urban policy and international relations, respectively. If targeted intervention has been a state strategy to solidify domination, its necessity has been crystallized in times of crisis, when there are cracks in the hegemony of imperialist capitalism. This is why the geo-political fear of the immigrant and the so-called race riots have been central to such state strategies, whether the subject of geo-political fear is the Black radicals in the Black ghettos of the 1960s and 1970s United States, the Indigenous activists in Canada in the 1960s, the former imperial subjects turned to post-colonial immigrant in the *banlieues* of Paris, the so-called sink estates of council housing in London and other British cities, or the immigrant in Toronto. Saying that ideology has been central to the ruling classes' geo-political fear of the non-White working-class populations does not mean that such fear is a delusion. As the worldwide urban upheavals of the last decade and the current Black Lives Matter movements have demonstrated, we are living in an extremely politically volatile time of the urban rage of the excluded (see Dikeç 2017; Taylor 2016).

The sociohistorical analysis that I provided here gives us a very complex, contradictory, and messy picture of the reality in Toronto. Still, this is only one aspect of our current conjuncture—that is, the aspect of the ideological dimension of actually existing urban policy in immigrant neighborhoods. Another important piece of the puzzle is to examine the on-the-ground resistance within and without immigrant neighborhoods and to historicize various forms of resistance across time, geography, and scale. I have touched upon some forms of resistance and appropriation of place-based policy by activists in Toronto. The question of what forms of resistance have managed to be born and survive has not been the primary analytical focus of this book as it deserves its own space. Subaltern struggles have been crucial in the formation of place-based urban policy in Toronto and elsewhere. While not systematically organized, there have always been pockets of resistance scattered across the city. Recall the timely intervention of Jane and Finch Action Against Poverty that pushed the City to add an extra consultation session for the Jane-Finch neighborhood, or the works of youth activists against police brutality in postwar suburbs. One of the impetuses of the current Black Lives Matter Toronto movement was the everyday contradictions and violence of place-based policing strategies such as TAVIS and racial profiling, the main subject matter of chapter 3. The choice in April 2015 of Mark Saunders as the first Black chief of police in Toronto and the second in Canada was the state reaction to the rise of Black activism in Toronto; albeit the reaction has been a cooptation of diversity similar to the presidency of Barack Obama in the United States. Ironically, Saunders resigned as Toronto's chief of police in July 2020 in the midst of the revival of the Black Lives Matter movement in the aftermath of the murder of George Floyd by the Minneapolis Police in May 2020. It remains to be seen and scrutinized how and to what extent the current popular and official focus on anti-Black racism would affect place-based urban policymaking.

In emphasizing the relational formation of urban policy and international relations, my aim is to direct attention to the governing of racialized ungovernability at the urban and international scales, and to underline the multifaceted relations of racialization, revolution, and state intervention. Such a relational framework helps us to bring together imperial governance, processes of racialization, and relations of resistance at a multiplicity of scales, territories, geographies, and temporalities. It pushes us to engage with how the geo-political fear of the immigrant is deeply ingrained in imperialist strategies and the changing relations of sovereignty, territory, and security in the twenty-first century. In our time of economic crisis, pandemics, intensified imperialist wars, the recurrent urban uprising of the excluded, and the electoral return of the hard-Right, paying attention to the relational formation of urban policy and international relations in governing racialized ungovernability is, in my view, an important political and intellectual task. *Fearing the Immigrant* aimed to make an opening for taking up such a task.

Acknowledgments

Like any intellectual work, this book is a collective product, even though its writing was a solitary affair. Many individuals, scattered across North America, Europe, and the Middle East, have been influential to my thinking through, starting, writing, and finishing this book. To do justice to their support, love, and camaraderie, I have to write a book-length of acknowledgments. I'd like to start with sending my deep gratitude to two fantastic women in my life, to whom I have dedicated this book.

To my mother, Farzaneh Vajihollahi, who taught me from an early age to stand for and believe in myself, to be generous and humble, and to ask difficult questions. Without her unconditional love and sacrifices, I would not have been able to live and change my life the way I have. Without her, neither I nor this book would have become a reality.

To my mentor and friend, Himani Bannerji (York University), whose work, life, and friendship I admire dearly. Her works have been fundamental not only to the development of my thinking and politics but also to navigating my everyday life in Canadian society. Himani is a giant intellectual, a militant anti-racist, feminist marxist, an enthusiastic teacher, and an extremely down-to-earth, kind-hearted person. I am forever grateful to have her in my life.

This book has its genesis in my doctoral dissertation, which I defended in January 2017 at the Faculty of Environmental and Urban Change at York University in Toronto, Canada. I am indebted to my PhD supervisor, Stefan Kipfer (York University), and my committee advisors, Liette Gilbert (York University) and Emily Gilbert (University of Toronto), for their close reading of my work, constructive critiques, and constant support. They read all or parts of the earlier drafts of this manuscript, and their insights were imperative to the making of this book.

Soon after defending my PhD, I left for Europe to take postdoctoral positions, first at the Brussels Centre for Urban Studies at the Vrije Universiteit Brussel (VUB) in Brussels, Belgium, and later at the Department of Politics and International Studies at the University of Warwick in Coventry, United Kingdom, as a British Academy International Newton Fellow. Halfway through my postdoctoral research in Europe I embarked on writing this book. During my time in Europe, I greatly benefited from fascinating dialogues with a small group of critical academics and intellectuals. In Brussels, I am forever indebted to my friends, colleagues, and comrades Line Algod (VUB) and Nadia Fadil (KU Leuven). It is impossible to think about my time in Belgium without these two amazing women scholars from whom I have learned tremendously. I am also thankful to Bas van Heur (VUB) at the Brussels Centre for Urban Studies for his support during my time as a coordinator and researcher there. In the UK, I am particularly grateful to Stuart Elden (University of Warwick), Charlotte Heath-Kelly (University of Warwick), Nick Vaughn-Williams (University of Warwick), Anthony King (University of Warwick), and Asim Qureshi (CAGE). I extremely benefited from Stuart's mentorship at the University of Warwick. Stuart's support of this book project and his engagement with and valuable comments on the initial book proposal and earlier drafts of this manuscript were invaluable.

Many other academics and scholars influenced the shape and direction of the research that has gone into this book. I would particularly like to thank Colleen Bell, Mustafa Dikeç, Arun Kundnani, Mark Neocleous, Tyler Shipley, Deborah Cowen, Tyler Wall, Ferruh Yılmaz, David McNally, Greg Albo, Thorben Wieditz, and Ilan Kapoor.

Special thanks to Pieter Martin, senior editor at the University of Minnesota Press, who trusted me and the book project. Without his support and patience, this book would not have seen the light of day. I am grateful to Pieter's editorial comments and his kind support, particularly as the Covid-19 pandemic severely delayed the review process of the manuscript.

Behind every published book lies the essential and yet invisible labor of editors. I am indebted to my friend, colleague, and comrade Stephan Dobson, whose copyedits have allowed my voice to rise above typos, occasional grammatical mistakes, and misplaced commas. I have learned a lot about writing and editing from limitless hours of conversation with Stephan and have benefited from his grounded knowledge of left politics in Toronto and Canada. I am also thankful for the care Wendy Holdman gave to the production process of the book and for the editors who made the manuscript ready for print.

I owe my sanity in the troubled neoliberal academic world and my energy to finish this book to my amazing friends, whose irreplaceable companionship, love, and trust have been oxygen to my blood and have helped me navigate my life across three continents. My sincere thanks go to Yasmin Ali, Sanaz Mehranvar, Hajar Moradi, Niloofar Golkar, Yasmine Hassan, Tina Mazhari, Leila Mazhari, Laili Soleimani, Baran Nosratpour, Dale Shin, Baolinh Dang, Wendy Glauser, Gülay Kılıçaslan, Sardar Saadi, Sonya Scott, Yasaman Adldoust, Sepideh Bagheri, Parmys Bahiraie, Panthéa Bahiraie, Greg Bird, Farzin Manouchehrian, and Nadi Naderi. I am extremely blessed to have them in my life.

I am incapable to adequately express my gratitude to my parents, Farzaneh Vajihollahi and Akbar Saberi, and my brother, Ali Saberi, for their unconditional love and support even when we have been a continent and an ocean apart for close to two decades.

I am deeply indebted to Pablo Vivanco, for his love, friendship, and support throughout the ups and downs of writing and life. Pablo generously read earlier drafts of this manuscript, helped with taking drone pictures, and shared his insights on politics and policy in Toronto. Misha (my cat) and Rosie (Pablo's cat) were amazing fluffy writing buddies during the long pandemic lockdown periods, keeping me company as they napped either on the couch or on the desk right beside my laptop.

Last but not least, I would like to thank my anonymous interviewees, who shared their time, insights, and doubts with me. Without their generosity, this book would not have been realized. The fact that all of them (with the exception of activists) preferred to remain anonymous speaks a lot about the state of freedom of speech in Canada.

I acknowledge the support I received from the British Academy in the United Kingdom in the form of an International Newton Fellowship (NIFBA19\190709), which gave me the opportunity to be a postdoctoral fellow at the University of Warwick Department of Politics and International Studies from October 2019 to September 2021, and without which I would not have had the time and resources to start and finish this book.

The strengths of this book are due to the company, influence, and support of all these great people and many others. The shortcomings, errors in details, and lacunae of judgment are obviously due to my faults.

Appendix A

SELECTED INTERVIEWEES

I1   Member of Toronto Police Accountability. Interviewed February 27, 2014.

I2   City councilor, City of Toronto. Interviewed September 13, 2013.

I3   Manager, Social Development, Finance & Administration, City of Toronto. Interviewed January 13, 2014.

I4   Public policy researcher, Woodgreen Community Services. Interviewed October 7, 2013.

I5   Retired staff, policy researcher, City of Toronto. Interviewed October 16, 2013.

I6   Activist, Jane and Finch against Poverty. Interviewed June 24, 2013.

I7   Activist, Ontario Coalition against Poverty. Interviewed March 10, 2014.

I8   Landlord, Greenwin Inc., San Romanoway. Interviewed October 23, 2013.

I9   Senior staff, Scarborough Housing Help Center. Interviewed November 6, 2013.

I10 Architect, E.R.A. Architects, Center of Urban Growth & Renewal. Interviewed September 27, 2013.

I11 Senior police officer, TAVIS, Crime Prevention Co-coordinator, FOCUS, Toronto Police Services. Interviewed October 11, 2013.

I12 Community justice consultant for the OPP and the TPS. Interviewed October 15, 2013.

I13 City staff, Youth Development Unit, Prevention and Intervention Toronto, City of Toronto. Interviewed September 16, 2013.

I14 Activist, Ontario Coalition against Poverty. Interviewed February 7, 2014.

I15 Member of Toronto Police Accountability. Interviewed February 5, 2014.

116 Youth activist, anti-police-brutality campaign. Interviewed June 26, 2013.

117 Neighbourhood lead officer, United Way Toronto. Interviewed September 25, 2013.

118 Community development officer, Neighbourhood Action Team, City of Toronto. Interviewed July 23, 2013.

119 Senior manager, Social Policy, Analysis & Research, City of Toronto. Interviewed October 24, 2013.

120 City councilor executive assistant, City of Toronto. Interviewed August 7, 2013.

121 Tower Renewal staff, City of Toronto. Interviewed August 27, 2013.

122 Community activist. Interviewed June 7, 2013.

123 Executive team member, United Way Toronto. Interviewed September 18, 2013.

124 Community development officer, Crisis Response Unit, City of Toronto. Interviewed August 20, 2013.

125 Senior staff, policy development officer, City of Toronto. Interviewed November 27, 2013.

126 Senior staff, Community Development Unit, FOCUS, City of Toronto. Interviewed September 24, 2013.

127 Senior staff, Public Interest. Interviewed November 22, 2013.

128 Senior staff, San Romanoway Revitalization Association. Interviewed October 4, 2013.

129 Senior staff, Action for Neighbourhood Change, United Way Toronto. Interviewed September 8, 2013.

130 Senior staff, Newcomer Strategy, City of Toronto. Interviewed December 3, 2013.

131 Youth Justice staff, St. Stephen's Community House. Interviewed October 25, 2013.

132 Landlord, Greenwin Inc., Farm Chalk. Interviewed October 23, 2013.

133 Senior police officer, Toronto Police Services. Interviewed October 11, 2013.

134 Academic, York University. Interviewed July 15, 2013.

Appendix B

PARTICIPANT OBSERVATIONS

Tower Renewal: Update from Toronto & Melbourne (Innis Town
Hall, University of Toronto, December 11, 2012)

Mobilizing Private Investment in Affordable Housing: Lessons from
the United States (Institute on Municipal Finance and Governance, Toronto, April 16, 2013)

Sweden: Low-Carbon Neighbourhood Design (OISE, University of
Toronto, April 16, 2013)

Closing the Gaps: Toronto's 13 Priority Neighbourhoods (Innis
Town Hall, University of Toronto, April 25, 2013)

Family Homelessness in Jane & Finch (Finch Community & Family
Centre, Toronto, July 17, 2013)

Toronto Strong Neighbourhood Strategy 2020 Community Conversation (Cedarbrook Community Centre, October 3, 2013)

Toronto's Growing Sociospatial Divide: What's Racism Got to Do
with It? (Innis College Town Hall, University of Toronto, October 17, 2013)

Toronto Strong Neighbourhood Strategy 2020 Community Conversation (City Hall Rotunda, October 21, 2013)

Toronto Strong Neighbourhood Strategy 2020 Community Conversation (Northern Secondary School, October 22, 2013)

Regent Park: After the Mix (Toronto Reference Library, Toronto,
April 29, 2014)

Incremental Strategies for Vertical Neighbourhoods—Design Workshop & Lecture (Ryerson University, May 3, 2014)

Precarious Housing among Migrant Communities: A Multi-sectoral
Discussion (OISE, University of Toronto, May 15, 2014)

Arrival Cities: Global Framework + Local Discourses (Centre for
City Ecology & Cities of Migration, Toronto, December 9, 2014)

Youth Violence, Communities and Faith (Idealogue Forum, Toronto, January 26, 2015)

Arrival Cities: How Immigration Succeeds and Fails on the Edge of the City (Ismaili Centre, Toronto, April 11, 2015)

Notes

BEGINNINGS

1. For major texts in this regard, see Hamlin's *Public Health and Social Justice in the Age of Chadwick: Britain, 1800–1854* (2009); Bator, Artibise, and Taylor's "Public Health Reform in Canada and Urban History: A Critical Survey" (1980); Neocleous's *The Fabrication of Social Order: A Critical Theory of Police Power* (2000); and Rabinow's *French Modern: Norms and Forms of the Social Environment* (1995).

2. What is now referred to as *place-based urban policy* emerged in the conjuncture of decolonization, first in the United States, to deal with the threat of the "racial break" that Black radicalism and urban rebellion had brought to the White establishment of that country. Urban policy was born through President Lyndon B. Johnson's War on Poverty—the Economic Opportunity Act (1964) and the Model Cities Act (1966)—which in turn were formed in relation to the U.S. counterinsurgency in the Philippines and Vietnam (Roy, Schrader and Crane 2014; Immerwahr 2015; Light 2003; Cochrane 2007). At its moment of emergence in the United States, urban policy had explicitly racialized and geo-political dimensions. It was meant to tackle the question of race and revolution in the "Black ghetto" by injecting development and security initiatives into those communities. In the UK, urban policy emerged in the 1960s under the lofty title of Urban Aid as a response to the 1958 urban unrest of mostly Black residents in Nottingham and London (Notting Hill). With the rise of Black Power in the 1970s and following the nationwide urban rebellions of 1980–81, community development and policing became more systematically used as urban policy (Bridge 1981; Solomos 2003; Field et al. 2019; Sivanandan [1999] 2019). In the aftermath of the 2001 urban uprising associated with South Asian youths in the country's northern cities, the New Labour government of Tony Blair rolled out the most systematic place-based urban policy in the UK history, called Community Cohesion (Kundnani 2007; Flint and Robinson 2008; Husband and Alam 2011). On the other side of the Channel in France, the Minguettes Hot Summer of 1981, the fear of which was reinforced by the images of Black unrest in Brixton, London, turned into the impetus for French *politique de la ville* (urban policy) in the *banlieues*. In the aftermath of the 1991 unrest in the *banlieues,* the French state rolled out the *Grands projects urbains* (1991) and the *Grands*

project de la ville (1998) (Dikeç 2007). The fear of the unrest in the *banlieues* was essential to the Jacques Chirac government's passing of *La Loi d'orientation et de programmation pour la ville et al renovation urbaine* in 2003 (Kipfer 2015). For a short analysis of of the links between these geographies, see Saberi (2018).

3. The exceptions here are the work of Roy, Schrader and Crane (2014) on the relational formation of community development in Johnson's War on Poverty and the U.S. counterinsurgency in Vietnam, as well as the work of Immerwahr (2015) on the long history of place-based intervention and community development in the history of the U.S. state interventions, domestically and internationally.

4. I use *post-colonial* as a temporal reference to the period after the official end of European colonialism in the late twentieth century. It is not a reference to the postcolonial school of thought.

5. I say *historically White* because the shift in the immigration policy to facilitate the migration of owners of capital from across the world has also changed the demography of wealth in downtown Toronto, albeit much slower than that of poverty. This relative changing color of the bourgeoisie has also caused panic among the White bourgeois establishment of Toronto and Canada; see the March 2013 issue of *Toronto Life.*

6. The category of *non-White* in this book does not include the Indigenous populations in Canada. The lack of focus on the Indigenous question is mostly due to the fact that none of the policies under study directly target the Indigenous populations living in Toronto.

7. The genealogy of the figure of the immigrant as the internal enemy in Europe (and later in North America) has a long history. In England, Bridget Anderson (2013) traces this history to the attempts of the ruling class to control the mobility of the poor, thus linking the figure of the immigrant to that of the vagrant and the history of labor mobility since the dawn of capitalism. Racializing the internal enemy as the immigrant goes back to at least the nineteenth century, to the figures of the Gypsy, the Jew, the Irish, the Communist, etc., figures that most often would overlap with each other into the twentieth century (Lucassen 2005; Virdee 2014, 142–87).

8. Any reference hitherto to "the state" is a reference to the integral state in the Gramscian sense.

1. MAKING THE IMMIGRANT

1. These included the Chinese Immigration Act of 1885, amended in 1887, 1892, 1900, and 1903.

2. In June 2002, the Liberal federal government replaced the 1976 Immigration Act with the 2001 Immigration and Refugee Protections Act.

3. The introduction of the bill took place against the background of two incidents involving Black men in Toronto in late 1994. The first was the Just Desserts café case, where four Black males attempted to rob the café and a young White woman was killed in the process. The second was the shooting of a White police officer on patrol from the 12th Division in the Black Creek area by a young Black Jamaican male who was living in Canada without status and had been previously ordered deported.

4. Throughout the book, I have used City as a reference to the City of Toronto (the municipality).

5. Broadbent is an influential figure in Toronto's philanthrocapitalist circles and is the cofounder of a series of related philanthropic organizations in Toronto. In 1982, Alan and Judy Broadbent established the Maytree Foundation, and he has since been the chairman of the foundation. Through the Maytree Foundation, Broadbent cofounded in 1992 and chairs the Caledon Institute of Social Policy; Tamarack—An Institute for Community Engagement, Diaspora Dialogues in 2001; and the Institute for Municipal Finance and Governance at the Munk Centre, University of Toronto. Broadbent is also chairman and CEO of Avana Capital Corporation, chairman of the Tides Canada Foundation, advisor to the Literary Review of Canada, cochair of Happy Planet Foods, member of the Governor's Council of the Toronto Public Library Foundation, senior fellow of Massey College, a member of the Order of Canada, and a recipient of the Queen's Jubilee Medal. In 2008, Broadbent published *Urban Nation: Why We Need to Give Power Back to the Cities to Make Canada Strong.*

6. Build Toronto is a City agency created on the recommendation of the City's Fiscal Review Panel, an ad-hoc mayor's committee dominated by power brokers and representatives of finance capital that also proposed privatization of Enwave, Toronto Hydro, and the Toronto Parking Authority.

2. THE "PARIS PROBLEM" IN TORONTO

1. For the list of interviews see Appendix A.

2. The changing demography was mentioned in reference to "the top 10 countries of origin for new immigrants—Sri Lanka, China, Philippines, Hong Kong, India, Jamaica, Poland, Guyana, Vietnam" (UWT 1999, 14).

3. Currie also served as United Way Toronto campaign director from 1989 to 1991.

4. Two maps identified youth as the main social problem across the postwar suburbs. Maps were also used in *A Decade of Decline* (UWT 2002, 85–90), but they were general maps of Toronto showing street boundaries, neighborhoods, and so on, rather than social problems.

5. The UK place-based policy reference points are the *Single Regeneration*

Budget (1994–2000), *New Deal for Communities* (1998–2008), and *National Strategy for Neighbourhood Renewal* (2001–2009). In the United States, the main place-based policy reference points are *The Empowerment Zones and Enterprise Communities* of the 1990s, the Department of Housing and Urban Development's *HOPE VI* (1992–2010), and the *Choice Neighborhoods* (2011–present). In 2012, United Way commissioned the for-profit research institute Public Interest to do a comprehensive research on the "best practices" of place-based urban policy. Public Interest was also the major third party that the City of Toronto hired to do community consultation in Regent Park prior to the demolition of the public housing project (Meagher, Lee, and Tolia 2012).

6. Richard Florida, mentioned earlier in the chapter, is the head of the Martin Prosperity Institute at the University of Toronto.

3. POLICING IMMIGRANT NEIGHBORHOODS

1. In September 2015, the Ontario government announced dramatic cuts to the annual funding of TAVIS as of 2016. The Ministry of Community Safety and Correctional Services cut the TAVIS budget from $5 million to $2.63 million effective January 2016. The ministry's spokesperson stated that rather than in the current form of TAVIS, the Ontario government is interested in focusing on "a proactive, collaborative, and community-based model of policing" (quoted in Gillis 2015). While the sudden cut to TAVIS funding was celebrated by many liberal and left critics, what has not gained attention is that the government will keep the Rapid Response Team, the militarized part of the force that is responsible for raids.

2. By 2017, the then Ontario Liberal government provided more than $31 million for PAVIS across the province. The strategy has grown to seventeen communities: Amherstberg Police Service, Brantford Police Service, Durham Regional Police Service, Greater Sudbury Police Service, Halton Regional Police Service, Hamilton Regional Police Service, Kingston Police Service, Lasalle Police Service, London Police Service, Niagara Regional Police Service, Nishnawbe-Aski Police Service, Ottawa Police Service, Peel Regional Police Service, Thunder Bay Police Service, Waterloo Regional Police Service, Windsor Police Service, and York Regional Police.

3. The college is located at 70 Birmingham Street, near Islington Avenue and Lakeshore Boulevard in South Etobicoke.

4. Criticizing police in Toronto has been a risky business even for members of the Toronto Police Services Board. See the *Hogtown: The Politics of Policing* documentary by Min Sook Lee (2005).

5. The Safer City Task Force recommended CAP to the city council in early summer 1999. It received the nearly unanimous support of the city coun-

cil in July of that year. With a budget of $1.9 million, the program was to run for eleven weeks in the summer of 1999. CAP received support from some organizations in low-income neighborhoods, including community–police liaison committees, business improvement associations, and ratepayer groups. For more information and critique, see *Who's the Target?* (CSTP 2000).

6. Toronto Community Housing is Toronto's public housing authority.

7. Eventually, the increasing public criticism of TAVIS resulted in the provincial announcement that the funding for the strategy would not be renewed as usual for 2016.

8. Toronto Police documented people on forms called Field Information Reports, which included personal details including skin color, the reason for the interaction, location, and names of others or "associates" who were involved in the stop (see Rankin and Winsa 2012a).

9. On Chief Blair's position, see the *Toronto Star*'s interview "The Chief on Race, Crime and Policing" (*Toronto Star* 2010). Then police chief Blair's reaction was very different from that of former police chief Fantino in 2003, who countered allegations of racism in the Toronto police force with a 337-page testimony (see TPS 2003) to the force's "proud tradition" of race relations.

10. The racialized dimension of policing is not limited to Black people or other non-White populations; Indigenous peoples are also one of the major targets of racial policing in Toronto and Canada. See Razack (2011) and Comak (2012).

11. For more information, see the whole *Race Matters* series in the *Toronto Star*, www.thestar.com/news/gta/raceandcrime.html.

12. For more information, see the whole *Known to Police* series in the *Toronto Star*, www.thestar.com/news/gta/knowntopolice.html.

13. The *Toronto Star* continued updating its contact-cards data. The paper undated its *Race Matters* series in 2013, this time with information about how many cardings an individual TAVIS officer would do. One high-ranking TAVIS officer, for example, received credits on 6,600 contact cards from 2008 to 2012; this was the second highest count of all officers (Rankin and Winsa 2013).

14. Initially known as the Institute for Strategic International Studies (ISIS), the institute was conceived in 2001 in the wake of the War on Terror. It is owned and operated by the Canadian Association of Chiefs of Police. Every year, police services from across Canada nominate a midlevel or senior officer to spend a year going around the world and studying what other services are doing to deal with issues that police forces also face in Canada (I12 2013). The goal is to "introduce new competencies and global perspective to Canada's current and future leaders in policing" ("About Us," cacpglobal.ca). Given the similarities between the acronym for the Institute (ISIS) and the English acronym of Daesh (the Islamic State of Iraq and Syria, ISIS), in 2015

the institute changed its name to Executive Global Studies Program. For more information, see http://cacpglobal.ca.

15. Quoted from the Ontario Provincial Police pamphlet on community policing.

16. The Neighbourhood Organized Coalition Opposed to Police in Schools (NO COPS)—a coalition of concerned parents, students, teachers, and community members, became a vocal voice. The coalition publicly criticized the ineffectiveness of the program and Toronto police evaluation of it and the decision to make it permanent (see NO COPS 2009; Benitah 2009).

17. Aside from the Toronto Police Service, other sponsors included Ontario Trillium Foundations, Ontario Arts Council, Toronto Arts Council, CIBC Bank, and the Catherine and Maxwell Meighen Foundation.

18. Throughout its five-year existence, 312 youth, aged 13 to 24 years (72% male and 28% female), attended the program.

19. Toronto Police delegate Sgt. Greg Watts heard about the Hub Model in the 2011 Ontario Association of Chiefs of Police conference, where McFee presented the strategy (Haggen 2012).

20. While TAVIS as a force was not involved with FOCUS, Greg Watts, who was the lead person in initiating the Prince Albert visit and the formation of FOCUS, was a high-ranking member of TAVIS at the time.

21. David Kennedy's model in Boston was taken up by other cities in the United States, including Chicago, New Orleans, Baltimore, and Oakland. Kennedy is currently the director of the National Network for Safe Communities, a project of John Jay College of Criminal Justice at CUNY in New York City (see www.jjay.cuny.edu/faculty/david-kennedy). In 2011, Kennedy published another book, *Don't Shoot: One Man, A Street Fellowship, and the End of Violence in Inner-City America*. The book received praise from politicians, chiefs of police, civic leaders, and academics. In the same year a documentary based on Chicago's adaptation of Kennedy's work was released: *The Interrupters*, which takes place in Englewood in Chicago's South Side. The documentary was broadcasted in Canada on the CBC News Network documentary series *The Passionate Eye* on January 28, 2012.

22. In 2008, the VRU established the Community Initiative to Reduce Violence (CIRV) to tackle gang violence in Glasgow. Soon it was extended to other jurisdictions and has been renamed the Scottish Violence Reduction Unit. For more information, see www.actiononviolence.org.uk/.

23. The VRU approaches gang members and invites them to attend a "call-in" meeting that is mainly used to communicate two messages: enforcement and social development—first, that there will be a zero-tolerance police response if the violence does not stop, which will impact every gang member, and second, a pledge from assorted agencies and charities that if youths do renounce violence, they can get help with education, training, and job finding.

24. Norm Taylor and Hugh Russell, two influential consultants for the Ontario Provincial Police and the Toronto Police Services on community policing, were the authors of the 2014 FOCUS evaluation report entitled *New Directions in Community Safety: Consolidating Lessons Learned about Risk and Collaboration* (Russell and Taylor 2014).

25. Colquhoun did not invent the idea of prevention. John A. Fielding (1721–1780) and Cesare Beccaria (1738–1794) had already emphasized that preventing crime is better than its punishment (see Rigakos et al. 2009). What was original to Colquhoun, as Neocleous (2000, 49–50) points out, was that he integrated "the general idea of prevention into a theory of police."

26. See the WHO's *World Report on Violence and Health* (2002) and a report of its commission *Closing the Gap in a Generation: Health Equity through Action on the Social Determinants of Health* (CSDH 2008).

27. Since 2000, Slutkin's public health approach (Cure Violence) has been used in many cities in the United States, including New York, Chicago, Baltimore, and Buffalo. It has also been used in Latin America and the Caribbean (Colombia, Honduras, Mexico, Jamaica, Guatemala, El Salvador), the Middle East (Iraq, Syria, the West Bank, Israel), as well as in South Africa, England, and Canada (Halifax). The WHO is among the "strategic partners" of Cure Violence; the latter organization is active in the WHO Global Campaign for Violence Prevention. For more information, see http:// cureviolence.org/partners/ and www.who.int/violenceprevention/about/ participants/cure_violence/en/.

28. Halfdan Mahler, who became the director-general of WHO in 1973, proposed "Health for All by the Year 2000" as the new agenda of the organization at the 1976 World Health Assembly. "Health for all," Mahler (1981) argued, "implied the removal of the obstacles to health—that is to say, the elimination of malnutrition, ignorance, contaminated drinking water and unhygienic housing—quite as much as it does the solution of purely medical problems." This new agenda took center stage at the International Conference on Primary Health Care, sponsored by WHO and UNICEF at Alma-Ata, Kazakhstan, in September 1978 (WHO and the United Nations Children's Fund 1978). The conference embraced Mahler's goal of "Health for All by the Year 2000," with primary health care as the means. (Irwin and Scali 2007, 239–40).

29. As we will see in chapter 5, the City of Toronto's policymakers have picked up equity as the new foundation of place-based urban policy in the Strong Neighbourhoods 2020 strategy.

30. The Millennium Development Goals were initially adopted by 189 world leaders as part of the Millennium Declaration signed in 2000. In 2002, then UN secretary-general Kofi Annan established the UN Millennium Campaign and commissioned the Millennium Project to develop a correct action plan for the world to achieve the goals.

4. MAKING URBAN POLICY

1. Bill Blair served as the chair for the United Way Public Sector campaign from 2008 to 2010. Gerry McCaughery was the chair of the United Way 2012 fundraising campaign.

2. This list is based on donations of $10,000 and higher (UWT 2012b, 17).

3. The most influential among the nonprofit research institutions are Tamarack, Caledon Institute of Social Policy, Canadian Policy Research Networks, and Public Interest.

4. The Cities Centre was established in the fall of 2007. Its opening was part of the University of Toronto's strategic plan to include urban issues among the university's five strategic priorities. By the fall of 2013, the Cities Centre closed its doors mainly because the university cut its funding. Ironically, its closure too was part of the university's strategic plan for enhancing its role in the worldwide knowledge production industry about urban issues. The university instead opened the Global Cities Institute in September 2013. At the time of its closure, many pro-urban political figures contested the decision. Toronto's former mayor David Miller wrote a letter in support of the Cities Centre.

5. The University of Toronto is not the only academic institution involved in knowledge production about urban policy in Toronto. York University and Ryerson University, both in Toronto, are also involved in making immigrant neighborhoods a problem and object of urban policy. The City Institute at York University has been involved in joint community–university projects in immigrant neighborhoods. The activities of these university-based research institutions are deeply territorialized to the point that each institute has its own community-research turf, situated in the vicinity of its own geographical location. For example, the City Institute at York University is active in the Jane and Finch area (the very area that York University has stigmatized for the last twenty years [see James 2012a, 2012b]), while the Cities Centre and the University of Toronto academics have worked in Scarborough and Mount Dennis.

6. The Cities Centre mandate is no longer accessible from its own website after its closure in 2014. A version of it can be accessed through the Centre for Urban Growth and Renewal. See http://cugr.ca/partners/.

7. See TBOT 2010, 4–11. For analyses of Barnett's *The Pentagon's New Map,* see Elden 2009 and Dalby 2007.

5. REFORMING URBAN POLICY

1. The group Nomanzland is one example. Created in 2006, the loose group of youth and artists met once a week at the West-Side Arts Hub in Jane

and Finch to create theatre, poetry, music, and art that represent struggles related to marginalization and oppression.

2. Despite this decision, the City retained the territorial boundaries of the thirteen priority neighborhoods as the first Neighbourhood Improvement Areas (City of Toronto 2012c, 8–9).

3. United Way mentioned its involvement in the "revitalization of inner-suburban neighbourhoods" in its 2012 Annual Report (UWT 2012b).

4. The city council had already approved the use of Urban HEART@ Toronto in 2012, when it approved the first draft of the new TSNS 2020 policy. What was new in 2014 was the application of Urban HEART and the actual designation of the targeted neighborhoods.

5. These cities include Guarulhos (Brazil); Jakarta and Denpasar (Indonesia); Tehran (Iran); Nakuru (Kenya); State of Sarawak (Malaysia); Mexico City (Mexico); Ulaanbaatar (Mongolia); Davao, Naga, Olongapo, Paranaque, Tacloban, Taguig, and Zamboanga (Philippines); Colombo (Sri Lanka); and Ho Chi Minh City (Vietnam).

6. To back up this argument, *Investing in Development* quotes statesmen such as King Abdullah of Jordan (January 23, 2004), former British Prime Minister Tony Blair (October 7, 2004), former U.S. president George W. Bush Jr. (March 14, 2004), former French president Jacques Chirac (May 26, 2004), former Brazilian president Luiz Lula da Silva (September 21, 2004), and former German chancellor Gerhard Schroder (2001), among others (United Nations 2005, 7).

6. URBANIZING CONCRETE TOWERS

1. Given the different forms of ownership, in 2017, the public-housing component of Tower Renewal received its own structure and programs called Social Housing Apartment Improvement Program (SHAIP) and Social Housing Apartment Retrofit Program (SHARP). The program is funded by the Ontario government. In the spring of 2017, the Ontario government announced its contribution of $42.9 million to the City of Toronto for repairs and retrofits to twenty-six public housing buildings. In the winter of 2018, the Ontario government allocated another $350 million toward retrofitting public housing buildings through SHARP.

2. There are 1,925 (eight-story and above) apartment towers in the Greater Golden Horseshoe built between 1945 and 1985, and more than one million people currently live in these apartment units; 62 percent of this housing stock is in Toronto (1,189 apartment towers), 77 percent of Toronto's apartment towers are rental (915 apartment towers), and the rest is public housing.

3. *Hidden homelessness* is the preferred term in the current research on

overcrowded housing; see Murdie and Logan (2010); Preston et al. (2011); and Paradis, Wilson, and Logan (2014).

4. Rental agreements are under the jurisdiction of the Province of Ontario. Under the Ontario Residential Tenancies Act, it is illegal for a landlord to demand or to collect a rent deposit of more than one month, or if it is less than a month, than for one rental period. A landlord can, however, demand a last month's rent deposit on or before the landlord and tenant enter into the tenancy agreement. This deposit may only be applied to the last month's rent. The landlord must pay tenants interest on the rent deposit every twelve months.

5. *Vertical Poverty*'s survey of 2,803 residents was developed by Public Interest, a private company, which since 2002 has been involved in community engagement, research, policy, and nonprofit capacity building. The company is funded on a fee-for-service basis (I27 2013). Public Interest was also the major player in organizing community engagement in the Regent Park Revitalization project. In 2012, Public Interest also did a research policy paper for the United Way on why place-based intervention is the solution to deconcentrating poverty; see Meagher, Lee, and Tolia (2012).

6. In 2012, the Social Housing Services Corporation was replaced by the Housing Services Corporation.

7. For more information, see http://cugr.ca/.

8. On the neoliberal dimension of Tower Renewal, see also Poppe and Young (2015).

9. Derek Ballantyne, the principal of DKGI Inc., is also the chair of the Canada Mortgage and Housing Corporation Board.

10. For more information, see http://towerrenewal.com/partners/.

11. *Arrival City* won the Donner Prize (an award given by the conservative Donner Canadian Foundation) for the best book on public affairs in Canada. The book was among the five finalists for the 2011 Lionel Gelber Prize for the world's best nonfiction book in English on foreign affairs. It was also nominated for the Shaughnessy Cohen Prize for Political Writing.

12. For more information, see Chief Planner Roundtable Report (City of Toronto 2013c).

13. Speakers included Doug Saunders, Emily Paradis (University of Toronto), and Alina Chatterjee (United Way).

14. For more information, see Cities of Migration 2015.

15. Nowhere in the 351-page book that claims to cover migration stories in twenty cities in countries as diverse as India, Bangladesh, Iran, Turkey, Kenya, Brazil, China, France, Germany, the United States, and Canada does one come across capitalism, colonialism, imperialism, and war as forces of migration. Instead, we are told, urbanization—characterized as a natural force sprung from Europe—and its benefits are what have attracted the villagers to voluntarily move to cities.

Bibliography

Abu-Laban, Yasmeen. 1998. "Welcome/Stay Out: The Contradiction of Canadian Integration and Immigration Policies at the Millennium." *Canadian Ethnic Studies* 30 (3): 190–211.

Agnew, John. 2007. "Know-Where: Geographies of Knowledge of World Politics." *International Political Sociology* 1: 138–48.

Agnew, John, and Stuart Corbridge. 1995. *Mastering Space: Hegemony, Territory and International Political Economy*. New York: Routledge.

Ahmad, Fahad. 2019. "Securitization and the Muslim Community in Canada." Broadbent Institute. July 19, 2019. https://www.broadbentinstitute.ca.

Ahmed, Sara. 2012. *On Being Included: Racism and Diversity in Institutional Life*. Durham, N.C.: Duke University Press.

Aidi, Hisham. 2014. *Rebel Music: Race, Empire and the New Muslim Youth Culture*. New York: Vintage.

Akers, Timothy, and Mark Lanier. 2009. "'Epidemiological Criminology': Coming Full Circle." *American Journal of Public Health* 99 (3): 397–402.

Allahwala, Ahmed M. 2011. "Civic Metropolitan Regionalism and the Politics of Competitive Multiculturalism: The Toronto Experience." PhD diss., Department of Political Science, York University.

Amin, Samir. 1973. *Le développement inégal: Essai sur les formations sociale du capitalisme périphérique*. Paris: Les Editions de Minuit.

Amin, Samir. 1974. *Accumulation on a World Scale: A Critique of the Theory of Underdevelopment*. New York: Monthly Review.

Anderson, Bridget. 2013. *Us and Them? The Dangerous Politics of Immigration Control*. Oxford: Oxford University Press.

Andrews, Allen G. 1992. *Review of Race Relation Practices of the Metropolitan Toronto Police Force*. Toronto: Metropolitan Toronto Police Services Board.

Armstrong, Laura. 2015. "United Way's Toronto and York Region Chapters Set to Merge." *Toronto Star*, January 9, 2015.

Arrighi, Giovanni. 2007. *Adam Smith in Beijing: Lineages of the 21st Century*. London: Verso.

August, Martine. 2014. "How 'Revitalization' Is Leading to Displacement in Regent Park." *Toronto Star*, May 5, 2014.

August, Martine, and Alan Walks. 2012. "The Redevelopment of Toronto's

Public Housing and the Dilution of Tenant Organization Power." In *Mixed Communities: Gentrification by Stealth,* edited by Gary Bridge, Tim Butler, and Loretta Lees, 273–97. Bristol, UK: Policy.

Austin, David. 2013. *Fear of a Black Nation: Race, Sex and Security in Sixties Montreal.* Toronto: Between the Lines.

Bachmann, Jan, Colleen Bell, and Caroline Holmqvist, eds. 2015. *War, Police and Assemblages of Intervention.* New York: Routledge.

Baldwin, Andrew, Laura Cameron, and Audrey Kobayashi. 2012. *Rethinking the Great White North: Race, Nature, and the Historical Geographies of Whiteness in Canada.* Vancouver: University of British Columbia Press.

Baldwin, Jeffrey. 2014. "A New Measurement of Health Equity: Urban HEART Toronto." *Belonging Community* (blog), February 26, 2016. https://belongingcommunity.wordpress.com/.

Balestra, Filipe, and Sara Göransson. 2009. "Incremental Housing Strategy." *Dezeen Magazine,* May 5, 2014. www.dezeen.com.

Bannerji, Himani. 1995. *Thinking Through: Essays on Feminism, Marxism, and Anti-racism.* Toronto: Women's Press.

Bannerji, Himani. 2000. *The Dark Side of the Nation: Essays on Multiculturalism, Nationalism and Gender.* Toronto: Canadian Scholars' Press.

Bannerji, Himani. 2011. *Demography and Democracy: Essays on Nationalism, Gender and Ideology.* Toronto: Canadian Scholars' Press.

Bannerji, Himani. 2014. "Marxism and Anti-Racism in Theory and Practice: Reflections and Interpretations." In *Theorizing Anti-Racism: Linkages in Marxism and Critical Race Theories,* edited by Abigail B. Bakan and Enakshi Dua, 127–44. Toronto: University of Toronto Press.

Bannerji, Himani. 2016. "Ideology." In *Keywords for Radicals: The Contested Vocabulary of Late-Capitalist Struggle,* edited by Kelly Fritsch, Clare O'Connor, and Andrew K. Thompson, 207–14. Oakland, Calif.: AK.

Barnes, Annmarie. 2009. "Displacing Danger: Mapping Crime through Deportation." *Journal of International Migration and Integration* 10: 431–45.

Barnett, Thomas. 2004. *The Pentagon's New Map.* New York: Berkley.

Bator, Paul A., Alan Artibise, and John H. Taylor. 1980. "Public Health Reform in Canada and Urban History: A Critical Survey." *Urban History Review* 9 (2): 87–102.

Bauder, Harald. 2002. "Neighbourhood Effects and Cultural Exclusion." *Urban Studies* 39: 85–93.

Bell, Colleen. 2011a. *The Freedom of Security: Governing Canada in the Age of Counter-terrorism.* Vancouver: University of British Columbia Press.

Bell, Colleen. 2011b. "Civilianising Warfare: Ways of War and Peace in Modern Counterinsurgency." *Journal of International Relations and Development* 14: 309–32.

Bellamy, Alex J. 2009. *Responsibility to Protect.* London: Polity.

Benitah, Sandie. 2009. "Police School Program: Hit-and-Miss with Teens." *CTV Toronto News.* October 24.

Best, Jacqueline. 2013. "Redefining Poverty as Risk and Vulnerability: Shifting Strategies of Liberal Economic Governance." *Third World Quarterly* 34 (1): 109–29.

Black, Jeremy. 1997. *Maps and Politics.* London: Reaktion.

Black, Jeremy. 2016. *Maps of War: Mapping Conflict through Centuries.* London: Bloomsbury.

Blanchard, Emmanuel. 2011. *La police parisienne et les algériens (1944–1962).* Paris: Nouveau Monde.

Block, Sheila. 2013. *Who Is Working for Minimum Wage in Ontario?* Toronto: Wellesley Institute.

Block, Sheila, and Grace-Edward Galabuzi. 2011. *Canada's Colour Coded Labour Market.* Toronto: Wellesley Institute.

Blomley, Nicholas. 2003. "Law, Property, and the Geography of Violence: The Frontier, the Survey, and the Grid." *Annals of the Association of American Geographers* 93 (1): 121–41.

Bloom, Joshua, and Waldo E. Martin Jr. 2013. *Black against Empire: The History and Politics of the Black Panther Party.* Berkeley: University of California Press.

Boudreau, Julie-Anne. 2000. *The Megacity Saga.* Montreal: Black Rose.

Boudreau, Julie-Anne, Roger Keil, and Douglas Young. 2009. *Changing Toronto: Governing Urban Neoliberalism.* Toronto: University of Toronto Press.

Bozikovic, Alex. 2017. "Lessons of the Grenfell Blaze: How Can Canada's Thousands of Aging Towers be Kept Safe?" *Globe and Mail,* June 23, 2017.

Bradburn, Jamie. 2011. "There's A Riot Goin' on Down Yonge Street." *Torontoist,* August 11, 2011. https://torontoist.com.

Bradford, Neil. 2005. *Place-Based Public Policy: Towards a New Urban and Community Agenda for Canada.* Research Report F|51. Ottawa: Canadian Policy Research Network.

Brenner, Neil. 2004. *New State Spaces.* Oxford: Oxford University Press.

Brenner, Neil, and Nick Theodore. 2005. "Neoliberalism and the Urban Condition." *City* 9 (1): 101–7.

Bridge, Lee. 1981. "Keeping the Lid On: British Urban Social Policy, 1975–81." *Race & Class* 23 (2/3): 171–85.

Broadbent, Alan. 2013. "Target the Poor, Not the Rich, for Real Solutions to Income Inequality." *Globe and Mail,* November 27, 2013.

Brown, Jim. 1998. "Squeegee People: Urban Guerrillas." *Our Toronto Free Press,* August, 1–2.

Bruser, David. 2010. "Troubled Neighbourhoods Desperate for Change." *Toronto Star*, February 7, 2010.

Burt, Geoff, Mark Sedra, Bernard Headley, Camille Hernandez-Ramdwar, Randy Seepersad, and Scot Wortley. 2016. *Deportation, Circular Migration and Organized Crime: Jamaica Case Study*. Ottawa: Public Safety Canada.

Burton, C. Emory. 1992. *The Poverty Debate*. Westport, Conn.: Greenwood.

CACP (Canadian Association of Chiefs of Police). 2003. *Towards a Crime Prevention Coalition: The Police Role in Crime Prevention through Social Development*. Ottawa: PSC.

CACP (Canadian Association of Chiefs of Police). 2008. *Building Community Resilience to Violent Ideologies*. Ottawa: CACP Prevention of Radicalization Study Group.

Callimachi, Rukmini, and Jim Yardley. 2015. "From Amateur to Ruthless: Jihadist in France." *New York Times*, January 17, 2015.

Camfield, David. 2000. "Assessing Resistance in Harris' Ontario, 1995–1999." In *Restructuring and Resistance: Canadian Public Policy in an Age of Global Capitalism*, edited by Mike Burke, Colin Mooers, and John Shields, 306–17. Halifax: Fernwood.

Canada Revenue Agency. 2016. "United Way of Greater Toronto." http://www.cra-arc.gc.ca.

Caulfield, Jon. 1994. *City Form and Everyday Life: Toronto's Gentrification and Critical Social Practice*. Toronto: University of Toronto Press.

CBC (Canadian Broadcasting Corporation). 2006. "Toronto's Gang Leaders 'Surgically' Removed in 60 Police Raids." *CBC News*, May 18, 2006.

CCLA (Canadian Civil Liberties Association). 2015. "Key Sections of Bill C-51 Violate Canadian Charter of Rights and Freedom." July 21, 2015. https://ccla.org.

CCSD (Canadian Council on Social Development). 1999. *Summary Statistics on Poverty in Toronto*. Kanata, ON: CCSD.

CERA (Centre for Equality Rights in Accommodation). 2000. *Early Intervention Pilot Project: Final Report*. Toronto: CERA.

CERA (Centre for Equality Rights in Accommodation). 2009. *Sorry It's Rented: Measuring Discrimination in Toronto's Housing Market*. Toronto: CERA.

Chandler, David. 2008. "Human Security: The Dog that Didn't Bark." *Security Dialogue* 39 (4): 427–38.

Chandler, David. 2012. "Resilience and Human Security: The Post-interventionist Paradigm." *Security Dialogue* 43 (3): 213–29.

Chariandy, David. 2018. *Brother*. New York: Bloomsbury.

Charity Intelligence Canada 2013. *Canada's 10 Largest Charities*. www.charityintelligence.ca.

Choudry, Aziz, Jull Hanley, Steve Jordan, Eric Shragge and Martha Stiegman. 2009. *Fight Back: Workplace Justice for Immigrants.* Winnipeg: Fernwood.

Chrisafis, Angelique. 2015. "Charlie Hebdo Attackers: Born, Raised and Radicalised in Paris." *Guardian,* January 12, 2015.

Church, Elizabeth. 2014. "Toronto to Debut 'Sophisticated' Way to Gauge Neighbourhood's Funding Needs." *Globe and Mail,* March 9, 2014.

Cities Centre. 2010. "Release of the 32-Page Report, *The Three Cities within Toronto.*" December 15, 2010.

Cities of Migration. 2015. *Webinar: Tower Renewal in the Arrival City.* March 13, 2015. http://citiesofmigration.ca/webinar/towerrenewal/.

City of Toronto. 2003. *Culture Plan for the Creative City.* Toronto: Culture Division, City of Toronto.

City of Toronto. 2004. *Community Safety Plan and Malvern Youth Employment Initiative.* Toronto: City of Toronto.

City of Toronto. 2005. *Toronto Strong Neighbourhood Strategy.* Toronto: City of Toronto.

City of Toronto (Tri-Level Committee on Guns and Violence). 2006. *Toronto's 13 Priority Areas: Research Methodology.* Toronto: City of Toronto.

City of Toronto. 2008a. *Culture Plan Progress Report II.* Toronto: Culture Division, City of Toronto.

City of Toronto. 2008b. *Mayor's Tower Renewal Project.* Toronto: City Planning Division.

City of Toronto. 2011a. *Tower Renewal: Implementation Book.* Toronto: City of Toronto.

City of Toronto. 2011b. *Priority Neighbourhood Designation.* Community Development and Recreation Committee consideration. June 29, 2011.

City of Toronto. 2011c. *Creative Capital Gains: An Action Plan for Toronto.* Toronto: Culture Division, City of Toronto.

City of Toronto. 2012a. *Toronto Strong Neighbourhoods Strategy 2020.* February 8, 2012. http://app.toronto.ca/tmmis/viewAgendaItemHistory .do?item=2012.CD10.3.

City of Toronto. 2012b. *Appendix A: Consultation Report, Toronto Strong Neighbourhood Strategy.* February 8, 2012. www.toronto.ca/legdocs/ mmis/2012/cd/bgrd/backgroundfile-45144.pdf.

City of Toronto. 2012c. "Staff Report: Final Report on Areas for Proposed Residential Apartment Commercial (RAC) Zone. May 2." Toronto: City Planning Division.

City of Toronto. 2013a. "Staff Report: Toronto Strong Neighbourhoods Strategy 2020 Implementation." Toronto: Social Development, Finance and Administration.

City of Toronto. 2013c. *Chief Planner Roundtable.* Toronto: City of Toronto.

City of Toronto. 2014a. *TSNS 2020 Consultation Summary.* Toronto: Social Development, Finance, and Administration.

City of Toronto. 2014b. *Areas for Proposed Residential Apartment Commercial (RAC) Zone.* January 31, 2014. www.toronto.ca/legdocs/mmis/ 2014/pg/bgrd/backgroundfile-66960.pdf.

City of Toronto. 2014c. *Toronto Strong Neighbourhoods Strategy 2020—Recommended Neighbourhood Improvement Areas.* Toronto: Social Development, Finance and Administration. March 4, 2014. www .toronto.ca/legdocs/mmis/2014/cd/bgrd/backgroundfile-67382.pdf.

City of Toronto. 2014d. *TSNS 2020 Consultation Summary.* Toronto: City of Toronto.

City of Toronto. 2016. "City of Toronto, Province of Ontario and Government of Canada Announce New Joint Initiatives to Increase Community Safety." June 30, 2016.

Coaffee, Jon, David Murakami Wood, and Peter Rogers. 2008. *The Everyday Resilience of the City: How Cities Respond to Terrorism and Disaster.* New York: Palgrave Macmillan.

Cochrane, Allan. 2007. *Understanding Urban Policy.* Malden, Mass.: Blackwell.

Cole, Desmond. 2015. "The Skin I'm In." *Toronto Life,* May, 39–42.

Colquhoun, Patrick. 1806. *The State of Indigence.* London: J. Hatchard.

Comack, Elizabeth. 2012. *Racialized Policing: Aboriginal People's Encounters with the Police.* Winnipeg: Fernwood.

Corbett, David. 1963. "Canada's Immigration Policy, 1957–1962." *International Journal* 18: 166–80.

Cosgrove, Denis. 2012. *Geography and Vision: Seeing, Imagining and Representing the World.* London: Bloomsbury.

Coulthard, Glen. 2014. *Red Skin, White Masks: Rejecting the Colonial Politics of Recognition.* Minneapolis: University of Minnesota Press.

Cowen, Deborah, and Vanessa Parlette. 2011. *Inner Suburbs at Stake: Investing in Social Infrastructure in Scarborough. Research Paper 220.* Toronto: Cities Centre, University of Toronto.

Cowen, Michael P., and Robert W. Shenton. 1996. *Doctrines of Development.* New York: Routledge.

CRICH (Centre for Research on Inner City Health). 2014. *Urban Heart @ Toronto.* Toronto: CRICH.

Crisanti, Vincent. 2011. "'Priority Neighbourhood' Designation." Letter to Councillor Mammoliti. www.toronto.ca/legdocs/mmis/2011/cd/bgrd/ backgroundfile-39079.pdf.

Cruikshank, Barbara. 1994. "The Will to Empower: Technologies of Citizenship and the War on Poverty." *Socialist Review* 23 (4): 29–54.

CSDH (Commission on Social Determinants of Health). 2008. *Closing the*

Gap in a Generation: Health Equity Through Action on the Social Determinants of Health. Geneva: World Health Organization.

CSTP (Committee to Stop Targeted Policing). 2000. *Who's the Target? An Evaluation of Community Action Policing.* Toronto: CSTP.

CUG+R (Centre for Urban Growth and Renewal). 2012. *Strong Neighbourhoods and Complete Communities: A New Approach to Zoning for Apartment Neighbourhoods.* Toronto: United Way Toronto.

CUG+R (Centre for Urban Growth and Renewal). 2018. *Growth and Resiliency in Tower in the Park Sites.* Toronto: CUG+R.

D'Arcy, Stephen. 2007. "The 'Jamaican Criminal' in Toronto, 1994: A Critical Ontology." *Canadian Journal of Communications* 32: 241–59.

Dalby, Simon. 1990. *Creating the Second Cold War: The Discourses of Politics.* New York: Guilford.

Dalby, Simon. 2007. "The Pentagon's New Imperial Cartography: Tabloid Realism and the War on Terror." In *Violent Geographies: Fear, Terror and Political Violence,* edited by Derek Gregory and Allan Pred, 295–308. New York: Routledge.

Dalby, Simon. 2008. "Imperialism, Domination, Culture: The Continued Relevance of Critical Geopolitics." *Geopolitics* 13: 413–36.

Dale, Stephen. 1999. *Lost in the Suburbs: A Political Travelogue.* Toronto: Stoddart.

Dauvergne, Peter, and Genevieve Lebaron. 2014. *Protest Inc.: The Corporatization of Activism.* Cambridge: Polity.

Davis, Alexander E., Vineet Thankur, and Peter Vale. 2020. *The Imperial Discipline: Race and the Founding of International Relations.* London: Pluto.

Deacon, Phil, Sylvia Novac, Joe Darden, David Hulchanski, and Anne-Marie Seguin. 2002. *State of Knowledge on Housing Discrimination.* Ottawa: Canada Mortgage and Housing Corporation (CMHC).

De Barros, Françoise. 2005. "Des 'Français musulmans d'Algérie' aux 'immigrés': L'importation de classifications coloniales dans les politiques du logement en France (1950–1970)." *Actes de la recherche en sciences sociales* 159 (4): 26–53.

de Goede, Marieke, and Stephanie Simon. 2013. "Governing Future Radicals in Europe." *Antipode* 45 (2): 315–35.

DeKeserdy, Walter, S. 2009. "Canadian Crime Control in the New Millennium: The Influence of Neo-conservative US Policies and Practices." *Police Practice and Research* 10 (4): 305–16.

De Souza, Marcelo Lopes. 2013. "NGOs and Social Movements: Convergences and Divergences." *City* 17 (2): 258–61.

DFAIT (Department of Foreign Affairs and International Trade). 1995. *Canada in the World: Government Statement.* Ottawa: Department of Foreign Affairs and International Trade.

Dikeç, Mustafa. 2007. *Badlands of the Republic: Space, Politics, and Urban Policy.* Malden, Mass.: Blackwell.

Dikeç, Mustafa. 2017. *Urban Rag: The Revolt of the Excluded.* New Haven, Conn.: Yale University Press.

Dillon, Michael, and Julian Reid. 2009. *The Liberal Way of War.* Abingdon, UK: Routledge.

DiManno. Rosie. 1994. "City's 'Innocence' Pillaged Long Ago." *Toronto Star,* April 8, 1994, A7.

DiManno. Rosie. 2005. "We're Now Paying Steep Price for Nihilism: City Takes Another Kick in the Gut." *Toronto Star,* December 28, 2005, A6.

Dodds, Klaus. 2005. *Global Geopolitics: A Critical Introduction.* London: Routledge.

Doolittle, Robyn. 2014a. "City Wants More Areas Added to 'Priority' List." *Toronto Star,* March 9, 2014.

Doolittle, Robyn. 2014b. "Toronto to Expand 'Priority' Neighbourhoods to 31." *Toronto Star,* March 9, 2014.

Dubber, Markus, and Mariana Valverde, eds. 2006. *The New Police Science: The Police Power in Domestic and International Governance.* Stanford, Calif.: Stanford University Press.

Duffield, Mark. 2001. *Global Governance and the New Wars: The Merger of Development and Security.* London: Zed.

Duffield, Mark. 2007. *Development, Security and Unending War.* London: Polity.

Edmonds, Penelope. 2010. "Unpacking Settler Colonialism's Urban Strategies: Indigenous Peoples in Victoria, British Columbia, and the Transition to a Settler-Colonial City." *Urban History Review* 38 (2): 4–20.

Elden, Stuart. 2009. *Terror and Territory: The Spatial Extent of Sovereignty.* Minneapolis: University of Minnesota Press.

El-Enany, Nadine. 2020. *(B)ordering Britain: Law, Race and Empire.* Manchester: University of Manchester Press.

Engels, Friedrich. (1845) 1992. *The Conditions of the Working Class in England.* Oxford: Oxford University Press.

Erickson, Bruce. 2013. *Canoe Nation: Nature, Race and the Making of a Canadian Icon.* Vancouver: University of British Columbia Press.

Esmonde, Jackie. 2002. "Criminalizing Poverty: The Criminal Law Power and the *Safe Street Act.*" *Journal of Law and Social Policy* 17: 63–86.

Evans, Bryan, and John Shields. 1998. *Shrinking the State: Globalization and Public Administration.* Winnipeg: Fernwood.

Fadil, Nadia, Francesco Ragazzi, and Martijn de Koning. 2019. *Radicalization in Belgium and The Netherlands.* London: I. B. Tauris.

Fair, Maureen, and David Hulchanski. 2008. *Policy Options for Maintaining*

Good-Quality, Socially Mixed, Inclusive Neighbourhoods. Discussion paper, Neighbourhood Change Project. Toronto: Cities Centre.

Fanon, Frantz. (1961) 1967. *Black Skin, White Masks.* Translated by Charles Lam Markmann. New York: Grove.

Fanon, Frantz. 2004. *The Wretched of the Earth.* Translated by Richard Philcox. New York: Grove.

Fassin, Didier. 2012. *Humanitarian Reason: A Moral History of the Present.* Berkeley: University of California Press.

FCM (Federation of Canadian Municipalities). 2001. *Early Warning: Will Canadian Cities Compete? A Comparative Overview of Municipal Governments in Canada, the United States and Europe.* Ottawa: FCM.

FCM (Federation of Canadian Municipalities). 2015. "Strengthening Canada's Hometowns: A Roadmap for Strong Cities and Communities." https://www.fcm.ca.

Feichtinger, Moritz, Stephan Malinowski, and Chase Richards. 2012. "Transformative Invasions: Western Post-9/11 Counterinsurgency and the Lessons of Colonialism." *Humanity: An International Journal of Human Rights, Humanitarianism, and Development* 3 (1): 35–63.

Feireiss, Lukas, ed. 2011. *Testify! The Consequences of Architecture.* Rotterdam: Nai.

Ferenc, Leslie. 2013. "United Way Toronto: 2012 Campaign Raised $116.1 Million and Exceeded Goals." *Toronto Star,* January 31, 2013.

Field, Paul, Robin Bunce, Leila Hassan, and Margaret Peacock. 2019. *Here to Stay, Here to Fight. A Race Today Anthology.* London: Pluto.

Filion, Pierre. 2000. "Balancing Concentration and Dispersion? Public Policy and Urban Structure in Toronto." *Environment and Planning C: Government and Policy* 18: 163–89.

Fiorito, Joe. 2014. "Regent Park's Growing Pains." *Toronto Star,* March 5, 2014.

Flint, John, and David Robinson. 2008. *Community Cohesion in Crisis? New Dimension of Diversity and Difference.* Bristol, UK: Policy.

Florida, Richard. 2002. *The Rise of the Creative Class: And How It's Transforming Work.* New York: Basic Books.

Florida, Richard. 2007. "Narrow Our Economic Disparities to Stay Competitive: Pity the Tri-City Toronto." *Global and Mail,* December 22, 2007.

Foley, Conor. 2010. *The Thin Blue Line: How Humanitarianism Went to War.* New York: Verso.

Forcese, Craig, and Kent Roach. 2015. "Bill C-51: What Fear Has Wrought." *Walrus.* September 18, 2015. https://thewalrus.ca/bill-c-51-what-fear-has-wrought.

Foucault, Michel. 1978. *The History of Sexuality, Volume 1: An Introduction.* Translated by Robert Hurley. New York: Vintage.

Foucault, Michel. 1995. *Discipline and Punish: The Birth of the Prison.* Translated by Alan Sheridan. New York: Vintage.

Foucault, Michel. 2003. *Society Must be Defended: Lectures at the College de France 1975–1976.* New York: Picador.

Foucault, Michel. 2004. *Security, Territory, Population: Lectures at the College de France 1977–1978.* New York: Palgrave Macmillan.

Frederickson, H. George. 1971. "Toward a New Public Administration." In *Toward a New Public Administration: The Minnowbrook Perspective,* edited by Frank Marini, 309–31. Scranton, Pa.: Chandler.

Friesen, Joe. 2005. "Despair and Frustration at Jane and Finch." *Globe and Mail,* November 11, 2005.

Friesen, Joe. 2006. "A Show of Community, Not Force." *Globe and Mail,* May 15, 2006.

Friis, Karsten. 2010. *The Politics of the Comprehensive Approach: The Military, Humanitarian and State-Building Discourse in Afghanistan.* Oslo: Norwegian Institute of International Affairs.

Frisken, Frances. 2007. *The Public Metropolis: The Political Dynamics of Urban Expansion in the Toronto Region, 1924–2003.* Toronto: Canadian Scholars' Press.

Galabuzi, Grace-Edward. 2006. *Canada's Economic Apartheid.* Toronto: Canadian Scholars' Press.

Gans, Herbert, J. 2018. *The Levittowners: Ways of Life and Politics in a New Suburban Community.* New York: Columbia University Press.

Gendron, Robin S. 2006. *Towards a Francophone Community: Canada's Relations with France and French Africa, 1945–1968.* Montreal: McGill-Queen's University Press.

Georgakas, Dan, and Marvin Surkin. 1998. *Detroit: I Do Mind Dying.* Chicago: Haymarket.

Gibson, Suzanne, and Katherine Macklem. 2008. *Leadership Solutions: Building Leadership in Toronto's Nonprofit and Voluntary Sector.* Toronto: United Way Toronto.

Gillis, Wendy. 2015. "Ontario Dramatically Cuts Funding for TAVIS Police Unit." *Toronto Star,* September 9, 2015.

Gilroy, Paul. 1987. *There Ain't No Black in the Union Jack: The Cultural Politics of Race and Nation.* London: Hutchinson.

Globe and Mail. 1969. "Militant Blacks Driving Whites from Youth Centers, Report Says." April 1, 1969.

Globe and Mail. 1970. "Sharp Calls Firebombings Work of Small Minority." March 10, 1970.

Gordon, Todd. 2006. *Cops, Crime and Capitalism: The Law-and-Order Agenda in Canada.* Halifax: Fernwood.

Government of Canada. 1966. *Canadian Immigration Policy. White Paper on Immigration.* Ottawa: Manpower and Immigration.

Government of Canada. 1974. *Canadian Immigration and Population Study. Three Years in Canada: First Report of the Longitudinal Survey on the Economic and Social Adaptation of Immigrants.* Ottawa: Manpower and Immigration.

Government of Canada. 2002. *Speech from the Throne to Open the Second Session of the 37th Parliament of Canada.* Privy Council Office: Ottawa . www.pcobcp.gc.ca.

Government of Canada. 2006. *Canadians Make a Difference in the World: Afghanistan.* Pamphlet. Ottawa: Government of Canada.

Government of Canada. 2008. *Counterinsurgency Operations: B-GL-323-004/FP-003.* Land Force. Ottawa: DND.

Government of Canada. 2018. *National Strategy on Countering Radicalization to Violence.* Ottawa: PSC.

Government of France. 2018. *Prévenir pour protéger: Plan national de prévention de la radicalisation.* Comité interministériel de prévention de la délinquance et de la radicalisation: Paris.

Graham, Peter, and Ian McKay. 2019. *Radical Ambition: The New Left in Toronto.* Toronto: Between the Lines.

Graham, Stephen. 2010. *Cities Under Siege: The New Military Urbanism.* New York: Verso.

Gramsci, Antonio. 1971. *Selections from the Prison Notebooks.* Edited and translated by Quintin Hoare and Geoffrey Nowell Smith. New York: International.

Guy, Mary E., and Sean A. McCandless. 2012. "Social Equity: Its Legacy, Its Promise." *Public Administration Review* 72, no. S1 (November–December): S5–S13.

Haffner, Jeanne. 2013. *The View from Above: The Science of Social Space.* Cambridge, Mass.: MIT Press.

Haggen, Ragnar. 2012. "Local PA Project Gets National Exposure." *paNOW.* July 21, 2012. www.panow.com.

Hajnal, Zoltan. 1995. "The Nature of Concentrated Urban Poverty in Canada and United States." *Canadian Journal of Sociology* 20 (4): 497–528.

Hall, Stuart. 1978. *Policing the Crisis: Mugging, the State and Law and Order.* London: Macmillan.

Hamlin, Christopher. 2009. *Public Health and Social Justice in the Age of Chadwick: Britain, 1800–1854.* Cambridge: Cambridge University Press.

Hamlin, Christopher, and Sally Sheard. 1998. "Revolutions in Public Health: 1848, and 1998." *BMJ* 317: 587–98.

Harcourt, Bernard E. 2001. *Illusion of Order: The False Promise of Broken Windows.* Cambridge, Mass.: Harvard University Press.

Hargreaves, Alec G. 1996. "A Deviant Construction: The French Media and the 'Banlieues.'" *New Community* 22 (4): 607–18.

Harley, J. Brian. 1988. "Maps, Knowledge, and Power." In *The Iconography of Landscape,* edited by Denis Cosgrove and Stephen Daniels, 277–312. Cambridge: Cambridge University Press.

Harrington, Michael. 1962. *The Other America: Poverty in the United States.* New York: Macmillan.

Hart, Gillian. 2009. "D/developments After the Meltdown." *Antipode* 41 (S1): 117–41.

Harvey, David. 1989a. "From Managerialism to Entrepreneurialism: The Transformation in Urban Governance in Late Capitalism." *Geographiska Annaler Serie B* 71B (1): 3–18.

Harvey, David. 1989b. *The Urban Experience.* Baltimore, Md.: Johns Hopkins University Press.

Harvey, David. 2005. *The New Imperialism.* New York: Oxford University Press.

Hawkins, Freda. 1974. "Canadian Immigration Policy and Management." *International Migration Review* 8 (2): 141–53.

Hawkins, Freda. 1991. *Critical Years in Immigration: Canada and Australia Compared.* Montreal: McGill-Queen's University Press.

Hayden, Dolores. 2003. *Building Suburbia: Green Fields and Urban Growth, 1820–2000.* New York: Vintage.

Hearn, Julie. 2007. "African NGOs: The New Comprados?" *Development and Change* 38 (6): 1095–110.

Henley, Jon. 2011. "Karen McCluskey: The Women Who Took on Glasgow's Gangs." *Guardian,* December 19, 2011.

Henry, Frances, and Effie Ginzberg. 1985. *Who Gets the Work?* Toronto: Urban Alliance on Race Relations and the Social Planning Council of Metropolitan Toronto.

Herb, H. Guntram, Jouni Häkli, Mark W. Corson, Nicole Mellow, Sebastian Cobarrubias, and Maribel Casas-Cortes. 2009. "Intervention: Mapping Is Critical." *Political Geography* 28: 332–42.

Heroux, Gaetan. 2011. "War on the Poor: Urban Poverty, Target Policing and Social Control." In *Anti-Security,* edited by Mark Neocleous and George Rigakos, 107–34. Ottawa: Red Quill.

Herzog, Ben. 2018. "Communicating Race: Canadian Foreign Correspondence on Citizenship 1945–1977." *Studies in Ethnicity and Nationalism* 18 (1): 38–56.

Hess, Paul, and Jane Farrow. 2010. *Walkability in Toronto's High-Rise Neighbourhoods.* Toronto: Jane's Walk.

Houdson, Peter James. 2010. "Imperial Designs: The Royal Bank of Canada in the Caribbean." *Race & Class* 52 (1): 33–48.

Hout, John. 1978. "Fight-Back against Racism." *Canadian Dimension,* 2–5.

Howell, Alison. 2005. "Peaceful, Tolerant and Orderly? A Feminist Analysis of Discourse of 'Canadian Values' in Canadian Foreign Policy." *Canadian Foreign Policy* 12 (1): 49–69.

Howell, Alison. 2015. "Resilience as Enhancement: Governmentality and Political Economy Beyond 'Responsibilities.'" *Politics* 35 (1): 67–71.

Hulchanski, David. 2007. *The Three Cities within Toronto: Income Polarization among Toronto's Neighbourhoods, 1970–2000.* Toronto: Centre for Urban & Community Studies.

Hulchanski, David. 2010. *The Three Cities within Toronto: Income Polarization among Toronto's Neighbourhoods, 1970–2005.* Toronto: Cities Centre.

Hume, Christopher. 2011. "London Riots a Long Way Off, but Closer Than We'd Like." *Toronto Star,* August 10, 2011.

Hume, Christopher. 2015a. "Suburbs of Paris and Toronto More Alike Than You'd Think." *Toronto Star,* January 15, 2015.

Hume, Christopher. 2015b. "It's Time to Transform the Suburbs." *Toronto Star,* February 13, 2015.

Husband, Charles, and Yunis Alam. 2011. *Social Cohesion and Counter-terrorism: A Policy Contradiction?* Bristol, UK: Policy.

Immerwahr, Daniel. 2015. *Thinking Small: The United States and the Lure of Community Development.* Cambridge, Mass.: Harvard University Press.

INCITE! Women of Color against Violence, ed. 2007. *The Revolution Will Not Be Funded: Beyond the Non-Profit Industrial Complex.* Cambridge, Mass.: South End.

Irwin, A., and E. Scali. 2007. "Action on the Social Determinants of Health: A Historical Perspective." *Global Public Health* 2 (3): 235–56.

ISIS (Institute for Strategic International Studies). 2008. *Policing Capacity in Canada: Scarce Resources or Infinite Potential?* Ottawa: ISIS.

ISIS (Institute for Strategic International Studies). 2009. *The Intervention Zone: Youth Violence and Its Extremes in Canada: Prevention and Enforcement in a New Zone of Opportunity.* Ottawa: ISIS.

Jackson, Peter. 1994. "Constructions of Criminality: Police–Community Relations in Toronto." *Antipode* 26 (3): 216–35.

James, Carl. 1998. "'Up to No Good': Black on the Streets and Encountering Police." In *Racism and Social Inequality in Canada: Concepts, Controversies and Strategies of Resistance,* edited by Vic Satzewich, 157–76. Toronto: Thompson.

James, Carl. 2012a. *Life at the Intersection: Community, Class and Schooling.* Winnipeg: Fernwood.

James, Carl. 2012b. "Students 'At Risk:' Stereotypes and the Schooling of Black Boys." *Urban Education* 47 (2): 464–94.

James, C. L. R. 1958. "Lectures on Federation. West Indies and British Guiana." https://www.marxists.org/archive/james-clr/works/1958/06/federation.htm.

Jardine, Lisa. 1997. *Worldly Goods: A New History of the Renaissance.* London: Macmillan.

Jeannotte, Sharon. 1999. *The Different Facets of Diversity and Social Cohesion.* Ottawa: Department of Canadian Heritage.

Jeannotte, Sharon. 2003. "Social Cohesion: Insights from Canadian Research." Paper presented at the Conference on Social Cohesion, Hong Kong, November 29.

Jessop, Bob. 2002. "Liberalism, Neoliberalism, and Urban Governance: A State-Theoretical Perspective." *Antipode* 34 (3): 452–72.

JFAAP (Jane and Finch Action against Poverty). 2013. *An Open Letter to the City of Toronto.* https://jfaap.wordpress.com/2013/10/08/jfaap-denounces-citys-phony-consultation/.

JFAAP (Jane and Finch Action against Poverty). 2014. *JFAAP Objects to the City Consulting Methods.* https://jfaap.wordpress.com/2014/01/24/jfaap-objects-to-the-city-consulting-methods/.

Johnson, Andrew F., and Andrew Stritch. 1997. *Canadian Public Policy: Globalization and Political Parties.* Toronto: Pearson Canada.

Joshi-Vijayan, Kabir. 2008. "Police Raids: How Cops and Landlords Work Together to Destroy Toronto Hoods." *Basics.* May 9, 2008. http://basicsnewsletter.blogspot.com.

Jouanneau, Daniel. 2005. "Lessons from Violence in Paris." *Toronto Star.* November 30, 2005, A21.

Kaldor, Mary. 1999. *New and Old Wars.* Cambridge: Polity.

Kaldor, Mary, and Shannon Beebe. 2010. *The Ultimate Weapon Is No Weapon: Human Security and the New Rules of War and Peace.* New York: Public Affairs.

Kaplan, Robert D. 1994. "The Coming of Anarchy." *Atlantic* (February): 44–76.

Karim, Karin H. 2002. "The Multiculturalism Debate in Canadian Newspapers: The Harbinger of a Political Storm?" *Journal of International Migration and Integration* 3–4: 439–55.

Katznelson, Ira. 2005. *When Affirmative Action Was White: An Untold History of Racial Inequality in Twentieth Century America.* New York: W. W. Norton.

Kazemipur, Abdolmohammad, and Shivalingappa S. Halli. 2000. *The New

Poverty in Canada: Ethnic Groups and Ghetto Neighbourhoods. Toronto: Thompson Educational.

Keating, Dan, Ariana Eunjung Cha, and Gabriel Florit. 2020. "'I Just Pray God Will Help Me': Racial, Ethnic Minorities Reel from Higher COVID-19 Death Rates." *Washington Post,* November 20, 2020.

Keesmaat, Jennifer. 2013. "Chief Planner Roundtable." In *Chief Planner Roundtable, Volume 2.* Toronto: City of Toronto.

Keil, Roger. 2002. "'Common-Sense' Neoliberalism: Progressive Conservative Urbanism in Toronto, Canada." *Antipode* 34 (3): 578–601.

Kennedy, David M. 2011. *Don't Shoot: One Man, A Street Fellowship, and the End of Violence in Inner-City America.* New York: Bloomsbury.

Kesik, Ted, and Ivan Saleff. 2005. "Differential Durability, Building Life Cycle and Sustainability." Paper presented at the 10th Conference on Building Science and Technology, Ottawa, May.

Kesik, Ted, Ivan Saleff, Robert Wright, Graeme Stewart, Nick Swerdfeger, and Jan Kroman. 2008. *Tower Renewal Guidelines: Project Brief.* Toronto: City of Toronto.

Khosla, Punam. 2003. *If Low Income Women of Colour Counted in Toronto.* Toronto: Community and Social Planning Council of Toronto.

Kibry, Tony. 2020. "Evidence Mounts on the Disproportionate Effect of COVID-19 on Ethnic Minorities." *Lancet* 8: 547–48.

Kierylo, Małgorzata. 2012. "'Equality Now!': Race, Racism and Resistance in 1970s Toronto." PhD diss., Department of History, Queen's University, Kingston, Canada.

Kilcullen, David. 2013. *Out of the Mountains: The Coming Age of the Urban Guerrilla.* Oxford: Oxford University Press.

Kipfer, Stefan. 1998. "Urban Politics in the 1990s: Notes on Toronto." In *Possible Urban Worlds,* edited by International Network for Urban Research and Action (INURA), 172–79. Basel: Birkhaeuser.

Kipfer, Stefan. 2015. "Neocolonial Urbanism? La renovation urbaine in Paris." *Antipode* 48 (3): 603–25.

Kipfer, Stefan, and Roger Keil. 2002. "Toronto Inc.? Planning the Competitive City in the New Toronto." *Antipode* 34 (2): 227–64.

Kipfer, Stefan, and Joan Petrunia. 2009. "'Re-colonization' and Public Housing: A Toronto Case Study." *Studies in Political Economy* 83: 111–39.

Kipfer, Stefan, and Parastou Saberi. 2014. "From 'Revolution' to Farce? Hard-Right Populism in the Making of Toronto." *Studies in Political Economy* 93: 127–51.

Kishman, Gary, Dieter K. Buse, and Mercedes Steedman, eds. 2000. *Whose National Security? Canadian State Surveillance and the Creation of Enemies.* Toronto: Between the Lines.

Kjellstrom, Tord, Susan Mercado, and Françoise Barten. 2008. *Our Cities, Our Health, Our Future: Acting on Social Determinants for Health Equity in Urban Settings.* Kobe, Japan: World Health Organization.

Klassen, Jerome, and Greg Albo, eds. 2013. *Empire's Ally: Canada and the War in Afghanistan.* Toronto: University of Toronto Press.

Knight, Gavin. 2011. "The Woman Taking the Fight to Glasgow's Gangs." *Telegraph,* September 24, 2011.

Knowles, Valerie. 2007. *Strangers at Our Gates: Canadian Immigration and Immigration Policy, 1540–2006.* Toronto: Dundurn.

Kundnani, Arun. 2007. *The End of Tolerance: Racism in 21st Century Britain.* London: Pluto.

Kundnani, Arun. 2009. *Spooked! How Not to Prevent Violent Extremism.* London: Institute of Race Relations.

Kundnani, Arun. 2014. *The Muslims Are Coming! Islamophobia, Extremism, and the Domestic War on Terror.* London: Verso.

Kundnani, Arun, and Ben Hayes. 2018. *The Globalization of Countering Violent Extremism Policies.* Amsterdam: Transnational Institute.

Lankin, Frances. 2002. *Two Solutions for Urban Poverty.* Toronto: Cities Centre.

Lankin, Frances. 2003. "A Message from the President." In United Way, *Torontonians Speak Out: On Community Values and Pressing Social Issues,* 1–3. Toronto: United Way.

Lee, Jong-Wook. 2003. *Speech to the Fifty-Sixth World Health Assembly.* Geneva: World Health Organization. https://apps.who.int/iris/handle/10665/78361.

Lee, Min Sook, director. 2005. *Hogtown: The Politics of Policing.* Mississauga, ON : McNabb Connolly. DVD.

Lefebvre, Henri. 1976. *De l'etat II.* Paris: Union generale d'editions.

Lefebvre, Henri. 1991. *The Production of Space.* Translated by Donald Nicholson-Smith. Oxford: Blackwell.

Lefebvre, Henri. 2009. *State, Space, World: Selected Essays.* Edited by Neil Brenner and Stuart Elden. Minneapolis: University of Minnesota Press.

Lehrer, Ute, and Thorben Wieditz. 2009. "Condominium Development and Gentrification." *Canadian Journal of Urban Research* 18 (1): 140–61.

Leighton, Barry. 1991. "Visions of Community Policing: Rhetoric and Reality in Canada." *Canadian Journal of Criminology* 33: 485–522.

Leong, Melissa. 2010. "Mixed Company Theatre Takes Action against Youth Issues." *National Post.* May 28, 2010.

Lerner, Jaime. 2014. *Urban Acupuncture: Celebrating Pinpricks of Change that Enrich City Life.* Washington, D.C.: Island.

Lester, Alan, and Fae Dussart. 2014. *Colonization and the Origins of Humanitarian Governance.* Cambridge: Cambridge University Press.

Levitt, Cyril, and William Shaffir. 2018. *The Riot at Christie Pits.* Toronto: New Jewish Press.

Leviten-Reid, Eric. 2006. *Asset-Based, Resident-Led Neighbourhood Development.* Toronto: Caledon Institute of Social Policy.

Lewis, Bernard. 2002. *What Went Wrong?* New York: Oxford University.

Lewis, Stephen. 1992. *Report of the Task Force on Race Relations and Policing.* Toronto: Solicitor General's Office.

Light, Jennifer S. 2003. *From Warfare to Welfare: Defense Intellectuals and the Urban Problems in Cold War America.* Baltimore, Md.: John Hopkins University Press.

Linebaugh, Peter. 2003. *The London Hanged.* London: Verso.

Lippens, Ronnie. 2004. "Viral Contagion and Anti-terrorism: Notes on Medical Emergency, Legality and Diplomacy." *International Journal of the Semiotics of Law* 17 (2): 125–39.

Long, Austin. 2006. *On "Other War:" Lesson from Five Decades of RAND Counterinsurgency Research.* Santa Monica, Calif.: RAND Corporation.

Lucassen, Leo. 2005. *The Immigrant Threat: The Integration of Old and New Migrants in Western Europe since 1850.* Urbana: University of Illinois Press.

Lydon, Mike, and Anthony Garcia. 2015. *Tactical Urbanism: Short-Term Action for Long-Term Change.* Washington, D.C.: Island.

Magnusson, W. 1983. "Toronto." In *City Politics in Canada,* edited by Warren Magnusson and Andrew Sancton, 94–139. Toronto: University of Toronto Press.

Mahler, Halfdan. 1981. *The Meaning of Health for All by the Year 2000.* Geneva: World Health Forum.

Mamdani, Mahmood. 2004. *Good Muslim, Bad Muslim.* New York: Random House.

Mamdani, Mahmood. 2020. *Neither Settler nor Native: The Making and Unmaking of Permanent Minorities.* Cambridge, Mass.: Harvard University Press.

Martin, Paul. 2005. "Address by Prime Minister Paul Martin to the Conference of the Federation of Canadian Municipalities." St. John's, Newfoundland. June 5, 2005.

Martin Prosperity Institute. 2009. *Ontario in the Creative Age.* Toronto: Martin Prosperity Institute.

Marx, Karl. (1844) 1992. *Capital: A Critique of Political Economy. Volume I.* London: Penguin.

Marx, Karl, and Frederick Engels. (1848) 1976. *The German Ideology.* Moscow: Progress.

Marx, Karl, and Frederick Engels. (1848) 2002. *The Communist Manifesto.* New York: Penguin.

Mayer, Margit. 2003. "The Onward Sweep of Social Capital: Causes and Consequences for Understanding Cities, Communities and Urban Movements." *International Journal of Urban and Regional Research* 27: 110–32.

Maynard, Robin. 2017. *Policing Black Lives: State Violence in Canada from Slavery to the Present.* Winnipeg: Fernwood.

Mbembe, Achille. 2001. *On the Postcolony.* Berkeley: University of California Press.

McBride, Stephen. 2005. *Paradigm Shift: Globalization and the Canadian State.* Halifax: Fernwood.

McCann, Eugene. 2011. "Urban Policy Mobilities and Global Circuits of Knowledge: Towards a Research Agenda." *Annals of the Association of American Geographers* 101 (1): 107–30.

McCann, Eugene, and Kevin Ward. 2015. "Thinking Through Dualisms in Urban Policy Mobilities." *International Journal of Urban and Regional Research* 39 (4): 828–30.

McFee, Dale, and Norman Taylor. 2014. *The Prince Albert Hub and the Emergence of Collaborative Risk-Driven Community Safety.* Ottawa: Canadian Police College Discussion Paper Series.

McGrath, John Michael. 2010. "Could the London Riots Happen in Toronto? The Star's Christopher Hume Says Yes." *Toronto Life,* August 10, 2010.

McGregor, Janyce, and Kady O'Malley. 2015. "Stephen Harper Makes His Case for New Powers to Combat Terror." *CBC News,* January 30, 2015. https://www.cbc.ca/news/politics.

McIsaac, Susan. 2011. "Letter from Susan McIsaac." In UWT (United Way Toronto), *Vertical Poverty.* Toronto: United Way.

McKercher, Asa. 2014. "The Centre Cannot Hold: Canada, Colonialism and the 'Afro-Asian Bloc' at the United Nations, 1960–62." *Journal of Imperial and Commonwealth History* 42 (2): 329–49.

McKnight, Zoe. 2014. "Regent Park Residents Find Relocation Unfair." *Toronto Star,* May 3, 2014.

McMurtry, Roy, and Alvin Curling. 2008. *The Review of the Roots of Youth Violence.* Toronto: Service Ontario.

Meagher, Sean, Angela Lee, and Nehal Tolia. 2012. *Evidence Review of Place-Based Approaches.* Toronto: Public Interest Strategy & Communication Inc.

Micallef, Shawn. 2017. "Grenfell Tower Fire a Warning for Toronto on Housing Crisis." *Toronto Star,* June 23, 2017.

Ministry of Community Safety and Correctional Services. 2011a. "A History of Coordinated Effort to Stop Guns and Gangs." July 12, 2011. http://news.ontario.ca.

Ministry of Community Safety and Correctional Services. 2011b. "Police and Province Working Together to Rid Ontario Streets of Guns and Gangs." January 27, 2011. http://news.ontario.ca.

Mondon, Aurélien, and Aaron Winter. 2017. "*Charlie Hebdo,* Republican Secularism and Islamophobia." In *After Charlie Hebdo: Terror, Racism, and Free Speech,* edited by Gauan Titley, Des Freedman, Gholam Khiabany, and Aurélien Mondon, 31–45. London: Zed.

Morrison Park Advisors. 2010. *Tower Renewal Financing Options Report.* Toronto: Morrison Park Advisors.

Murdie, Robert A. 2002. "A Comparison of the Rental Housing Experiences of Polish and Somali Newcomers in Toronto." *CUCS Research Bulleting #9.* Toronto: Centre for Urban and Community Studies, University of Toronto.

Murdie, Robert, and Jennifer Logan. 2010. *Precarious Housing and Hidden Homelessness among Refugees, Asylum Seekers, and Immigrants: Bibliography and Review of Canadian Literature from 2005 to 2010.* Toronto: CERIS–Ontario Metropolitan Centre.

Murphy, Chris. 1988. "Community Problems, Problem Communities, and Community Policing in Toronto." *Journal of Research in Crime and Delinquency* 25 (4): 394–10.

Nagl, John A. 2014. *Knife Fights: A Memoir of Modern War in Theory and Practice.* New York: Penguin.

National Post Editorial Board. 2010. "Toronto's Angry (Non-White) Voters." *National Post.* October 27, 2010.

Navaro, Vicente. 2009. "What We Mean by Social Determinants of Health." *International Journal of Health Services* 39 (3): 423–41.

Neocleous, Mark. 2000. *The Fabrication of Social Order: A Critical Theory of Police Power.* London: Pluto.

Neocleous, Mark. 2003. "Off the Map: On Violence and Cartography." *European Journal of Social Theory* 6 (4): 409–25.

Neocleous, Mark. 2006. "Theoretical Foundations of the 'New Police Science.'" In *The New Police Science: The Police Power in Domestic and International Governance,* edited by Markus D. Dubber and Mariana Valverde, 17–41. Stanford: Stanford University Press.

Neocleous, Mark. 2008. *Critique of Security.* Edinburgh: Edinburgh University Press.

Neocleous, Mark. 2016. *The Universal Adversary: Security, Capital and "The Enemies of All Mankind."* New York: Routledge.

NO COPS (Neighbourhood Organizing Coalition Opposed to Police in Schools). 2009. "Newly Released SRO Report Gets Failing Grade." *Basics News,* November 30, 2009. http://basicsnewsletter.blogspot.ca/.

Normandeau, Andre, and Barry Leighton. 1990. *The Future of Policing in Canada.* Ottawa: Ministry of the Solicitor General of Canada.

OACP (Ontario Association of Chiefs of Police). 2010. *Partnership for a Safe Community: Ontario's New Community Policing Model.* Presentation. Kingston, Ontario.

OCCC (Ontario Crime Control Commission). 1998. *Report on Youth Crime.* Toronto: Queen's Printer for Ontario.

OECD (Organization for Economic Co-operation and Development). 2002. *Territorial Reviews: Canada.* Paris: OECD. www.oecd-ilibrary.org.

OHRC (Ontario Human Rights Commission). 1977. *Life Together: A Report on Human Rights in Ontario.* Toronto: OHRC.

O'Malley, Pat. 2010. "Resilient Subjects: Uncertainty, Warfare and Liberalism." *Economy and Society* 39 (4): 488–509.

Ong, Aihwa. 2011. "Introduction: Worlding Cities, or the Art of Being Global." In *Worlding Cities: Asian Experiments and the Art of Being Global,* edited by Ananya Roy and Aihwa Ong, 1–26. Chichester: Blackwell.

Ontario Attorney General. 2009. "A History of Coordinated Crime Fighting." February 26, 2009. https://news.ontario.ca/en/

Ornstein, Michael. 2000. *Ethno-racial Inequality in the City of Toronto: An Analysis of the 1996 Census.* Toronto: Access and Equity Unit, City of Toronto.

Ó Tuathail, Gearoid, and Simon Dalby. 1998. *Rethinking Geopolitics.* London: Routledge.

Paperny, Anna Mehler. 2012. "Toronto Tries Saskatchewan's Method for Stopping Crime before It Starts." *Globe and Mail,* July 19, 2012.

Paradis, Emily, Ruth Maries Wilson, and Jennifer Logan. 2014. *Nowhere Else to Go: Inadequate Housing & Risk of Homelessness among Families in Toronto's Aging Rental Buildings.* Toronto: Cities Centre.

Paradis, Emily, Sylvia Novac, Monica Sarty, and David Hulchanski. 2008. *Better Off in a Shelter? A Year of Homelessness & Housing among Status Immigrant, Non-status Migrant, and Canadian-Born Families.* Toronto: Cities Centre.

Parsons, Christopher, Lex Gill, Tamir Israel, Bill Robinson, and Ronald Deibert. 2017. *Analysis of the Communications Security Establishment Act and Related Provisions in Bill C-59.* Toronto: University of Toronto.

Patrick, Stewart, and Kaysie Brown. 2007. *Greater Than the Sum of Its Parts? Assessing "Whole of Government" Approaches to Fragile States.* New York: International Peace Academy.

Pattilo, Mary. 2009. "Revisiting Loïc Wacquant's *Urban Outcasts.*" *International Journal of Urban and Regional Research* 33 (3): 858–64.

Pecaut, David. 2003. "Here Are Their Ideas." *Toronto Star,* April 12, 2003.

Pecaut, David. 2007. "Toronto Summit 2007: The Big Challenges." *Toronto Star,* February 25, 2007.

Peck, Jamie. 2004. "Geography and Public Policy: Constructions of Neo-liberalism." *Progress in Human Geography* 28 (3): 392–405.

Peck, Jamie, and Adam Tickell. 2002. "Neoliberalising Space." *Antipode* 34 (2): 380–404.

Peckham, Robert, ed. 2014. "Introduction: Pathologizing Crime, Criminalizing Disease." In *Disease and Crime: A History of Social Pathologies and the New Politics of Health,* edited by Robert Peckham, 1–21. New York: Routledge.

Pendakur, Kishna, and Ravi Pendakur. 2011. "Colour by Numbers: Minority Earnings in Canada 1995–2005." *International Migration & Integration* 12: 305–26.

Perrons, Diane, and Sophia Skyers. 2003. "Empowerment Through Participation? Conceptual Explorations and a Case Study." *International Journal of Urban and Regional Research* 27 (2): 265–85.

Pithouse, Richard. 2011. "Fidelity to Fanon." In *Living Fanon: Global Perspectives,* edited by Nigel C. Gibson, 225–34. New York: Palgrave Macmillan.

Pitman, Walter. 1977. *Now Is Not Too Late. Report Submitted to the Council of Metropolitan Toronto by the Task Force on Human Relations.* Toronto: Metro Toronto.

Poppe, Will, and Douglas Young. 2015. "The Politics of Place: Place-Making versus Densification in Toronto's Tower Neighbourhoods." *International Journal of Urban and Regional Research* 39 (3): 613–21.

Powell, Betsy. 2010. *Bad Seeds: The True Story of Toronto's Galloway Boys Street Gangs.* Mississauga, ON: Wiley.

Prasad, Amrit. 2018. "The Urban Health Equity Assessment and Responses Tool (HEART)—A Decade of Development and Implementation." *Journal of Urban Health* 95: 609.

Preston, Valerie, Robert Murdie, Silvia D'Addario, Prince Sibanda, and Ann-Marie Murnaghan with Jennifer Logal and Mi Hae Ahn. 2011. *Precarious Housing and Hidden Homelessness among Refugees, Asylum Seekers, and Immigrants in the Toronto Metropolitan Area.* Toronto: CERIS–Ontario Metropolitan Centre.

Prime Minister's Task Force on Urban Issues. 2002. *Canada's Urban Strategy: A Vision for the 21st Century.* Ottawa: Prime Minister's Task Force on Urban Issues.

PSC (Public Safety Canada). 2013a. *Toronto Anti-Violence Intervention Strategy (Synopsis).* www.publicsafety.gc.ca.

PSC (Public Safety Canada). 2013b. *Youth in Policing Initiative (Synopsis).* www.publicsafety.gc.ca.

PSC (Public Safety Canada). 2013c. *School Resource Officer Program (Synopsis).* www.publicsafety.gc.ca.

PSC (Public Safety Canada). 2013d. *Community Mobilization Prince Albert.* www.publicsafety.gc.ca.

PSC (Public Safety Canada). 2018a. *Departmental Plan, 2018–19.* Ottawa: PSC.

PSC (Public Safety Canada). 2018b. *Federal Funding for Toronto Police to Expand Counter Radicalization to Violence Initiative.* Ottawa: PSC.

Public Health Ontario. 2020. *COVID-19 in Ontario: A Focus on Diversity: January 15, 2020 to May 14, 2020.* Toronto: Ontario Agency for Health Protection and Promotion.

Qureshi, Asim. 2018. "Experiencing the War on Terror: Bringing Experiential Knowledge into Critical Terrorism Studies." PhD diss., School of Politics and International Studies, Kent University.

Rabinow, Paul. 1995. *French Modern: Norms and Forms of the Social Environment.* Chicago: University of Chicago Press.

Rachlis, Chuck, and David Wolfe. 1997. "An Insider's View of the NDP Government of Ontario: The Politics of Permanent Opposition Meets the Economics of Permanent Recession." In *The Government and Politics of Ontario,* edited by Graham White, 331–64. Toronto: University of Toronto Press.

Rankin, Jim. 2010. "Race Matters: Blacks Documented by Police at High Rate." *Toronto Star,* February 6, 2010.

Rankin, Jim. 2012. "How *The Star* Analyzed Toronto Police Stop and Arrest Data." *Toronto Star,* March 9, 2012.

Rankin, Jim. 2013. "'Excuse Me Officer, Why Are You Stopping Me?'" *Toronto Star,* September 27, 2013.

Rankin, Jim, and Patty Winsa. 2012a. "Known to Police: Toronto Police Stop and Document Black and Brown People Far More Than Whites." *Toronto Star,* March 9, 2012.

Rankin, Jim, and Patty Winsa. 2012b. "Police Board Chair Seeks Race-Based Probe to Stop." *Toronto Star,* March 15, 2012.

Rankin, Jim, and Patty Winsa. 2013. "One Officer, Five Years, 6,600 Contact Cards." *Toronto Star,* September 27, 2013.

Rawls, John. 1971. *A Theory of Justice.* Cambridge, Mass.: Harvard University Press.

Rawls, John. 1999. *The Law of Peoples.* Cambridge, Mass.: Harvard University Press.

Razack, Sherene. 2000. "From the 'Clean Snows of Petawawa': The Violence of Canadian Peacekeepers in Somalia." *Cultural Anthropology* 15 (1): 127–63.

Razack, Sherene. 2004. *Dark Threats and White Knights: The Somalia Affair, Peacekeeping and the New Imperialism.* Toronto: University of Toronto Press.

Razack, Sherene. 2011. "The Space of Difference in Law: Inquests into Aboriginal Deaths in Custody." *Somatechnics* 1 (1): 87–123.

Rigakos, George, John McMullan, Joshua Johnson, and Gülden Özcan. 2009. *A General Police System: Political Economy and Security in the Age of Enlightenment.* Ottawa: Red Quill.

Rigouste, Mathieu 2011, *L'ennemi intérieur.* Paris: La Découverte.

Roach, Kent, and Stephane Carvin. 2017. "We Need Real, Honest Debate on Bill C-59." *Globe and Mail,* December 4, 2017.

Robinson, Jennifer. 2015. "'Arriving at' Urban Policies: The Topological Spaces of Urban Policy Mobilities." *International Journal of Urban and Regional Research* 39 (4): 831–34.

Rodriguez, Dylan. 2007. "The Political Logic of the Non-Profit Industrial Complex." In *The Revolution Will Not Be Funded: Beyond the Non-profit Industrial Complex,* edited by INCITE! Women of Color against Violence, 21–40. Cambridge, Mass.: South End.

Rowe, Mary W., ed. 2000. *Toronto: Considering Self-Government.* Owen Sound, ON: Ginger Press.

Roy, Arundhati. 2004. "Public Power in the Age of Empire." *Socialist Worker,* September 3. http://socialistworker.org.

Roy, Ananya, Stuart Schrader, and Emma S. Crane. 2014. "'The Anti-poverty Hoax': Development, Pacification and the Making of Community in the Global 1960s." *Cities* 44 (April): 139–45.

Ruddell, Rick, and Nicholas Jones. 2014. *The Economics of Policing: Five Years into the Great Recession.* Collaborative Centre for Justice and Safety. Regina: University of Regina Press.

Russell, Bob. 2000. "From the Workhouse to Workfare: The Welfare State and Shifting Policy Terrains." In *Restructuring and Resistance: Canadian Public Policy in the Age of Global Capitalism,* edited by Mike Burke, Colin Mooers, and John Shields, 26-49. Halifax: Fernwood.

Russell, Hugh, and Norman Taylor. 2014. *New Directions in Community Safety.* Ottawa: Ontario Association of Chiefs of Police.

Saberi, Parastou. 2017. "Humanizing Pacification: On the Role of Urbanism in French Colonial Pacification Strategies." In *Destroy, Build, Secure: Readings on Pacification,* edited by Tyler Wall, Parastou Saberi, and William Jackson, 88–106. Ottawa: Red Quill.

Saberi, Parastou. 2018. "Urban Geopolitics and 'The Immigrant': Lessons from Toronto." *Salvage #6: Evidence of Things Not Seen,* 237–52.

Saberi, Parastou. 2019. "Preventing Radicalization in European Cities: A Geopolitical Question." *Political Geography* 74.

Satzewich, Vic. 1989. "Racism and Canadian Immigration Policy: The Government's View of Caribbean Migration, 1962–1966." *Canadian Ethnic Studies* 21 (1): 77-97.

Saunders, Doug. 2010. "Arrival City & Our Urban Futures." *The Agenda with Steve Paikin.* www.youtube.com/watch?v=mCEfo2yTFzs.

Saunders, Doug. 2011. *Arrival City: How the Largest Migration in History is Shaping Our World.* Toronto: Vintage Canada.

Saunders, Doug. 2013. "We're a Nation of Suburban Apartment-Dwellers, but Afraid to Admit It." *Globe and Mail,* March 30, 2013.

Saunders, Doug. 2018. "In the Dead Spaces between Buildings, An Architectural Revolution." *Globe and Mail,* May 25, 2018.

Scott, James C. 1998. *Seeing Like a State: How Certain Schemes to Improve the Human Condition Have Failed.* New Haven, Conn.: Yale University Press.

Sewell, John. 2010. *Police in Canada.* Toronto: James Lorimer.

Sharma, Nandita. 2006. *Home Economics: Nationalism and Making of "Migrant Workers" in Canada.* Toronto: University of Toronto Press.

Shepherd, Leslie. 2014. "Toronto Researchers Adapt World Health Organization Tool to Measure the Health and Well-Being of the City's Neighbourhoods." February 24, 2014. www.stmichaelshospital.com.

Shipley, Tyler. 2017. *Ottawa and the Empire: Canada and the Military Coup in Honduras.* Toronto: Between the Lines.

Shipley, Tyler. 2020. *Canada in the World: Settler Capitalism and the Colonial Imagination.* Halifax, NS: Fernwood.

Siciliano, Amy M. 2010. "Policing Poverty: Race, Space and the Fear of Crime After the Year of the Gun (2005) in Suburban Toronto." PhD diss., Department of Geography, University of Toronto.

Siddiqui, Haroon. 2011. "The Lessons of Britain's Rainbow Riots." *Toronto Star.* August 11, 2011.

Silverstein, Paul A. 2018. *Postcolonial France: Race, Islam, and the Future of the Republic.* London: Pluto.

Sivanandan, A. (1999) 2019. *Communities of Resistance: Writings on Black Struggle for Liberation.* London: Verso.

Skaburskis, Andrejs, and Diana Mok. 2000. "The Impact of Withdrawing Subsidies for New Rental Housing: Projections for Toronto and Ontario." *Housing Studies* 15 (2): 169–94.

Slater, Tom. 2004. "Municipally Managed Gentrification in South Parkdale, Toronto." *Canadian Geographer* 48 (3): 303–25.

Slutkin, Gary. 2011. "Rioting Is a Disease Spread from Person to Person—The Key Is to Stop the Infection." *Guardian,* August 14, 2011.

Slutkin, Gary. 2012. *Violence Is a Contagious Disease.* Washington, D.C.: National Academy Press.

Smith, Charles C. 2007. *Conflict, Crisis and Accountability: Racial Profiling and Law Enforcement in Canada.* Ottawa: Canadian Centre for Policy Alternatives.

Smith, Dorothy. 1990. *The Conceptual Practices of Power: A Feminist Sociology of Knowledge*. Boston: Northeastern University Press.

Smith, Neil. 1996. *The New Urban Frontier: Gentrification and the Revanchist City*. New York: Routledge.

Smith, Neil. 2002. "New Globalism, New Urbanism: Gentrification as Global Urban Strategy." *Antipode* 34 (3): 427–450.

SNTF (Strong Neighbourhood Taskforce). 2005. *Strong Neighbourhoods: A Call to Action*. Toronto: City of Toronto and United Way Toronto.

Social Planning Council of Metropolitan Toronto. 1997. *Merchants of Care? The Non-profit Sector in a Competitive Social Services Marketplace*. Toronto: SPC.

Solomos, John. 2003. *Race and Racism in Britain*. London: Palgrave.

Sorenson, André. 2010. *Tower Renewal and Transit City: Toronto Election 2010*. Discussion Paper # 9. Toronto: Cities Centre.

Spooner, Kevin. 2009. *Canada, the Congo Crisis and UN Peacekeeping, 1960–1964*. Vancouver: University of British Columbia Press.

Stanley, Dick. 2003. "What Do We Know about Social Cohesion: The Research Perspective of the Federal Government's Social Cohesion Research Network." *Canadian Journal of Sociology* 28 (1): 5–17.

Stapleton, John, and Jasmine Kay. 2015. *The Working Poor in the Toronto Region: Mapping Working Poverty in Canada's Richest City*. Toronto: Metcalf Foundation.

Stapleton, John, Brian Murphy, and Yue Xing. 2012. *The Working Poor in the Toronto Region: Who They Are, Where They Live, and How Trends Are Changing*. Toronto: Metcalf Foundation.

Stasiulis, Daiva. 1989. "Minority Resistance in the Local State: Toronto in the 1970s and 1980s." *Ethnic and Racial Studies* 12 (1): 63–83.

Stewart, Graeme. 2007. "Faulty Towers." *Toronto Star,* March 25, 2007.

Stewart, Graeme. 2008. "The Suburban Tower and Toronto's Legacy of Modern Housing." *Docomomo* 39 (September): 23–29.

Stewart, Graeme, Bryan Bowen, George Martin, Jason Thorne, and Michael McCelland. 2012. *Strong Neighbourhoods and Complete Communities: A New Approach to Zoning for Apartment Neighbourhoods*. Toronto: Centre for Urban Growth and Renewal (CUG+R).

Stewart, Graeme, and Jason Thorne. 2010. *Tower Neighbourhood Renewal in the Greater Golden Horseshoe: An Analysis of High-Rise Apartment Tower Neighbourhoods Developed in the Postwar Boom (1945–1984)*. Toronto: E.R.A. Architects, planningAlliance, and Cities Centre.

Strobel, Mike. 2014. "Give My Neighbourhood 'Priority' Designation." *Toronto Sun.* March 17, 2014.

Tator, Carol, and Frances Henry. 2006. *Racial Profiling in Canada: Challenging the Myth of "A Few Bad Apples."* Toronto: University of Toronto Press.

Taylor, Keeanga-Yamahtta. 2016. *From #BlackLivesMatter to Black Liberation.* Chicago: Haymarket.

TBOT (Toronto Board of Trade). 2002. *Strong City, Strong Nation: Securing Toronto's Contribution to Canada.* Toronto: TBOT.

TBOT (Toronto Board of Trade). 2003. *Affordable, Available, Achievable: Practical Solutions to Affordable Housing Challenges.* Toronto: TBOT.

TBOT (Toronto Board of Trade). 2009. *Vote Toronto 2010: Framework for a Better City.* Discussion Paper. Toronto: TBOT.

TBOT (Toronto Board of Trade). 2010. *Lifting All Boats: Promoting Social Cohesion and Economic Inclusion in the Toronto Region.* Toronto: TBOT.

TBOT and UWT (Toronto Board of Trade and United Way Toronto). 2014. *Closing the Prosperity Gap: Solutions for a More Liveable City Region.* Toronto: TBOT.

TCF (Toronto Community Foundation). 2010. *Toronto's Vital Signs 2010.* Toronto: TCF.

TCF (Toronto Community Foundation). 2011. *Toronto's Vital Signs 2011.* Toronto: TCF.

TCF (Toronto Community Foundation). 2012. *Toronto's Vital Signs 2012.* Toronto: TCF.

TCF (Toronto Community Foundation). 2013. *Toronto's Vital Signs 2013.* Toronto: TCF.

TCSA (Toronto City Summit Alliance). 2003. *Enough Talk: An Action Plan for the Toronto Region.* Toronto: TCSA.

TD Bank Financial. 2002a. *A Choice Between Investing in Canada's Cities or Disinvesting in Canada's Future.* Toronto: TD Bank Financial.

TD Bank Financial. 2002b. *The Greater Toronto Area (GTA): Canada's Primary Economic Locomotive in Need of Repair.* Toronto: TD Bank Financial.

TD Economics. 2003. *Affordable Housing in Canada: In Search of a New Paradigm.* Toronto: TD Bank.

TDRC (Toronto Disaster Relief Committee). 1998. *Homelessness in Toronto: State of Emergency, An Urgent Call for Emergency Humanitarian Relief and Prevention Measures.* Toronto: TDRC.

Teotonio, Isabel. 2012. "Fundraising for the United Way Has Professional Benefits, Too." *Toronto Star,* September 14, 2012.

Thobani, Sunera. 2000. "Closing Ranks: Racism and Sexism in Canada's Immigration Policy." *Race & Class* 42 (1): 35–55.

Thobani, Sunera. 2007. *Exalted Subjects: Studies in the Making of Race and Nation in Canada.* Toronto: University of Toronto Press.

Thrasher, Fredric. 1927. *The Gang.* Chicago: University of Chicago Press.

Torjman, Sherri. 2006. *Shared Space: The Communities Agenda.* Toronto: Caledon Institute of Social Policy.

Toronto Public Health. 2011. *Healthy Toronto by Design.* Toronto: City of Toronto.

Toronto Public Health. 2012a. *The Walkable City: Neighbourhood Design and Preference, Travel Choices and Health.* Toronto: City of Toronto.

Toronto Public Health. 2012b. *Toward Healthier Apartment Neighbourhoods.* Toronto: City of Toronto.

Toronto Star. 1933. "Draper Admits Receiving Riot Warning." August 17, 1933, 1, 3.

Toronto Star. 1972. "Government's Decision 'Is Defensible.'" August 25, 1972.

Toronto Star. 2005. "This Is What It's Come To." December 28, 2005.

Toronto Star. 2010. "The Chief on Race, Crime and Policing." February 6, 2010.

Toronto Star. 2013. "Toronto Police Must Reform 'Carding' System that Targets Minorities: Editorial." September 29, 2013.

Toronto Star. 2014a. "An Urban Checkup." March 5, 2014, A16.

Toronto Star. 2014b. "Let New Data Guide the Way." March 11, 2014, A14.

Tower Renewal Partnership. 2016a. *Green Finance and Tower Renewal.* Toronto: Tower Renewal Partnership.

Tower Renewal Partnership. 2016b. *Understanding the Tower Landscape.* Toronto: Tower Renewal Partnership.

Tower Renewal Partnership. 2018. *Growth and Resiliency in Tower in the Park Sites Across the GGH.* Toronto: Tower Renewal Partnership.

TPS (Toronto Police Service). 2003. *Policing a World within a City.* Toronto: TPS.

TPS (Toronto Police Service). 2009. *The Badge.* September–October.

TPS (Toronto Police Service). 2011. "School Resource Officer Program, 2011: Follow-Up Evaluation." Toronto: TPS.

TPS (Toronto Police Service). 2016. *TAVIS.* www.torontopolice.on.ca/tavis/.

Ungerleider, Charles, and Josette McGregor. 1991. "Police-Challenge 2000: Issues Affecting Relations Between Police and Minorities in Canada." *Canadian Journal of Criminology* 33: 555–63.

United Nations. 2000. 55/2/ United Nations Millennium Declaration. A/RES/55/2. September 18, 2000. https://digitallibrary.un.org/record/422015?ln=en.

United Nations. 2005. *Investing in Development: A Practical Plan to Achieve the Millennium Development Goals: Overview.* New York: United Nations.

Urban HEART@Toronto. 2014. *An Evidence-Based Standard for Measuring the Well-Being of Toronto's Neighbourhoods.* Toronto: St. Michael's.

UWT (United Way Toronto). 1997a. *Metro Toronto: A Community at Risk.* Toronto: UWT.

UWT (United Way Toronto). 1997b. *Beyond Survival: Homelessness in Metro Toronto.* Toronto: UWT.

UWT (United Way Toronto). 1997c. *Way Ahead: Focus on the Future.* Toronto: UWT.

UWT (United Way Toronto). 1999. *Toronto at a Turning Point: Demographic, Economic and Social Trends in Toronto.* Toronto: UWT.

UWT (United Way Toronto). 2002. *A Decade of Decline: Poverty and Income Inequalities in the City of Toronto in the 1990s.* Toronto: UWT.

UWT (United Way Toronto). 2003. *Torontonians Speak out on Community Values and Pressing Issues.* Toronto: UWT.

UWT (United Way Toronto). 2004. *Poverty by Postal Code: The Geography of Neighbourhood Poverty, 1981–2001.* Toronto: UWT.

UWT (United Way Toronto). 2011. *Poverty by Postal Code 2: Vertical Poverty: Declining Income, Housing Quality and Community Life in Toronto's Inner Suburban High-rise Apartments.* Toronto: UWT.

UWT (United Way Toronto). 2012a. *Building Strong Neighbourhoods: Closing Gaps and Creating Opportunities.* Toronto: UWT.

UWT (United Way Toronto). 2012b. *Working Together. 2012 Annual Report.* Toronto: United Way Toronto.

UWT (United Way Toronto) and City of Toronto. 2005. *Strong Neighbourhoods: A Call to Action.* Toronto: UWT.

Valpy, Michael. 1994. "Face to Face with a New Violence." *Globe and Mail,* April 12, 1994, A2.

Valpy, Michael. 2005. "Could It Happen Here?" *Globe and Mail,* November 12, 2005.

Valpy, Michael, and Daniel Leblanc. 2010. "Federal Political Parties Take Note of Rob Ford's Strategy." *Globe and Mail,* October 27, 2010.

Van der Pijl, Kees. 2014. *The Discipline of Western Supremacy: Modes of Foreign Relations and Political Economy.* London: Pluto.

Van Nostrand, John. 2014. "If We Build It, They Will Stay." *Walrus* (September): 34–39.

Vaughan, Laura. 2018. *Mapping Society: The Spatial Dimensions of Social Cartography.* London: UCL Press.

Vineberg, Robert. 2018. "The Winds of Change: Fairclough and the Removal of Discriminatory Immigration Barriers." In *Reassessing the Rogue Tory: Canadian Foreign Relations in the Diefenbaker Era,* edited by Janice Cavell and Ryan Touhey, 227–44. Vancouver: University of British Columbia Press.

Virdee, Satnam. 2014. *Racism, Class and the Racialized Outsider.* London: Palgrave.

Vitalis, Robert. 2015. *White World Order, Black Power Politics: The Birth of American International Relations.* Ithaca, N.Y.: Cornell University Press.

Wacquant, Loïc. 2008. *Urban Outcasts: A Comparative Sociology of Advanced Marginality*. Cambridge: Polity.

Wacquant, Loïc. 2009. *Punishing the Poor: The Neoliberal Government of Social Insecurity*. Durham, N.C.: Duke University Press.

Wacquant, Loïc, and Tom Slater. 2014. "Territorial Stigmatization in Action." *Environment and Planning A* 46: 1270–80.

Waddington, David. 2008. "The Madness of the Mob? Explaining the 'Irrationality' and Destructiveness of Crowd Violence." *Sociology Compass* 2 (2): 675–78.

Walcott, Rinaldo. 2003. *Black Like Who? Writing Black Canada*. Toronto: Insomniac.

Walker, Jeremy, and Melina Cooper. 2011. "Genealogies of Resilience: From System Ecology to the Political Economy of Crisis Adaptation." *Security Dialogue* 42 (2): 143–60.

Walks, Alan. 2004. "Suburbanization, the Vote, and Changes in Federal and Provincial Political Representation and Influence between Inner Cities and Suburbs in Large Canadian Urban Regions, 1945–1999." *Urban Affairs* 39 (4): 411–40.

Ward, Kevin. 2006. "'Policies in Motion,' Urban Management and State Restructuring: The Trans-local Expansion of Business Improvement Districts." *International Journal of Urban and Regional Research* 30 (1): 54–75.

Webster, David. 2009. *Fire and Full Moon: Canada and Indonesia in a Decolonizing World*. Vancouver: University of British Columbia Press.

Weizman, Eyal. 2011. *The Least of All Possible Evils: Humanitarian Violence from Ardent to Gaza*. New York: Verso.

Welsh, Moira. 2010. "Elite Toronto Police Squad Looks for Trouble." *Toronto Star*, February 8, 2010.

WHO (World Health Organization). 1948. *Constitution of the World Health Organization*. Geneva: WHO.

WHO (World Health Organization). 2002. *World Report on Violence and Health*. Geneva: WHO.

WHO (World Health Organization). 2010a. *Urban HEART: Urban Health Equity Assessment and Response Tool*. Kobe, Japan: WHO.

WHO (World Health Organization). 2010b. *Global Forum on Urbanization and Health, Report*. Kobe, Japan: WHO.

WHO (World Health Organization) and the United Nations Children's Fund. 1978. *Primary Health Care: Report of the International Conference on Primary Health Care, Alma-Ata, USSR, 6–12 September 1978*. Geneva: WHO. https://apps.who.int/iris/handle/10665/39228

Willsher, Kim. 2020. "In a Paris Banlieue, Coronavirus Amplifies Years of Inequality." *Guardian*, April 25, 2020.

Wilson, James Q., and George Kelling. 1982. "Broken Windows." *Atlantic Monthly* (March): 29–38.

Wilson, Kalpana. 2012. *Race, Racism and Development.* New York: Zed.

Wilson, William Julius. 1987. *The Truly Disadvantaged.* Chicago: University of Chicago Press.

Winsa, Patty, and Jim Rankin. 2013a. "Tense Times in Policing on TCHC Property." *Toronto Star,* September 27, 2013.

Winsa, Patty, and Jim Rankin. 2013b. "TAVIS Police Unit in Eye of the Storm." *Toronto Star,* September 27, 2013.

Winsa, Patty, and Jim Rankin. 2014. "Toronto Activists Move Forward with Human Rights Challenge to Police Carding." *Toronto Star,* February 3, 2014.

Wolch, Jennifer. 1990. *The Shadow State: Government and the Voluntary Sector in Transition.* New York: Foundation Center.

Wolfe, David. 1984. "The Rise and Demise of the Keynesian Era in Canada: Economic Policy, 1930–1982." In *Modern Canada, 1930–1980s,* edited by Michael S. Cross and Gregory S. Kealey. Toronto: McClelland and Stewart.

Wolff, Robert Paul. 1977. *Understanding Rawls: A Reconstruction and Critique of a Theory of Justice.* Princeton, N.J.: Princeton University Press.

Wolfowitz, Paul. 2005. "Foreword." In World Bank, *World Development Report 2006: Equity and Development,* xi–xii. Washington, D.C.: World Bank; Oxford: Oxford University Press.

Wood, Denis. 2010. *Rethinking the Power of Maps.* New York: Guilford.

Wood, Ellen Meiksins. 2005. *Empire of Capital.* New York: Verso.

World Bank. 2000. *Attacking Poverty.* Oxford: Oxford University Press.

World Bank. 2005. *World Development Report 2006: Equity and Development.* Washington, D.C.: World Bank; Oxford: Oxford University Press.

World Bank. 2012. *Resilience, Equity and Opportunity.* Washington, D.C.: World Bank.

World Bank. 2013. *Inclusion Matters: The Foundation for Shared Prosperity.* Washington, D.C.: World Bank.

World Bank. 2014. *Work Development Indicators.* Washington, D.C. World Bank.

Wortley, Scot. 2013. "Police Stops Damage Lives of Black Torontonians." *Toronto Star,* September 28, 2013.

Wortley, Scot, and Akwasi Owusu-Bempah. 2011. "The Usual Suspects: Police Stop and Search Practices in Canada." *Policing and Society: An International Journal of Research and Policy* 21 (4): 395–407.

Wortley, Scot, and Akwasi Owusu-Bempah. 2012. "Race, Ethnicity, Crime and Criminal Justice in Canada." In *Race, Ethnicity, Crime and Criminal*

Justice in the Americas, edited by Anita Kalunta-Crumpton, 11–40. New York: Palgrave.

Wyler, Liana Sun. 2008. *Weak and Failing States: Evolving Security Threats and U.S. Policy.* Report prepared for Members and Committees of Congress. Washington, D.C.: Foreign Affairs, Defense, and Trade Division.

Yılmaz, Ferruh. 2016. *How the Workers Became Muslims: Immigration, Culture, and Hegemonic Transformations in Europe.* Ann Arbor: University of Michigan Press.

Index

Illustrations are indicated by page numbers in italic.

Parastou Saberi is a visiting research fellow at the University of Warwick Department of Politics and International Studies.